The Universe of Design

Design is the fundamental act of intelligence; it is the making of plans to shape the world to our needs. This book examines the theoretical foundations of the processes of planning and design.

Different types of design—creating an urban plan, drawing a floorplan, or drawing up a business plan—share characteristics; their reasoning, processes, and problems all have similarities. For a long time, the dominant theories in these areas have attempted to use objective, mathematical methods for design. But as researchers in many fields are beginning to discover, design problems are "wicked": they cannot be brought under control by rational or scientific means.

Forty years ago, as Herbert Simon was writing his classic work on design, *The Sciences of the Artificial*, which argued for the general applicability of rational methods, Horst Rittel, professor at the University of California, Berkeley, and former head of the Hochschule für Gestaltung, Ulm, was describing the characteristics of design problems that make such rational methods inappropriate. Best known for his idea of "wicked problems," Rittel, who was trained as a mathematician and systems analyst, studied the process by which designers in many different fields worked and pioneered a school of design theories and methods that attempted to rehabilitate the use of rationality by recognizing its limits and developing practices that did not depend on demonstrably false assumptions about rationality.

Rittel's work is of relevance to any field planning for the future. He recognized the central nature of human values, and explored how to design when these questions of value are of primary importance.

Jean-Pierre Protzen is Professor of the Graduate School at the University of California, Berkeley. He was Horst Rittel's colleague and collaborator for over twenty years and since Rittel's death in 1990 has continued teaching Rittel's work at Berkeley.

David J. Harris was Protzen's student at Berkeley, and his dissertation, "Design Theory: From Scientific Method to Humanist Practice," relied heavily on Rittel's work. He currently works as an editor and writing coach.

The Universe of Design

Horst Rittel's Theories of Design and Planning

Jean-Pierre Protzen and David J. Harris

Routledge
Taylor & Francis Group

LONDON AND NEW YORK

First published 2010
by Routledge
2 Park Square, Milton Park, Abingdon, Oxon, OX14 4RN

Simultaneously published in the USA and Canada
by Routledge
270 Madison Avenue, New York, NY 10016

Routledge is an imprint of the Taylor & Francis Group, an informa business

© 2010 Jean-Pierre Protzen and David J. Harris

Typeset in Univers by Pindar NZ, Auckland, New Zealand
Printed and bound in Great Britain by TJ International Ltd, Padstow, Cornwall

British Library Cataloguing in Publication Data
A catalogue record for this book is available from the British Library

Library of Congress Cataloging-in-Publication Data
Protzen, Jean-Pierre.
The universe of design : Horst Rittel's theories of design and planning / Jean-Pierre Protzen and David J. Harris.
          p. cm.
      Includes bibliographical references and index.
          1. Engineering design–Management. 2. Industrial design–Methodology.
3. Industrial engineering–Methodology. 4. System theory. 5. Rittel, Horst W. J.
I. Harris, David J., 1965- II. Title. III. Title: Horst Rittel's theories of design and planning.
      TA174.P78 2010
      620'.0042—dc22   2009046228

ISBN10: 0–415–77988–X (hbk)
ISBN10: 0–415–77989–8 (pbk)
ISBN10: 0–203–85158–7 (ebk)

ISBN13: 978–0–415–77988–3 (hbk)
ISBN13: 978–0–415–77989–0 (pbk)
ISBN13: 978–0–203–85158–6 (ebk)

To the memory of Horst Rittel

Contents

Preface

In 1966 I obtained a research grant from the Swiss National Science Foundation to go to Berkeley to investigate cities as communication networks. My colleague at the Swiss Institute of Technology (Eidgenössische Technische Hochschule (ETH)) in Zurich, Lucius Burckhardt, exhorted me to introduce myself to Horst Rittel in Berkeley's Department of Architecture. Burckhardt had known Rittel at Ulm, where both had taught at the Hochschule für Gestaltung and therefore was well acquainted with Rittel's work in design and planning methodology. Burckhardt's recommendation proved to be one of the most consequential counsels I ever received.

Rittel, upon hearing about my project, not only took an immediate interest in it but also had many helpful suggestions with regard to literature to review, people to talk to, as well of how I could go about the project. In short, he became my mentor.

Rittel, at the time, had established, among others, an introductory course to Design Theories and Methods, Architecture 130. This course was an outgrowth of a seminar, Science and Design, he held for the faculty at the time he joined the Department of Architecture in 1963. It was a revelation to me. Rittel's portrayal of the work of designers explained many of the frustrations I had experienced in my earlier career as a practicing architect. I became interested in the topic and soon Horst asked me to teach the course in his absence.

From there on we became colleagues and friends. Our children played together; together we traveled the world, taught and worked. At Berkeley we expanded the Design Theories and Methods curriculum of the Department and taught a variety of related courses, including design studios with an emphasis on the procedural aspects of design. And over the years we collaborated on numerous projects dealing with information systems for planners and government agencies at the Studiengruppe für Systemforschung in Heidelberg and at the University of Stuttgart.

When Horst died in 1990, a few days before his 60th birthday, I promised myself that I would assemble his innumerable lecture notes and other unpublished material and try to write a synopsis of his work. Although I continued to teach the Design Theories and Methods material and have done so until today, the project dragged on for a variety of reasons, not the least of which was my research on ancient architecture in South America. The project, however, came back into focus when, through the intermediary of the head librarian of Berkeley's College of Environmental Design, Elizabeth Byrne, I met Hugh Dubberly, who, at the time, was assembling the most extensive bibliography of Horst Rittel's work (Rith and Dubberly 2007).

Animated by Dubberly's efforts, I joined forces with Dr. David Harris, a former student and teaching assistant of mine in the Design Theories and Methods program at Berkeley. Although David never met Horst, he is thoroughly familiar with his writings and teachings and used Rittel's work in a prominent role in his doctoral dissertation (Harris 2002). From the start of our project, David and I discussed how and with which manuscripts and lesser-known publications of Rittel's we could best represent the scope of his work and the development of his theories of design and planning over time to an English-speaking audience. We kept this discussion alive throughout the project, which has taken many turns before it found its final form. We are confident that we have reached our goal. However, we should remind the reader that what we present is only one aspect, albeit perhaps the most significant, of Rittel's work. His life work was multifaceted, encompassing such fields as chemistry, artificial intelligence, theory of technology, and information theory. Needless to say, a complete synopsis of his work would require another book.

Berkeley, June 2009
Jean-Pierre Protzen

Acknowledgments

We would like to thank Elizabeth Byrne, head librarian of the College of Environmental Design at Berkeley, for supporting our project. She has been most helpful with all kinds of library-related issues. In addition, it was she who put us in contact with Hugh Dubberly of Dubberly Design Office in San Francisco.

Hugh Dubberly recognized the significance of Horst Rittel's work for designers and set out to compile a complete bibliography of his writings. Hugh's effort led not only to our collaboration, but also inspired us to assemble the present book. We thank him for both.

Chapters 2.1 and 3.1 were originally published in *Bedrifts Økonomen* 8 (1972).

Chapters 1.1 and 4.1 were originally published in German as *Uberlegungen zur wissenschaftlichen und politischen Bedeutung der Entscheidungstheorie*, (1963 Karlsruhe: Gesellschaft für Kernforschung) and *Technischer Wandel und Stadtstruktur*, (in "Stadt, Kultur, Natur. Chancen zukünftiger Lebensgestaltung", edited by Rudolf Wildenmann, Baden-Baden 1989) respectively. Both have been translated into English by Jean-Pierre Protzen.

Every effort has been made to contact and acknowledge copyright owners, but the authors and publishers would be pleased to have any errors or omissions brought to their attention so that corrections may be published at a later printing.

Prologue

The study of the activities of design or planning is a relatively new field, dating back to the middle of the twentieth century, yet one that has gained significant influence in the practice of planning and building. Horst W. J. Rittel, a pioneering design theorist, contributed significant theoretical and practical ideas that have shaped the field. Some of them, such as the notion of "wicked problems," have gained either fame or notoriety, depending on whom you ask;[1] others are less well known, mainly because they were never published, have appeared in publications with limited distribution, or were published in German only. It is the purpose of this publication to bring some of these lesser-known ideas to a wider audience.

Brief History of Design Theories and Methods

A comprehensive history of the discipline of Design Theories and Methods (DTM) has yet to be written, but there is no doubt that Horst W. J. Rittel played a pivotal role in its formulation and development. DTM arose out of an era in which scientific and purely rational methods were revered, not least for the tremendous changes that had been brought by technological development and industrialization. DTM was born from the assumption and hope that by studying the activity of design and developing rational methods one could improve the process and thereby bring about better designs. At the core of the discipline are such questions as what is design? How is design possible? What is the nature of design problems? How do designers reason? What kind of knowledge do they use and how is that knowledge structured and acquired? What procedures do designers follow and what is the logic of these procedures? Can design be taught, and if so how?

Design here is to be understood in a very broad sense. Horst Rittel defined it as "an activity that aims at the production of a plan, which plan—if implemented—is intended to bring about a situation with specific desired characteristics without creating unforeseen and undesired side and after effects."[2]

Design so defined is a purposeful activity which implies thinking before acting. The outcome of design is not a thing or an object, but a plan or a set of instructions, which in most cases are left to others to execute, if they are executed at all. Designers worry about the potential consequences of their planned actions. To anticipate the consequences, they vicariously manipulate the world in simulations and models, asking "what if" questions. Designers do not have any direct feedback from the real world until after their plans are implemented; they do not have the luxury of trial and error in the real world.

Design, so defined, covers a wide range of activities and is not limited to any particular profession. The lawmaker drafting a new law, the city planner devising strategies to manage urban growth, the engineer proposing actions to reduce traffic jams, the scientist conceiving an experiment, the manager conjuring up a new advertising campaign—all are designing, but so is everybody else: we carry an agenda, plan our careers, establish college funds for the education of our children, and make shopping lists. Everybody designs at least some of the time; nobody designs all the time.

Some people hold that designing and planning are two distinct activities: an architect designs, a traffic engineer plans. Rittel made no such distinction; in fact, he considered the terms to be synonymous, which is consistent with common usage, both current and historical.[3] Rittel's use of the terms as synonymous is consistent with his general definition of design, and reveals his focus: he was looking at the nature of the problem and questions of how to solve the problems better.

Rittel always wondered why this human ability to plan for the future has not received the same attention as epistemology, that is, the study of the human ability to know, to know that we know, and to know what we know to be true, a field that has preoccupied philosophers since the dawn of time. In 1987, at a conference on Design Theories and Methods in Boston, Rittel mused that "[i]t is one of the mysteries of our civilization that the noble and prominent activity of design has found little scholarly attention until recently." Considering the real and practical impact of design on our world, and that it changes people's lives for better or worse, it is the more curious that design has not come under greater scrutiny.

The "activist" phase

In his book *Method in Architecture* (1984), Tom Heath argues that the discipline of Design Theories and Methods may have its origin in the recognition, perhaps first articulated by Viollet-le-Duc in 1872, that design problems are becoming so complicated that they escape the designer's intuitive grasp:

> It must needs be confessed that modern architects, surrounded as they are by prejudices and traditions and embarrassed by historical confusion in respect to their art, are neither inspired by original ideas or guided by definite and well understood principles; a fact the more plainly betrayed the more elaborate and complex are the monuments they are called upon to design and execute.
>
> (Heath 1984: 13)

Some 90 years later, Christopher Alexander, in his *Notes on the Synthesis of Form* (1964), echoes Viollet-le-Duc's concerns:

> Today functional problems are becoming less simple all the time. But designers rarely confess their inability to solve them. Instead, when a designer does not understand the problem clearly enough to find the order it really calls for, he falls back on some arbitrarily chosen formal order. The problem, because of its complexity, remains unsolved.
>
> (Alexander 1964: 1)

Alexander noted that, while there are "bounds to man's cognitive and creative capacity," it is also true that man has found means to overcome at least some of his limitations. He pointed to arithmetic, where we have developed algorithms that allow us quickly to perform operations on the back of an envelope that we could not do in our heads. We have devised means to represent the complication of, say, a long division, such that we can handle it. "But at present we have no corresponding way of simplifying design problems for ourselves" (Alexander 1964: 6).

In its modern form, the discipline may be traced back to World War II, when complex military logistical problems were in want of new planning and decision-making tools. For this purpose new mathematical procedures were developed that today are known by such names as *operations research*, *systems engineering*, and *systems analysis*. These new approaches owe much to the notion of "open systems," first formulated by the Austrian biologist Ludwig von Bertalanffy in the late 1920s and to Norbert Wiener's notion of "cybernetics" or the theory of feedback loops. As opposed to closed systems, open systems, as exemplified by biological systems, depend for their survival on the exchange of energy and information with their environment. Cybernetics provides the theoretical framework for studying and understanding how the interaction of an organism (or a mechanical system) with its environment affects its behavior.

After World War II these methods took hold of the field of design, as witnessed by such texts as *Introduction to Design* (1962), by Morris Asimow, Professor of Engineering at the University of California at Los Angeles; *Product Design and Decision Theory* (1963), by Kenneth Starr, Professor of Production Management at Columbia University; *The Sciences of the Artificial* (1969), by Herbert Simon, Professor of Political Science at Carnegie Mellon University; *Systematic Methods for Designers* (1965), by L. Bruce Archer, Professor of Design Research at the Royal College of Arts; *Vers une architecture scientifique* (1971), by the French architect Yona Friedman; and the already-mentioned *Notes on the Synthesis of Form* (1964), by Christopher Alexander. The emerging discourse on DTM crystallized and established itself as a discipline at the first conference on design methods, the "Conference on Systematic and Intuitive Methods in Engineering, Industrial Design, Architecture, and Communication," held in London in September 1962 (Jones and Thornley 1962). As the title of the conference suggests, design was then recognized as an activity that transcends professional boundaries.

The application of methods for design and planning, in fact, spread further than the conference would indicate. Other fields and professions had equally embraced the ideas and methods of systems thinking and operations research, most prominently City and Regional Planning, Education, and Public and Business Administration; such methods were applied to management techniques and organization design, and to concerns about the course of humanity.

In 1947 Herbert A. Simon first published his *Administrative Behavior: a study of decision-making processes in administrative organization*, which gave rise to what today is called management science. His work spawned other works, for example, Jacob Marschak's "Towards an Economic Theory of Organization and Information" (1954), or Horst W. J. Rittel's "Hierarchy vs. Team? Considerations on the Organization of Research of R&D Co-operatives" (1965), both texts searching for the most efficient work organization given a particular task.

1954 saw the founding of the Regional Science Association International, a group of multi-disciplinary researchers under the leadership of Walter Isard, dedicated to the rigorous scientific analysis of the "regional impacts of national or global processes of economic and social change" (RSAI 2008). Within this field one finds the work of a colleague of Rittel's at Berkeley, William Alonso, best illustrated by his *Location and Land Use: Toward a General Theory of Land Rent* (1964).

In the early 1970s Andreas Faludi wrote *Planning Theory* (1973), which he described as "a venture in establishing planning theory as an intellectual endeavor aiming at solving some of a whole range of problems which planners face" (1973: ix).

A dramatic and controversial application of systems analysis and modeling was Jay W. Forrester's *World Dynamics* (1971), which tried to predict what would happen to world resources as the population continued to increase. This model, commissioned by the Club of Rome, formed the basis for its first report, *The Limits to Growth* (Meadows *et al.* 1972), which, since publication in 1972, has been translated into 30 languages and sold over 30 million copies. Much maligned at the time, with the current revived concern with climate change and environmental degradation, the report is gaining new significance: "in hindsight, the Club of Rome turned out to be right. We simply wasted 30 years by ignoring this work" (Simmons 2000: 72).

The reflective phase

The "activist" phase, in which professions across the board imported and applied these techniques on small and large scales, was soon to be followed by a reflective phase, in which practitioners and researchers alike took stock of the successes and failures of these techniques and started to question their basic underlying assumptions and theories.

Prominent among those who questioned the basic assumptions of the new methods were C. West Churchman and Ida R. Hoos. The former, in his *Challenge to Reason* (1968), tried to answer the question: "How can we design improvement in a large system without understanding the whole system, and if the answer is that we cannot, how is it possible to understand the whole system?" (Churchman 1968: 2). The latter, in her *Systems Analysis in Public Policy: a critique* (1969), challenged the evaluation methods prevailing in education, waste management, and healthcare. She saw in these methods a "kind of quantomania," or as she put it later: "What you could not count did not count. The social and human aspects were systematically avoided in the rush to be scientific" (Hoos 2009). More specifically, Horst Rittel and Melvin Webber, in "Dilemmas of a General Theory of Planning" (1973), called attention to some of the mistaken beliefs of the "scientification" of planning, and explained how planning problems differ from scientific problems. At the same time, Aaron Wildavsky, in his article "If Planning is Everything, Maybe it is Nothing" (1973), argued that planners have become victims of planning; their creation has overwhelmed them. In a similar vein, John Friedmann, in his *Retracking America* (1973), proclaimed, "[o]ur inherited notions of planning are dead" (xiii).

He traced those inherited notions back to Frederick W. Taylor and his scientific management, and into the present day under the name of operations research and systems analysis.

Rittel, in another article, one included here, "On the Planning Crisis: Systems Analysis of the First and Second Generations," went beyond critique to propose a different approach, a second generation. Independent of Rittel and some years later, Donald Schön, through his critique of what he called the epistemology of technical rationality, reached similar conclusions and proposed a new kind of planner, *The Reflective Practitioner* (1983).

The reflective phase spawned its own political activism in the form of advocacy planning and participatory or community design. Suspicious of technocratic elites and critical of the logical positivism that guided urban planning, Paul Davidoff, in his "Advocacy and Pluralism in Planning" (1965), argued that just as a defendant in a court of law is represented by an attorney knowledgeable in the law and legal procedures, urban communities, the poor in particular, should be represented by planners that would argue their case before planning bureaucracies. These movements have the merit of having recognized planning problems to be neither technical nor scientific, but political—"political" in the sense that they are about the allocation and distribution of resources and that they should be dealt with in the political arena.

Yet these movements ran afoul of bureaucracies once they were co-opted by government agencies and institutionalized. In his *After the Planners* (1971), Robert Goodman provides a rather scathing criticism of advocacy planners and the system in which they operate.

The reflective phase in DTM was influenced by parallel developments in the philosophy of science in which the prevailing assumption of positive objectivity came under tight scrutiny. Karl Popper challenged positivism in his *The Logic of Scientific Discovery* (1959). In *The Structure of Scientific Revolutions* (1962), Thomas Kuhn convincingly argued that prevailing worldviews, his "paradigms," channel scientists' work. Michael Polanyi, in his *Personal Knowledge* (1958), showed how the work of scientists is not a purely rational enterprise, but that it is guided by unspoken assumptions, or "tacit" knowledge and skills, and Paul Feyerabend disputed the notion that there was such a thing as a specific method, of whatever kind, for scientific discovery. In his *Against Method* (1975), he argued that truth emerges from many aspects of existence.

The current state

Critiques, reflections, and new proposals continue to inform the discourse about DTM. At least two books have purported to lay "a new foundation for design": Terry Winograd and Fernando Flores's *Understanding Computers and Cognition* (1986), and, more recently, Klaus Krippendorff's *The Semantic Turn* (2006). Winograd and Flores "want to break with the rationalistic tradition [of problem solving], proposing a different language for situations in which 'problems arise'" (77). They argue that design problems do not have an objective existence, but that, following Heidegger, people encounter problems whenever their "habitual, standard, comfortable 'being-in-the world'" is interrupted, that is, when they experience a "breakdown" and their practices and equipment become "present-to-hand" (Winograd and Flores 1986: 77).

In the introduction to *The Semantic Turn*, Bruce Archer writes that Krippendorff's axiom of human-centered design is "that *humans do not respond to the physical properties of things*—to their form, structure and function—*but to their individual and cultural meanings*" (Krippendorff 2006: xix, italics in original). Based on this assumption, Krippendorff, a former student of Rittel's at Ulm, outlines the tenets of what he calls a science *for* design, as opposed to a science *of* design.[4] The science *for* design is meant to directly assist designers in their daily practice.

Explorations in Planning Theory (1996), edited by S. Mandelbaum, L. Mazza, and R. W. Burchell, demonstrates that the discourse on planning theory and methods is not only alive and well, but also contentious. Here we will mention only two texts to illustrate the diversity of approaches: Niraj Verma's *Similarity, Connections and Systems: the search for a new rationality for planning and management* (1998) and *The Argumentative Turn in Policy Analysis and Planning* (1993), edited by Frank Fischer and John Forester. Verma explores new ground; he notes that as scientists we are probing for differences, but as planners and designers we are looking for similarities. Addressing C. West Churchman's challenge to reason mentioned above, Verma argues that "[b]ecoming critical about the similarities between ideas can help to make useful links between them" (Verma 1998: 83). Similarity may not help us understand the whole system, but it will help us think about and better understand the systems we try to improve. In an earlier article, "Pragmatic Rationality and Planning Theory" (1996), Verma argues that, unlike earlier notions of rationality, the pragmatic rationality works towards consequences rather than causes, integrates facts and values and rejects the search for ultimate foundations.

In the introduction to *The Argumentative Turn*, the editors state that the book "explores . . . a simple but profound insight: Policy analysis and planning are practical processes of argumentation" (Fischer and Forester 1993: 2). Neither in this book, nor in a subsequent text by John Forester, *The Deliberative Practitioner* (1999), which elaborates on *The Argumentative Turn*, does one find any references to Rittel. This is surprising, because, as the reader will see, the notion that planning is an argumentative process was proposed, explored, and developed by Rittel some 20 years earlier, and has been at the core of much of his work.

Another turn in the study of design is the emergence of ethnographic investigations into the workings of practicing architects and engineers as exemplified by *Architecture: the story of practice* (1991) by Dana Cuff or Louis L. Bucciarelli's "An Ethnographic Perspective on Engineering Design" (1988). Both these texts lend substantial support to Rittel's understanding of the nature of planning problems and the argumentative nature of the planning process. Thomas Moran and John Carroll, in their *Design Rationale: concepts, techniques, and use* (1996), summarize what emerges from such ethnographic studies as follows:

> Design problems are almost always too large for one person. Many
> different technical disciplines are required, as well as management

discipline, in addition to creative and integrative skills. Design is a communication-intensive collaborative activity. The communication problem is heightened by the fact that the various stakeholders speak different disciplinary languages, are motivated by different values, see different issues when looking at the same design problem, and have different interests.

(Moran and Carroll 1996: 5)

Texts by other cognitive and computer scientists, like Moran, have at their core the development of tools meant to facilitate collaborative design, for example *Visualizing Argumentation* (2003) by Paul A. Kirschner *et al.*, and most recently, Jeffrey Conklin's *Dialogue Mapping: building shared understanding of wicked problems* (2006). In all these texts, the Issue-based Information System (IBIS) developed by Rittel, (which is presented in this publication), plays a central role.

Horst W. J. Rittel (1932–1990)

Horst Willhelm Jakob Rittel was born on 14 July 1930 in Berlin, where he attended elementary school followed by the Gymnasium Adolfinum. In 1949 he began the study of mathematics and theoretical physics at the University of Göttingen, knowledge that he later applied when he was first hired as mathematician and physicist by the Maschinenfabrik Deutschland in Dortmund. There he developed design aids for mechanical engineers to control vibrations and deformations and built cost-prediction tools, among other things. In 1958 Rittel joined the Sozialforschungsstelle at the University of Münster, where he not only became involved in the theory of predicting socio-economic processes and in the planning and evaluation of sociological field research, but also devoted time to the study of sociology and mathematical logic. That same year he followed a call to join the faculty of the Hochschule für Gestaltung (HfG) at Ulm.

Horst Rittel at Ulm

Founded in 1953 by the siblings Hans and Sophie Scholl, the HfG was to become one of the most innovative and influential, albeit short-lived, design schools of the twentieth century. Its first director, the Swiss architect and artist Max Bill, a former student of the Bauhaus, envisioned the HfG as a reincarnation of the ideas and methods of the Bauhaus. Bill was soon to be ousted by rebellious teaching assistants who were clamoring for a more rigorous, not to say scientific, approach to design. As a consequence, the content of the so-called Foundation Course, modeled after the Bauhaus and required of all students, was changed from its original engagement with materials and tools to a set of courses that were to impart to design students so-called "operational knowledge," the knowledge instrumental to the success of all kinds of designers, product designers, architects, graphic designers etc.:

- Sociology: designers have to have an understanding of the workings of the society in which they live and practice.

- Economics: designers must understand the workings of the economic system (capitalism) and be able to appreciate their role and position in this system.
- Cultural history: designers need to be aware of the history of ideas and material objects, and must know how they themselves and their work are connected to the past.
- Psychology: designers must understand the basics of perception and human behavior.
- Mathematics: mathematics, being a universal language of form and structure, as well as a generative tool for new forms and ideas, is essential for all designers.

Within this framework, Rittel taught courses in design methodology, mathematical operations analysis, communication theory, and epistemology. Shortly after he moved to Ulm he also was elected to the membership in a triumvirate of directors that shaped and ran the school from 1959 to 1963. Rittel was prominently involved in formulating and implementing the premises on which the teaching of design at Ulm was based. These premises, or "working hypotheses" as Rittel called them, he described as follows:

1. There exists basic knowledge that is common to designers of all stripes. (The application of this hypothesis is, of course, illustrated by the "operational knowledge" mentioned above.)
2. Today, the formation of universal geniuses is unthinkable; therefore, different types of designers must also acquire domain specific knowledge and skills.
3. The ability to communicate and present one's ideas can be taught.
4. Methods of working and work organization are equally subject to teaching.
5. The designer's competence to make judgments can be enhanced and made more explicit.
6. Similarly, the designer's decision-making ability, especially the courage to commit oneself to a plan, is subject to exercise and practice.
7. Last but not least, the designer's imagination can be augmented and trained.

(Rittel 1961)

At Ulm, Rittel mingled with illustrious designers and design theorists. Among them, and to name but a few, were Charles Eames, Buckminster Fuller, Konrad Wachsmann, Tomás Maldonado, and Bruce Archer. It is safe to say that Rittel's understanding of design deepened at Ulm and that it was there that he developed a vision of a theory of design that would gel once he joined the faculty of the Department of Architecture at the University of California at Berkeley in 1963.

Horst Rittel at Berkeley

In 1959 the Department of City and Regional Planning, the Department of Landscape Architecture, and the College of Architecture at the University of California at Berkeley, which had hitherto been independent academic units, merged to form a single integrated college, the College of Environmental Design. This union was more than just an administrative move; it was the product of a vision, held by many of the faculty in these departments, a view of interdisciplinary cooperation and inter-dependence among professional fields as the modern response to the complexity, even chaos, of the mechanized industrial world. As Dean William Wurster, who had suggested and engineered the merger, wrote in the first bulletin published for the combined college:

> In simpler times it was enough to be adept at one's own profession but in these complicated times it becomes necessary to be not only the master of one profession but also to have a real perception of other disciplines in order to know how these may be integrated with one's own to produce a harmonious result.

(Wurster 1960)

To contribute to the formulation and implementation of the new vision, Berkeley invited, among others, Christopher Alexander, who had just graduated from Harvard, and Rittel out of Ulm to join the Architecture Faculty. Shortly after his arrival, Rittel was asked to give a seminar for the faculty outlining the assumptions, tenets, and methods of what today we may call a science of design. This seminar, presented for the first time in this volume, was crucial for the future course of the Department of Architecture. In 1966, the Department adopted a new curriculum with a strong option in DTM, which included courses and seminars on the psychology of perception and communication, problem-solving procedures and operations research models, pro-gram development and evaluation procedures, methods of architectural research, the integrated specification of environmental structures, and design methods for specific environmental problems. The affinity here with the Ulm notion of "opera-tional knowledge" is unmistakable.

At Berkeley, Rittel's ideas not only fell on fertile ground; here he also found new colleagues and students who challenged and inspired him. Perhaps the most influential colleague was C. West Churchman, a philosopher and profes-sor in the School of Business Administration,[5] and author of many texts on the systems approach. Churchman, as director of the Social Sciences Program of the Space Sciences Laboratories, had organized what became known simply as the "Churchman Seminar," a seminar on design. The premises for this seminar were that design is a ubiquitous activity practiced by almost everybody, at least some of the time, and that there may be some generalizable observations to be made about how people go about it. To this effect, the seminar assembled people from across the campus and across the disciplines: Music, Engineering, Political Science, Public Health, Business Administration, Art, Education, Architecture, City and Regional Planning, and more. It was in one of these seminars that Rittel first presented his notion of design and planning problems as "wicked" in contrast to problems of math-ematics, chess, or puzzles, which he termed "tame" (Churchman 1967). Prodded by another colleague, Melvin Webber, professor of City and Regional Planning, Rittel elaborated the notion of "wicked problems," and jointly they published what arguably is the most influential and seminal paper in the field: "Dilemmas in a General Theory of Planning" (Rittel and Webber 1973).

The notion of "wicked problems" led Rittel to the formulation of what he called a "Second Generation Systems Approach." This approach signaled a departure from the earlier efforts to put design on a purely rational basis, which were based on the epistemology that Donald Schön later called "Technical Rationality" (Schön 1983). Already at Ulm, Rittel had

> argued that dichotomies purporting to distinguish systematic versus intuitive, and rational versus non-rational design are untenable. Rather, he asked, to what degree can and should design processes be made explicit, and to what extent can and should they be made communicable to others. For only communicable processes can be taught, and only explicitly formulated processes can be critically scrutinized and improved upon.
>
> (Churchman, Protzen, and Webber 1992)

The development of this second generation approach became the focus of Rittel's work and of the research and teaching agendas in the discipline at Berkeley. At the core of the second generation is the understanding of design as an argumentative, or deliberative, process. Designers are seen to argue with themselves and with others about the appropriateness of a course of action. Much research by both faculty and students concentrated on finding ways of making this deliberation explicit, on understanding its structure and its logic, on supporting it, and on strengthening the process in order to make it more powerful and more controllable. A significant outcome of this research agenda was the "Issue-Based Information System" (IBIS) and its related argumentation systems, which were used, for example, by German government agencies and the Organization for Economic Co-operation and Development (OECD).

Horst Rittel at Stuttgart

From 1973 on, Rittel commuted between Berkeley and the University of Stuttgart, where he was appointed Professor for the Foundations of Planning to the Faculty of Architecture and City Planning, and where he created and directed the Institut für Grundlagen der Planung. At that time serious efforts to reform higher education pervaded the Federal Republic of Germany, and new legislation was discussed and passed that called for, among other things, the reorganization of the entire system of architectural education. Thus, when elected Dean of the Faculty of Architecture and City Planning, Rittel, referring to an earlier article of his (Rittel 1966), remarked that "[t]his gave me the opportunity to involve myself another time in the 'design of an educational system for design.'" He feared that the reform would impose a rigid curriculum, which he compared to a mess hall with a single menu for everyone. Instead, he argued for an educational system that promotes the co-existence of competing ideas and which stimulates their rivalry, and in which students are invited to find their own standpoint in this field of positions.

How could such an educational philosophy be justified in the formation of state-certified, accredited professionals, Rittel asked? On the one hand, he invoked the great divergence among planners and architects about what are, or should be, common qualifications. On the other hand, he saw such a great differentiation in the problems professionals were asked to solve that a standardized formation could no longer be justified: no curriculum could possibly impart all the knowledge and all the skills necessary for the whole spectrum of tasks in professional life. In departure from the "operational knowledge" notion of Ulm, Rittel now thought that one could not even define a "sufficient minimum for all [types of designers]." Furthermore, it is to be expected that the future problem-scape and the knowledge necessary to cope with it will continue to change. Under these circumstances, a curriculum can at most hope to transmit basic principles of how one copes with the inherent difficulties of planning and design, of how, in a sea of ever-changing knowledge and situations, one can keep informed, that is, of how one learns to learn.[6]

Horst Rittel at the Studiengruppe für Systemforschung

About the time Rittel joined the faculty at Ulm, he also linked up with the "Studiengruppe für Systemforschung" (Study Group for Systems Research) in Heidelberg. This group, at first a loose association of young scientists that later became institutionalized as a government-sponsored "think-tank," was inspired by the understanding "that science and technology achieve not only good ends, but also produce the horrors of war, the threat of nuclear conflict, and damage to the natural environment." With this insight the Studiengruppe strived "for an open, public democratic control of the development of research and technology" (Krauch 2006: 131–132). In the early 1960s the Studiengruppe counted among its members, and again to name but some, the sociologist Hans Paul Bahrdt, the psychiatrist Paul Matussek, the philosopher Jürgen Habermas, the chemists Helmut Krauch and Werner Kunz, the economist Walter Baur, and later the philosopher and systems analyst C. West Churchman. Rittel's collaboration with the Studiengruppe is of great significance because, as Wolf Reuter wrote, Rittel's work on DTM is embedded in a spectrum of activities and publications that far transcends that work. The Studiengruppe was the catalyst for many of his works that went against the grain of entrenched disciplinary boundaries (Reuter 1992: 4).

The Spectrum of Horst Rittel's Work

Though his work covered a wide range of specific fields, we can see it as revealing his interest in the nature of problems, and in how we think about and deal with them. By their very nature, Rittel's interests were focused on fundamental human activities: understanding problems and the processes by which people approach those problems are issues relevant across the span of human activity. Rittel's work spanned a large part of that spectrum.

Whatever the field, he focused on the structure, representation, and reasoning related to the problem—whether management of information, research in chemistry, or urban design. The unifying thread was the search for how people understood, reasoned about, learned about, and dealt with the real-world problems and issues they faced.

In its concern for research, the generation and management of knowledge and information, and the political aspects associated with knowledge, Rittel's work necessarily encompassed the full range of human life, just as he believed that design became a part of most aspects of human life.

This wide scope of his vision can be seen in a single article, "The Reasoning of Designers" (which is included in this collection). Because design is a ubiquitous activity, Rittel's reasoning of the designer applies ubiquitously. The article reveals an unstated epistemology and moral system, recognizing that the questions of what is understood and what is valued are the ones important to one who intends to change the world. Rittel probably wouldn't have thought to state it in those terms: he wasn't interested in knowledge as knowledge; he would have simply focused on the project at hand—be it information systems, architecture and planning, chemistry—which may explain why the principles stated in "The Reasoning of Designers" were used, but not explicitly stated, in his work with IBIS.

"The Reasoning of Designers" presents a world dominated by different personal perspectives of what is, and what could and should be (not to mention the different perspectives of how to make those changes and how those changes came about). The IBIS and the systems derived from it were intended to capture and represent those perspectives so they could be shared and communicated. Of course, a world of differing perspectives is one of the fundamental ideas behind the idea of "wicked problems."

Rittel's vision of design shows a world where the important questions are what we should do, and what we want to do—where the deontic issues dominate the factual—in contrast to the world of the first generation, where the search for an objective truth prevailed.

Rittel was concerned not only with what could be determined "objectively," but also with values, especially personal values. This becomes the linchpin for many of his later concerns, such as the IBIS, wicked problems, and the reasoning of the designer.

One can see the influence of Karl Popper's theories of knowledge—science built on testing and rejecting hypotheses, and the truth and knowledge determined by the best-tested hypotheses. There is no objective truth to be found with certainty; we have, at best, theories that have not been proven wrong. Therefore, we must work with and manage the disparate ideas, and use them—though they do not always agree—to come to an overall decision.

It is this overarching vision that led Rittel's ideas to be appropriate in many fields—fields of great diversity with little obvious connection.

He did work that might be called practical epistemology—studies of how people did and could manage information, such as studies of research processes and research institutes, studies of how to know what is known.

He looked at the processes of research institutes, at knowledge in chemistry research, and at development of information systems, including his own development of the IBIS, which is included in this volume, and gives an alternate (but compatible) perspective of the argumentative process described in "The Reasoning of Designers." With Werner Kunz he wrote a series of articles looking at management of information and documentation both generally ("Training in the Information Sciences," and "Documentation and the Transfer of

Knowledge," both 1971), and in some specific fields (e.g. chemistry and foreign affairs). This volume does not look at these information management issues, focusing primarily on the theoretical issues that make such information systems so important.

Rittel was studying how people understand and solve different sorts of issues—how they plan, how they learn. The practical side of that was studying how they tried to track ideas, and how they could better track ideas, to facilitate design processes and research processes—which, as far as information management is concerned, share characteristics, for all that designers and researchers are involved in different tasks. The theoretical side of that was developing and explaining the issues and structures of knowledge and problems on a more general level, which is what his work on wicked problems and the reasoning of designers does.

One way to look at tame problems is that they require a specific perspective and framework. In a world of science like that described so variously by Popper, Kuhn, Feyerabend, Foucault, or Latour, one in which social factors determine the context and conceptual framework for science, one cannot easily reduce the practical issues of scientific research to tame problems, one must manage different research and personal agendas among the research scientists; one must manage differences in perspective among researchers (e.g. different views of what constitutes science, such as those different theories of science mentioned above). On a practical level, even the work of researchers is dominated by the wicked design questions of how to manage resources and design new studies. Tame problems require a specific perspective; Rittel's work revealed that real world problems, across fields, are not defined by single perspectives.

Evolution of Rittel's Work in Design Theories and Methods

There are two dimensions of particular note to the evolution of Rittel's work: the evolution of the tone and the evolution of the focus.

The tone of Rittel's earlier work—notably the "Science and Design" seminars—is one of optimism; it is a guarded optimism, but his focus is on the positive potential. He has a grand vision: near the beginning of the second seminar, he states: "At the end of this seminar series an overall innovating system, including an enquiring device and a direction-determining device as well, will be proposed." And, in this idea of an overall innovating system, it should be kept in mind that in the first seminar Rittel defines innovation as a concept that embraces both design and science. We have Rittel's handwritten notes (mostly in German) for the overall innovating system.

This optimism about the ability of the theoretician to develop an overarching theory begins to dwindle. Although Rittel's later work does present a fuller picture of the overall process of design—a maturity and confidence of statement and theory that contrasts with the more tentative nature of the early seminars—the fullness of the theory is not matched by a corresponding overarching system. As his understanding of the overall picture of the design process became more detailed and more mature, there was a diminution in his belief that it could be contained in a single system. By the end of his career, he could see the process from an overall perspective, but from that perspective he could also see that the process could not be unified into a complete system, and the IBIS, though it could capture all of the argumentative structure of the design process, was a limited system: it was nothing more than a reflection of the ideas of the design participants; IBIS was not intended to synthesize, evaluate, or otherwise generate new information that was not put there by the users; it was not intended to be an expert system or any sort of artificial intelligence. Rittel was an insistent critic of artificial intelligence research which aims at simulating, or better yet, surpassing human intelligence. He saw in such efforts a direct parallel with Goethe's Faust and his homunculus. Rather than pursue artificial intelligence (AI), Rittel proposed that we focus on "natural intelligence-enhancement" (NIE) as a less ambitious, yet more promising strategy. He would say "as my eyeglasses don't see on my behalf but help me see better, one might use the computer not to think on one's behalf, but to reinforce and enhance one's ability to think."

With respect to the focus, we can see a shift from the attempt to create an overarching theory of design, based on the abstract view of the process, to a more personalized view—one where the abstract theory gets subordinated to the personal and political issues at the heart of the design process. This parallels the shift of focus, mentioned above, from the Ulm perspective of "operational knowledge" to the concern with the developing designers' ability to cope with the unknown and unexpected—the principle underlying his curriculum development at Stuttgart. Thus the search for the large-scale systems—which can be seen in the seminar series, and in the issues faced by "On the Planning Crisis"—gets replaced by a search for the understanding of an individual, and an attempt to record, understand, and work with the varying views of the different individuals.

Continued Relevance of Horst Rittel's Work

Design—as Rittel defined it, the making of plans to bring about desired situations in the world—is basically intertwined with the concept of intelligence. The chance creation of order or beauty is not design: snowflakes and other crystals are not designed—unless our beliefs suggest that all of creation was the act of an intelligent being. Design is purpose, intention, and plan; it is the precursor to intelligent action. Design is, if we look at it in this broad sense, one of the primary characteristics of the human race. It is the foundation of our adaptivity that we can learn about situations and plan for them in the future. It is the foundation of civilization, of art, of science. Rittel observes that everybody designs some of the time,[7] so the concern of his work can hardly be limited.

Rittel's work explored the fundamental issues of planned human endeavor—issues central to any vision for a future—whether to envision a single product or an entire city, or even, indeed, any world we can dream of creating. His work looked at the interplay of human needs and interests, at the basic logical conflicts that will plague our decision-making processes and complicate the ability to plan when many people are involved.

We can see Rittel's work as transcending all fields of human endeavor.[8] Though Rittel had a very specific definition of design, a great majority of Rittel's work has significance beyond the activities qualified under his definition. His definition excluded many activities that might, under another perspective, be considered design. For example, he said that the sculptor was not a designer because of the immediate feedback available as the piece is created. But the sculptor faces wickedness: there is no definitive formulation of the sculptor's problem, but, to the sculptor at least, it is a problem. Similarly, we can see that the sculptor, too, engages in an argumentative process. These issues that Rittel strove to describe are fundamental in intelligent action.

Rittel said it was the designer's responsibility to avoid the unforeseen and undesirable side and aftereffects of design, and his work was aimed at trying to avoid such outcomes (though he admitted the logical impossibility of preventing such side and aftereffects with any certainty).

In a world where unforeseen and undesirable side and aftereffects seem to be the issue of the moment—what with global climate change and mass extinctions, and other problems too numerous to list—this concern for eliminating (or at least reducing) the undesirable side and aftereffects of our designs is necessary. And as the scale of our interventions increases, the impact of the undesirable side and aftereffects grows. From the so-called "green revolution" and its use of agricultural chemicals, to the development and deployment of nuclear power—whose foreseeable, and undesirable effects can be seen in the Chernobyl disaster—to the unknown, uncertain results of new, rapidly deployed technologies like genetic engineering and wireless communication systems, which have already been implicated in many problems, though without certainty, it can be seen that humanity's survival may very well depend on adopting new paradigms for design—paradigms that balance the relentless optimism shown by previous generations of scientists with a much greater level of caution.

It has been a common belief of the past century that new technologies can be developed to solve all problems, and that new technologies should be used because whatever problems they may cause (e.g. the creation of radioactive waste), these problems will ultimately be solved by further technology.

Rittel would have scorned such attitudes as reckless and short-sighted. But his scorn was not an emotional reaction; it was the product of careful study. Indeed, as noted, he started with optimism, and despite the conclusions of his later work, the belief in human ability to productively plan remained. Despite the impossibility of knowing all possible outcomes of a plan, he did not advocate inaction.

Rittel's caution is not a pessimistic one: he does not argue that there is no possible solution that will do well, or that we should stop trying to design. He argues that we must continue trying, but with a new perspective—one that is sensitive to issues that are typically left outside the concerns of the developers of technology and other large-scale design endeavors.

It is this blend of caution mixed with optimistic ambition, this balance between the extremes that we hope to present here.

While we have been teaching Rittel's work consistently at the University of California since his death, little work has been done beyond that to bring to the public those ideas of his which were not already published—and this despite continued interest in his work. Hugh Dubberly, teaching cybernetics at Stanford, began a project to compile a comprehensive bibliography of Rittel's work when he saw the relevance of the work to his own courses, and it was his inquiries that provided the spark that has been turned into this book.[9]

Rittel's work has not been widely published in English. Here we have an opportunity to bring some little-known and little-available English articles to a wider public.

Rittel's approach to planning and design teaches much of value in these times. His interest in revealing motivations is crucial for many reasons. His interest in hearing all the different interests and needs of those impacted by projects becomes more important as growing cultures are forced to live in closer and closer contact.

Rittel did not attempt to simplify the richness and difficulty of the world—an approach necessary for the creation of practical solutions, and one with the greatest possibility of successful outcomes. His work is an honest view of the problems faced in design and a sketch of an approach to dealing with these problems more effectively.

Our Intentions and Method
About the making of the book

Four decades ago, when the transcript of the Science and Design seminars (in Part One of this volume) was put into the CED library, it was titled "Universe of Design," but the source of the title is uncertain. We don't know the full story behind the seminar transcripts. Who authorized them? Who managed the recording? We have the name of the transcriber, and beyond that we know nothing about the making of the transcript. We have a copy of the seminar transcript annotated in Rittel's handwriting; on its cover he wrote, "Who invented this title?" Perhaps one of the seminar participants heard Rittel use this phrase in some passing remark; perhaps it was a construction of the editor, James Harris. We just don't know; if Rittel discovered who was responsible, it is not noted on his copy.

Rittel's notes indicate that he would have titled the seminars, "Science and Design," as we named them in this volume. Having decided not to use the title, "The Universe of Design," for the seminar series, and having a larger purpose of showing the range of Rittel's ideas, we felt that it would serve well as the title for the whole collection of works—a collection that spans over two decades of Rittel's work, and which spans the range of his ideas. Rittel's work always tried to encompass the whole of design—design in all its aspects and manifestations in different fields. His efforts were not directed at solving small aspects of design—though he saw a place for such studies—his efforts were directed at constructing a whole coherent framework in which to understand, explain, and improve design, at least partly by recognizing design's paradoxes and internal contradictions. From the questions on decision theory and the general issues addressed in the 1964 seminars, through the work on wicked problems and the reasoning of designers, to his thoughts about design pathologies, Rittel's perspective encompassed the entire universe of design. The pieces included in this collection present that wide range of ideas. The works included in this volume look at design in the widest scope: these are not questions of urban planning or chemistry or information systems, these are fundamental issues that characterize the human act of design, that indeed characterize the whole Universe of Design.

Our selection of materials and the structure of the work

There are four main sections to this book in addition to the introduction and conclusion: foundations, wicked problems, reasoning about design, and consequences of design. We wished to use works that could show both the range of his concerns as well as give some sense of the historical progression of the work, and the insight that comes from seeing the relationship between early works and later works.

The first section begins by examining two works that lay out the general questions and premises that concerned Rittel. We start with an article on decision theory, and this is, in a way, the predecessor to all that follows: how do we make a decision?

The decision theory article was translated from German. Its concern with the most basic or general question for design is a good place to start a discussion of the more general process of design. Ultimately design is about the decisions that we make: which course of action will we choose in response to the situation that we face? What will our choice be for our design? The decision theory article also serves as a good starting place, because more than any of the other work, it is closely aligned with what Rittel comes to call "the first generation of design methods." We can see in this piece the attempt to find rational foundations—an attempt that will later be abandoned as Rittel proves to his own satisfaction that such rationality is logically impossible.

This is followed by the Science and Design seminars, which cover a lot of territory by laying out many of the basic questions and perspectives that Rittel used throughout his career. These two early pieces are characterized, somewhat more than the later ones, by the optimism that first-generation designers had been feeling throughout their heyday following World War II. The seminar transcript that forms the bulk of this work was never published and was available only in the UC Berkeley CED archives. In preparing the seminars we used a copy of the transcript that Rittel himself reviewed, and made comments and corrections on about half of it. In addition, we have available a large set of notes that Rittel made while working on the seminar—some notes are preparatory and merely review what was said in the seminars, but others are retrospective—Rittel's own notes following the seminars whose transcripts are presented here.

The seminar series was widely attended by the faculty of the CED, as recalled by seminar attendee Donald Olsen, a professor of architecture and colleague of Rittel's (whose introduction to the seminar series is included). It is, essentially, a snapshot of Rittel's overall idea of design at the time he first came to Berkeley.

The second section, which is also the shortest, looks at Rittel's best-known idea: that of wicked problems, and places in it the context of his reasoning. The well-known article on wicked problems does not cover some of the important related ideas like the paradoxes of rationality. "On the Planning Crisis," in addition to discussing the properties of wicked problems, also examines a number of other ideas that were central to his work—most notably the idea of the first and second generations of design theory, but also such ideas as the paradoxes of rationality, and the symmetry of ignorance.[10] It is a minor curiosity that this article suggests 11 distinct properties that define tame/wicked problems, in contrast to the more famous Rittel and Webber article "Dilemmas in a General Theory of Planning," which lists ten properties. This variation helps reveal that Rittel was himself unsure to what extent it was possible to define different aspects of the issues that define problems.

The third section considers the structure of the reasoning involved in design projects. Rittel, in trying to develop systems to handle the problems relevant to wicked problems, begins to specify the different aspects of the reasoning that informs a design process, and starts to look at ways to understand and characterize this reasoning that allows it to be better understood and better communicated. The three articles in this section look at the same basic issues from three different angles. The first—the "Structure and Usefulness of Planning Information Systems" article gives a theoretical overview of the issues involved. It was a companion piece to the publication of "On the Planning Crisis," and as such has a similar level of generality. Second in the section, we present "Issues as Elements of Information Systems." This article takes a more technical perspective—that of trying to introduce the IBIS, a system "meant to support coordination and planning of political decision processes." It is a practical article for a practical system, intended for implementation and practical purposes. But underlying the practical system is a theory that describes the design process as consisting of a process of argumentation structured by the use of issues, positions, and arguments.

The third article in the section looks at the same ideas from the perspective of the individual reasoner/designer. In "The Reasoning of Designers," Rittel uses the same argumentative structure that he developed in the IBIS, but the focus is now on what is inside the designer's head. This is a later work, presented near the end of his career. It shows much of the same logic that was used to develop the IBIS, but the logic has been turned inwards: it is no longer a tool by which to work with design—it is the fundamental process by which design proceeds.

The fourth and final section looks at the consequences of design: what happens when plans are implemented? In this section there are two articles: one that looks at the impact of technological change on urban structure and culture, and another that looks at the failures or pathologies of design.

Written near the end of his life, the article on technological change explores the ramifications of employing new technologies throughout society, with an interest to show how the implications of new designs and new technologies can reach far beyond the simple performance of the design itself.

The second piece is an article written by J. P. Protzen on Rittel's pathologies of design. No longer is the focus on how to create a design system that guarantees success (the optimistic underpinning of his earliest work). Instead we see the effort to recognize the various personal aspects of the design process—the types of reasoning designers use that lead to significant failures.

A brief Epilogue closes the book with a discussion of where these ideas will take us.

A few notes on editorial practices

Firstly, as concerns the use of notes: in most of Rittel's work, Rittel himself used notes sparingly. All of Rittel's notes are identified as his; unmarked notes are ours.

Second, in editing, we have taken the liberty of correcting obvious errors and rehabilitating incomplete or incoherent sentences, without indicating every alteration. While a purist might wish to see every word that we saw in reviewing the seminar transcripts and old typescripts, we opted for ease and flow of reading, as well as expression of Rittel's ideas as best we understood them.

Third, Rittel often cited works or authors in his work without giving complete references; this is especially true for the seminar series, but affects the unpublished works as well. We have attempted to find appropriate references for these citations or exemplary works from cited authors who are not well known. While we have retained as separate the reference lists that Rittel himself generated, we have also attempted to find sources that match Rittel's references that are not complete citations, and included these citations as part of Rittel's reference list.

Fourth, in the seminar series, in which our source was a written transcript of an audio recording, we have attempted to leave in the emphases as placed by the original transcriber—sometimes all capitals, sometimes underlining, sometimes exclamation marks—as these seem to give a better sense of Rittel's voice.

Finally, in the translations, where a word in Rittel's original German does not translate well into English, it has been retained (in parentheses) in parallel with the proposed translation.

Notes

1 As one measure of their currency as an idea, we note that "wicked problems" have an entry in Wikipedia.
2 This is how Rittel defined it in his lecture notes for the course Architecture 130, Introduction to Design Theories and Methods, in the Department of Architecture at The University of California, Berkeley, in 1968. Rittel continued using that definition in his work and in his teaching (including Arch. 130) until the end of his life.
3 For example, in the *Oxford English Dictionary*, the first definition of "design" given is "a mental plan."
4 The reader will find that Horst Rittel early on made a distinction between science *of, for,* and *in* design in Seminar 1 of *Science and Design* included in this collection.
5 Today's Haas School of Business.
6 From a speech at the opening of an exhibit on the "Study of Architecture" at Stuttgart on 24 October 1979.
7 In "The Reasoning of Designers," found in this volume.
8 A perspective that is reflected both by Rittel's own bibliography and a list of works that cite his ideas.
9 See Rith and Dubberly 2007.
10 Rittel's symmetry of ignorance: "nobody knows better by virtue of his degrees or his status" (see "On the Planning Crisis" in this volume).

Part One

Foundations

This first section is the longest in the text. Its work is to lay the foundations—the basic premises—for Rittel's research. Though there is a clear evolution in Rittel's work as he develops new ideas and changes old ones, there is yet a basic foundation that is consistent. Rittel, throughout, is committed to the use of clear, sound logic—conscious rationality in all its strengths. Indeed, it is his careful use of rationality and logic that guides him to his later conclusions. Throughout his career, he considers the same basic question: what can we learn from a rational examination of the process of design? We can see the basic answers laid out in a schematic form in the first article in the section, "Reflections on the Scientific and Political Significance of Decision Theory," which is also the earliest work in this collection, and then explored in much greater detail in the seminar series, another early work. The seminar series also presents many of the philosophers and philosophical perspectives that influenced Rittel: it defines his basic questions, and the primary sources that shaped them.

In a way, these articles are Rittel's history; they provide both a foundation and a beginning. More generally, we can see these works of Rittel as paralleling the history of the study of design methods; in the terminology of the prologue, we can see them as defining the beginning of the reflective phase of design theories. The first conference in the field was held one year after the decision theory article was published, and just two years before the seminar series was held. For Rittel, and others, design had become the object of study, thus initiating the reflective phase.

This section starts by looking at the basic ideas that are necessary to consider how decisions are made, and how this interacts with the basic propositions of the first generation. The first article by Rittel that we discuss (mentioned above) is rooted in Rittel's assumption of the value of science, and his commitment to apply those rational principles that he sees as lying beneath the progress that has been made in practical applications (he is not yet speaking of design theory at the time of writing this article).

But, he says, this use of scientific reasoning ought to be amenable to scientific study. And this reasoning is what drives his practice as he moves forward to his later works. Here, in this early article, he is just starting down this path. He can see that there may be significant issues in the "scientification" in decision-making. This is seen in his concern for politics, reflected in the title of the article. And so his aim in this article is to lay out the concerns that he sees in this use of science in the realm of decision-making. As he notes, when one is no longer looking only to describe, but rather is looking to create and change, it is no longer pure science.

In addition to presenting the fundamental issues that he will examine through his career, he also describes the basic method that he intends to use, and will use through his career, to drive his examination: the scientific method as applied to the study of scientific design. He is looking at design as if the process itself was the subject of his scientific study.

In the "Science and Design" seminars, he has begun to explicitly consider design rather than decision-making. It is here that he lays out in great detail both his intended program of research—to which he remains fundamentally true during the rest of his career—as well as many of the ideas that provided the context according to which he reasoned about the problems of design. In the seminars we can see him bring in the ideas of many of those who influenced him, most notably Karl Popper and Kenneth Boulding.

We can also see an optimism that matches the mood of the decision theory article. This optimism is reserved—he can already see potential problems—but it is an optimism that is still present—a belief that the scientific systems will be of great value, and that rationality will guide the way out of the difficulties.

There is no reason to believe he lost this belief in the possibility that scientific systems would add great value, nor that we should do our best to use rationality whenever possible. But as his studies took him further, he began to see that the area in which rationality was applicable began to shrink, as he realized that more and more—and ultimately all—decisions had a political element. Even in the 1961 article he struggles with this, but the full ramifications are not yet apparent. It is, perhaps, a parallel to Wittgenstein's conclusion to the *Tractatus*, a conclusion that so reduces the value of work on one path that we must be silent, and thus the work that follows is forced to take a different path and to work from different conclusions. But in these early works he is not yet envisioning the "second generation" of design theories that he will propose later; he is still setting the groundwork that will eventually lead him to the conclusion that such new design theories are necessary.

Chapter 1.1

Reflections on the Scientific and Political Significance of Decision Theory[1]

Horst W. J. Rittel

I

The sciences of operations research, cybernetics, information theory, game theory, and systems engineering—to name only the most important ones—developed in the last two decades, share common approaches and overlap in many ways. This is no surprise if we think about their origin. They all are children of World War II. It started with the enrollment of scientists to solve the novel organizational and technological problems of modern warfare, which exceeded the competence of the military and engineers. The development of radar, the support and supply of continental battlefields and the planning of strategies created planning and decision problems that could not be solved with a sufficiently high guarantee of success using conventional techniques. The results of this scientific cooperation are not only new technologies—for example technologies of communication, data processing, or astronautics—but these first efforts also led to new, independent sciences that not only find increasingly "peaceful" applications but also have become important and necessary tools in planning, politics and development. In the USA, for example, there are today tens of thousands of scientists engaged in these new fields and several hundreds of millions of dollars are spent every year in the promotion and, especially, the application of these technologies.

   The commonalities of the named disciplines may be explained by the situation that gave rise to them: they were invented for situations with a pressing need for action in which the scientist acted not only as consultant in the traditional way, but became a co-responsible decision maker. There are several motivations for this:

- Too much is at stake: the costs of failure are so high that it is well worth the cost of using the very best means to justify[2] one's decisions, or even to develop new methods to do so (e.g. in problems of defense strategies, development of third world countries, projects of atomic technologies and space travel).

- The problem cannot be solved by conventional means: it is too large and too complex (e.g. the space program).
- One seeks more rational and cheaper ways (e.g. automation).
- One seeks to shield a system against catastrophes caused by inadequacies and mistakes (e.g. a defense system against Herostratos and randomness, an economy against crisis).
- One wants to know which goals reasonably to pursue; one realizes that the political and ideological goals are too coarse and too pat to yield instructions for concrete and far-reaching decisions: historical philosophical programs less and less provide practicable norms for political decisions (e.g. development planning or defense policies).

In addition there is the conviction that, in view of these difficulties, the scientific methods are useful and promising. This assumption is inherent in the age of "scientification," even though it smacks of a positivist philosophy: science that claims objectivity in the name of a last authority is dangerously close to an uninhibited belief in progress. The justification of the scientification can be inferred from its effects: the scientific method, especially that of the natural sciences, has become the most effective tool for shaping reality:

> Science spread like a disease . . . Precise methods can never again be shaken off
>
> (O. Morgenstern)[3]

> The attitude that places the rational sciences and technology at the heart of thinking offers a better chance for survival than the sullen annoyance over technology that often characterizes the western intellectual!
>
> (Steinbuch 1961: 3)

The scientific method is the modern equivalent of Spinoza's program to investigate the world "more geometrico."

The new tendency towards an "engaged science" has, however, not been without consequences for science and its ideology. The classic ideal of science gave it a single task: to gain knowledge (*Erkenntnisse*), for only new knowledge signifies progress in an absolute sense and it therefore becomes desirable "for its own sake." The applicability of this knowledge is not a problem for the sciences; it will show itself. Science forms its own reality; it is an autonomous province separate from the "extra scientific" world.

This ideal has proven quite effective. The institution of science as a generator of "innovation" isolated from the vagaries of events has become an important element of modern social systems.

The new disciplines to be discussed here, however, represent a type of science that does not fit the classical program:

- Knowledge is no longer sought for its own sake—without any consideration of its later uses—but in view of concrete tasks;
- Its results should be to generate recommendations for action;
- The scientist is an active participant in planning and decision-making.

The decision-making process thus becomes itself an object for scientific investigation. One could doubt whether such an activity deserves to be called a science. If one does it anyway, this means a revision of the concept of science that makes the traditional ideal an extreme case. The basis of such a theory of science cannot simply be an epistemology, because knowledge is only one component of action. Neither can a linguistic theory of science (*sprachanlytische Wissenschaftstheorie*) fulfill that role. What would be required here as a foundation is a theory of action (*Handlungslehre*), which recognizes knowledge as a presupposition for action. A science in this broader sense, however, would lose many of its hitherto typical characteristics:

> A science that goes that far gives up its objectivity as well as its immunity
> . . . The science of tomorrow will not be objective . . . the future science
> will not be politically immune.[4]

The above expressed apprehension of a camouflaged positivism is invalidated—or at least moderated—by such a concept of science. If the institution of science abandons its apodictic claim to objectivity and if it accepts that it, including its goals and values, is subject to historical change and the play of forces, it loses the character of a patent ideology and of a rigid, absolute authority.

II

Efforts to draw the consequences, to systematize the above-mentioned new disciplines according to their commonalities and singularities, and to relate the whole to the system of the traditional sciences, are not lacking. There is a whole series of proposals for overarching concepts and collective terminologies, but none of them has imposed itself thus far. Contrary to the specification of the domain of objects of the traditional sciences (physics, economics), the new disciplines are characterized by the arbitrariness (*Beliebigkeit*) of their objects (cybernetic considerations are appropriate for economic as well as for biological phenomena), wherefore, a classification according to approaches and methods seems to be more appropriate. One can suspect that collective names such as "general methodology," "systems sciences," or "praxeology" (Kotarbinski, Lange) might impose themselves. One could argue that the naming is irrelevant, what counts are the results. But names are programs. In the name is that which is named. And on the name for this theory of action (*Handlungslehre*) depends its role. A negative example may prove the point: if it has become the norm in German to translate "operations research" as "*Unternehmungsforschung*" (the science of firms), one can understand this in times of economic growth, but the designation obscures, if not excludes, the non-economic application of this discipline (e.g. its application to city and regional planning, to research planning, to politics).

The science to be discussed here is a science of action, specifically of rational action (*"zweckrationales"* Handeln, Max Weber). Such a science is at the same time:

- deductive (as mathematics is), in that it draws conclusions from an axiomatic system and construes models for types of actions;
- inductive (as physics is) in that it hypothesizes from empirical observations, which become the foundation for the formation of theories;
- instrumental (as is engineering) in that it develops means and methods for applications for concrete situations;
- pragmatic, in that it continuously considers the applicability and participates itself in its application (as in medicine).

Such a science has a "meta-scientific" character in that:

- it belongs to none of the existing sciences;
- it concerns many of the existing sciences;
- it may include as its object the approaches of the sciences;
- it develops new methods;
- it provides an adequate language to speak about science and to conduct research on research;
- it occasionally allows the transfer of indications from one science to another;
- it uncovers structural relationships of diverse sciences;
- it investigates the relations between research, development and implementation, mediates between science and application, and dissolves the opposition of theory to practice.

Such a science is by its nature interdisciplinary. From the beginning on, representatives from the most diverse backgrounds participated in the new disciplines: engineers, mathematicians, biologists, economists, sociologists, political scientists, physicists, and philosophers. Apart from graduate programs in Operations Research, there exists today hardly any education for these new disciplines, such that they are carried on and developed by the most diverse group of specialists. Optimists and enthusiasts may see in this development the chance for the restoration of the much mourned *universitas litterarum*.

III

As intimated, there does not exist today such a meta-science in a rigorous and closed form. There are only trials and tendencies. The current state-of-the-art reveals two major directions, two areas of concentration, which one can subsume under the designations of "systems research" and "decision theory."

The object examined by systems research is the behavior of systems. A system is a multi-variable entity (an information system, a production process, an ecology, a biological organism, a military organization). The behavior of systems is described by the temporal succession of their states. Systems are made of components that are linked together, that is, they exchange effects. This interaction of effects is not represented as material or energy flows; in contrast to the classical physical or technological systems, one considers information flows. Information is the substratum that is transported and transformed (e.g. a message, not an energy flow). This peculiarity results from the intention to study primarily the organization, governance, control, and regulation of any particular system. Systems research does not limit itself to the observation of existing systems. Its primary intention is to design new systems, which are to accomplish a given purpose or mission. In this, the determination of an adequate division of labor between humans and mechanical components in so-called "human-machine systems" is an important consideration. The categories of systems theory such as "determination," "stability," "feed-back," "complexity," "self-organization," and "learning," are in fact such that they allow characterization of the most diverse systems. Theories of design and planning and of heuristics belong equally to systems theory. Systems research encompasses large parts of cybernetics, operations research, communication theory, and parts of game theory, as well as results from human engineering, psychology, information technology and modern statistics.

Decision theory, on the other hand, can be understood as comprising all those activities that are concerned with the problem of selecting appropriate means to transform a given situation into another situation which satisfies the goals and intentions of an "actor" as best as possible. The class of decision-making situations so described reaches from that of the politician, the economist or the military to that of the researcher, or even the chess player. "Risk," "strategy," "utility," "rationality," "expectation," and "goal" are concepts that are relevant for all these situations.

This dichotomy of today's state of "praxeology," as already mentioned, refers to only its foci of development. It goes without saying that a decision maker, including his or her environment, can also be considered a system; and that the design of a system involves a sequence of decisions.

What follows will primarily concentrate on what here has been called decision theory.

IV

The study of decision-making was until now in the domain of philosophy, theology history, and, to a certain extent, also psychology. The question about the "nature" of decision relegated the problems of technique and practice of decision-making into the background. The philosophy of "practical reason" has found little interest in the last decades. The reaching of a decision was rarely the object of scientific consideration. The ability to reach difficult decisions was considered the privilege of an endowed personality. It was thought that this ability could hardly be learned; that there could not be any rules or recipes for it. Farsightedness, reflectivity, sense of responsibility were factors that defied all specification. Decision rules as proposed by Machiavelli were considered immoral and cynical, the maxims of moral philosophy as trivial and self-evident. For the daily use the "common sense" was seen as entirely sufficient. Athletes who make consequential and difficult decisions and the hero of solitary judgments are held in high esteem, the "decision happy" personality with decades of experience is in high demand, as demonstrated by the job advertisements in big daily newspapers.

In the face of this opinion, anyone who approaches the phenomenon of decision-making scientifically, specifically in the manner of the natural sciences, is suspected of defining decision as something that in no way corresponds to its "essence" or "true nature." Obviously, it is not a question of simply transferring natural science concepts—even if there are tempting analogies. One would too easily arrive at proscribed biologisms. Such notions as the "battle of survival," "natural growth," and so forth, should at least be kept out of the basic considerations. As already mentioned above, only the modes of thinking and of drawing conclusions of natural science should be transferred and used.

However, the question, whether the objects of such an approach actually, or even only possibly, correspond to decisions as commonly understood, cannot be ignored. The use of natural science concepts often involves shifts and narrowing of meanings (think of how during the last century the concepts of force and energy have gained in precision). The clarification of concepts is necessary, be it only to avoid endless arguments about whether the concepts really capture what they stand for.

In fact, the object "decision" brings about some curious consequences for its scientific treatment. For one thing, each scientific activity is itself a sequence of decisions. These decisions depend on value systems that are proper to science. Already the choice of research objects deemed "scientifically interesting," the formation of concepts, the establishment of norms for scientific correctness, all rest on "pre-scientific" conventions and traditions that are nothing but established value systems. Since a science of decision necessarily contains a science of values, is it possible to methodologically isolate a specific value system, namely that of science? In that case, does one not—in unexpressed or even unadmitted ways—assign superiority to this special value system over all other value systems, a superiority, which, by its own standards is unjustified?

Without resolving this paradox one may say that the "scientifically more appropriate" point of view is one which also includes the scientific value system in its consideration and which foregoes its claim to absolute objectivity. Even the scientific value system is subject to change, has its place in the conflicts of value systems, and the scientist *nolens volens* is a political player in the resulting disputes. This, of course, applies to any science, but even more so to a Science of Decision.

In view of more recent political developments, there is a lot of discussion about the increasing influence of scientists on politics. In particular the influence of "consultants" on world-political decisions of the USA has triggered many critical remarks about academic "know-alls." This development, nevertheless, will continue, as there is no alternative in view. The institution of science has changed. The inevitable consequence of the scientification of politics is the politicization of science.

V

Before addressing the question of what should be understood by a decision, one needs to take a stand on one of the following two points of view:

(a) the point of view of the external observer, who studies the behavior of a decision-making system from "outside" without participation;

(b) the point of view of the "decision maker": the scientist has to decide her or himself, or she or he has to take the side of the decision maker.

Both cases are about the determination of an object system (O-System); in the first case one wants to understand that is, predict, the behavior of the decision-making system. In the second case the object system is to be transformed in some intended fashion through active behavior. Determination means reduction of uncertainty. This can be achieved through the improvement of the predictive abilities or through active intervention.

In case (a) it is the question of empirically ascertaining the rules of the decision behavior of an O-system. This is done by constructing a model of a given object that contains the knowledge about the system. This model is sufficient if, from the knowledge of past situation, it allows the derivation, that is, prediction, of the object's behavior in future situations. For this purpose one must seek the determinants that govern the behavior of the O-System. If one takes the behaviorist—or more neutrally expressed—the behavior-theoretical point of view, this information can be gleaned from the observed behavior. Under these circumstances, when is it possible to say that a behavior pattern is driven by decisions? Is decision not a concept that is derived from introspection, which only by analogy may be transferred onto subjects we are used to considering "the likes-of-us"? There are light and heavy decisions, yet the energy consumption is small and hardly noticeable to an external observer. The energetic determination of an act of decision is as good as impossible; there remains only the communication-theoretical approach. Decision processes, therefore, must be derived from the object behavior's order and structure that describes the state succession, the so-called behavior trajectory. If one imagines the manifold of possible states as a geometric space, then the behavior of a system can be mapped as a path in this space. The individual stations of this path are parametrically marked by time. Seen in retrospect, it is clear that this path forms a simple trajectory without branches. However, this is different if the behavior trajectory is to be extrapolated into the future. The expected prolongations of the already realized trajectory will then fan out. This fan will be the narrower the more precise the knowledge about the observed system is. With increasing distance from the starting point, that is, with the increasing length of the time interval over which the forecast is to be made, the more divergent the fan becomes. These forecasting fans are the consequences of imperfect determination.

There also exist cases in which the prognostic fan consists of only a few branches, which can easily be distinguished and considered alternative branches of the already covered trajectory.

If in the previous case each trajectory could be weighted with various degrees of expectation (there exists a "most probable" path), now each path has a high expectation. The experimenter or observer cannot possibly derive the path that will be followed from the past behavior. Such branching points in future trajectories will be called decision situations. They are singular points in the model of the object behavior.

If one accepts this interpretation, it follows that dice and the rat in the laboratory of the psychologist are making decisions. Their behavior shows such singularities of choices out of a discrete number of alternatives. That is not surprising. The die is designed to have six stable balance states, which are reached over a great manifold of trajectories. These trajectories, however, depend unstably and in complicated ways on the initial conditions of the throw of the die, so that one has the worst preconditions for a forecast. For this reason, a die is well suited as a partner in social games or also as an oracle. And the labyrinth is purposefully arranged to impose on the rat discrete alternatives. The biologist is playing against the rat. In some ways he is betting on its behavior. The rat loses its decision-making system as soon as it has learned its task and thus behaves predictably. There are a number of behaviorist's jokes: the rat, after having learned its task, can say that from "its point of view" it has conditioned the experimenter. For then the rat "has brought the experimenter so far" that every time it runs through the labyrinth he will provide it with food.

The points of decisions of the object system are thus determined by the model of the observer; they are the points of alternative expectation of behavior. If the model contains such points, then every decision of the object system programs a piece of its behavior trajectory by executing a single trajectory among those offered, or considered possible, by the observer. From the point of view of (a) decision theory seeks the motivation for this behavior, that is, the determinants to correct the object model. The better it succeeds, the more the object loses for the observer its ability to "decide."

VI

In case (b) the circumstances are different. An "actor system" (A-System) finds itself in a position where it must program an "object system's" (O-System) behavior. One may say it is forced to act, especially if one considers non-action, "passing," as a behavior or action. A decision-making situation exists when a choice has to be made among a variety of alternatives. When such a situation arises depends again on the A-System; it can stop at any time and search alternatives, or it can let itself carried away by the inertia of its prior behavior. It appears that it is a psychological characteristic of a decision process that it is performed "consciously" and not blindly.

Once the alternatives are established, one could leave the burden of decision to a mechanism, say a die or an oracle. Such is, however, rarely to be recommended, only when there are absolutely no reasons to decide in favor of a specific alternative. Otherwise, one searches for, and weighs, arguments until the symmetry of helplessness in face of the alternatives dissolves itself in favor of one of them. It is precisely one of the characteristics of conscious decisions that its preparation is determined by the construction of its own problematic. This process of "motivation" continues, until it becomes clear that the final choice has to be made that way and no other. It would be "irrational" to choose another alternative than this one.

Decisions without motive seem hardly to exist. In André Gide's *Les*

Caves du Vatican,[5] its hero, Lafcadio, tries in vain to perform the "acte gratuit." The enterprise to plant an unmotivated crime into this world fails. As long as no perpetrator is unmasked, society will search for motives until a plausible perpetrator is found—even if it is not the "true" perpetrator. He will be considered the true perpetrator until society's legal authorities find a more plausible perpetrator. The whole of criminology and history is based on this.

It is the task of decision theory to elaborate adequate alternatives and to reduce the uncertainty of choice until an unequivocal advantage emerges for a specific alternative. It goes without saying that this, of course, does not exclude faulty decisions. Naturally, the motivation process can rely only on the existing knowledge of what the A-system deems worthwhile pursuits and the existing knowledge of O-system's behavior. The latter may be gained from point-of-view (a).

For what follows point-of-view (b) will be adopted. Of course, all real cases are a mixture of (a) and (b), for there are no purely uninvolved observers (almost no observation is without repercussion on the [thing] observed) and any action is based on experience, which was gained from observation.

VII

To arrive at models of decision processes one appeals to a methodological trick. One imagines that one delegates the decision-making to a "machine" and asks what such a machine would be like, what data one would have to feed it, etc. This is to be understood as a paradigm only and does not mean to actually delegate the decision to a machine. This mental model has become a useful tool for elucidating what is meant by "learning," "intelligence," "perception," or "decision." Such a "machine" reflects the state of knowledge about these processes and properties. It shows behaviors that are "homomorphous" to our representations as formulated. By comparing the machine's behavior with the "intended" one can refine the representations and formulations of the intended. What can be formulated as rules of behavior trajectories can—at least in principle—be mechanized.

Yet the actual delegation to a machine is also gaining in significance. One programs a computer according to a decision model and lets it reckon the consequences of the various strategies (e.g. sequences of actions). Or one lets the machine take over the role of the object system and one "plays against it." Even in cases in which one cannot entrust the machine with the task of determining the "optimal" decision—this is at this time only possible for standard types of decision tasks—there exists a large class of problems in which machines can be used with success to simulate "cases of emergency." The simulation techniques are the modern version of the sandboxes of the classical military general staff. They have become a valuable tool for training and education (business games, simulation of air-traffic controls or of a pilot's cockpit, teaching machines, etc.).

VIII

Hence, a decision model is a homomorphous representation of a decision situation or a class of such situations. It consists of the following components:

- an actor system (A-System) that must make a decision;
- an object system (O-System) that is influenced by the decision.

The A-System may be an individual, a group, or an organization that is understood as a system of people, machines and rules.

The O-System is the opposite side, the object, the contracting party, the enemy, or also a friend with whom the A-System must collaborate. Sometimes it is useful to attribute active agency to the O-System, especially when O has such reactions vis-à-vis the measures taken by A that could be interpreted as "interest oriented".

As a rule, all the elements (people, machines, etc.) that are under the control of A (i.e. that can be relied on to implement A's decisions) belong to the A-System. (The issue of unreliability within A's own ranks creates special problems.)

The data and relationships that enter the model can be classified as follows:

- the variables under the control of A. These variables determine the decision space, i.e. the manifold of alternatives. For a decision situation to exist it must contain more than just one alternative. Of course, the decision space contains only those alternatives that have been identified by, and that lie within the finite potential of A;
- the variables of O that are of significance to A, and whose states are observable or can be indirectly established;
- the regularities (constrictions) in the behavior of O as a function of the observables. These encompass e.g. all the scientific knowledge about O's behavior and represent A's "image" of O;
- the expectations about the effect of A's actions. It represents all the knowledge about the influence of the variables controlled by A on the essential variables of O, that is, the functional relationships that connect the two types of variables. These expectations are mostly marred by uncertainties;
- a goal or an intention of A, which determines which states of O are to be achieved or avoided, or which establishes ranking of desirability of possible states of O. Here one must distinguish a gross goal function, which evaluates only the states of O, from a net goal function, in which the costs of achieving a certain state of O are deducted from the value of that state;
- a point of view or an attitude of A vis-à-vis the decision situation that can be formulated as a so-called decision criterion. A can act cautiously, recklessly, pessimistically, skeptically, etc. This reflects A's attitude towards risk, uncertainty and his own ignorance. The decision criteria are relationships between degrees of regarding the expectations about effects and the assessment of the situation. The decision criteria bring the "psychology" of A into play;
- rules of behavior that exclude certain of A's actions, even though they would be within the realm of A's potential, or promise some direct benefits. This includes social norms, ethical principles, and the like. Such restrictions can also be construed as limitations of A's action space. If, nevertheless, these restrictions are mentioned separately, it characterizes them as independent factors of influence.

Each of the above mentioned determinants has its own difficulties. The variables may be measured on a variety of scales (nominal, ordinal, difference, or ratio scales); the relationships may be logical relations, probability distributions, differential functions and so on.

A mathematical model at this level of consideration is not very useful. At best one can arrive at some conditions for the formulation of singular entities and relationships. Mathematical models become useful only when investigating specific classes of decision situations (two-person, zero-sum games; transportation problems; problems of regulation).

Mathematics start only after all the named variables and relationships are appropriately determined. The process of identifying the determinants, that is, the construction of a model, is based on empirical investigations; that is to say, one needs adequate concepts and methods of measurement. Thus, serious and numerous problems arise with the specification of each determinant. The efforts made in this direction to date alone justify decision theory, since they allow the description of very complicated and realistic decision situations—even if a subsequent mathematization is not yet possible. This anatomy of decision processes brings their properties to attention. It permits the discrimination between cases and their characteristics. For example, strict antagonistic two-person games will rarely be found in reality. Most conflict situations also show co-operative traits. Nevertheless, the mathematical models of these extreme cases, together with other extreme cases, set a range within which one finds the real situations in mixed forms, with the possibility of assigning them a "degree of agonality."

In what follows, some considerations along these lines will demonstrate the ways of thinking and the difficulties of decision theory.

IX

Let us take the question of A's goals or intentions. It will be answered as soon as it is known what values are to be attributed to the individual states of the O and A systems. Add to this the imperative: "seek to achieve the state that according to this scale yields the highest value." Apart from the fact that an actor quite often "does not know himself what he wants," there remain numerous difficulties:

- What point in time is to be considered? Or is it a sequence of situations, a time frame that is to be evaluated? How are this year's expected results (profits) to be offset against those expected next year? How much hardship are the presently living willing to bear for a higher expectation of happiness for their great-grandchildren? What is a reasonable planning interval? How are the values of different states at different times to be compared?
- Real situations distinguish themselves by their multi-variability, i.e. by the manifold of aspects by which they are evaluated. Apartments are not only evaluated according to their rent, but also by their layout (plan), location, thermal insulation, etc. A military situation is not only assessed by one's own and the enemy's losses. Each dollar of a fixed amount that is spent in support of a research project necessarily is withheld from all other projects. And the economic success

of a firm is not measured only by its profits, but also its liquidity, market share, order portfolio, competition, etc. Most of the time a situation is characterized by "but—but" statements: "but with regard to this other aspect, it is the reverse that holds". Which situation is to be preferred? How can the "vector" of evaluations under different aspects be mapped on a linear scale?

- Another difficulty arises because the—necessarily subjective—conceptions of utility of different people are not additive. The reason for this is that the "degree" of pain or of well-being is not communicable. There is no way to compare the degree of satisfaction of different people. In measurement, theoretically speaking, utility scales are difference scales with arbitrarily set units and zero points, and therefore without any means to compare the fixed points of two subjective scales (as opposed to the Fahrenheit and Celsius scales).

- This is especially significant when establishing social utility functions. How does the utility of the individual weigh in with the utility of the collective? How is the utility function of an institution derived from the utility functions of its members? The decades-long efforts of economists to define a "social welfare function" were not very successful.

- Yet social utility functions are needed to establish the value of a research institute, an urban park, a public transport system. A given situation always has utility for a given A-system. In the examples given above, the A-system certainly is not an individual nor a profit-oriented institution.

- A goal has the form: "A wishes to accomplish X," where X usually is only a partial aspect of an overall situation. The other aspects of this situation are by no means indifferent, unless X is to be accomplished "at any price." A positively formulated goal implies a whole range of unexpressed conditions which exclude many ways to attain the goal. To establish a goal function, all the implicit conditions need to be formulated. An example will demonstrate this difficulty. If the goal is to "augment the per capita agricultural food production," this goal can be achieved by raising productivity, by expanding the acreage devoted to agriculture, but also by the reduction of the population. To exclude the last two possibilities, many more conditions and sub-goals are necessary.

- Political and ideological goals (raising the general standard of living, promotion of private property, establishment of a communist society, securing world peace, the greatest good for the greatest number, completion of history) generally lack in the precision and enumeration of their conditions and sub-goals. They demand the fulfillment of certain demands made of an end-situation without mentioning what path will lead there, and without specifying the "costs" of this path. One may, at times, deviate from the direct path, or even increase the distance to the goal, only to reach the goal more efficiently, or only because the circumstances demand it: the restriction of freedom for the sake of preserving freedom, limited warfare to avoid an unlimited war, today's deprivation for tomorrow's happiness. Goals of the mentioned type contain no instruction about the means to accomplish them. One cannot derive from them any advice for the behavior here and now. That is the reason for the astonishing fact that states with fundamentally divergent ideologies show—*in concreto*—very similar behaviors. The same problematic points to the numerous historical examples of terror in the name of the noblest ideals.

- Even moral systems considered as situation-independent norms of behavior are not sufficient to specify the path to reach the goals. First, they provide primarily prohibitions and not commandments; second, decision situations—especially the problematic ones—are such that moral principles come into conflict. That is the drama of the Schiller type (the obligations towards the home land and the family, and towards humanity and its individual representative create contradictory demands), or the Sartre type (the problem of "dirty hands": there is no alternative without blemish).

Many of these difficulties have been treated by the modern decision theory. There are methods, models, and conceptual frameworks aplenty to discover goals, to measure utility and to analyze value systems. Yet we are still far away from having satisfactorily researched and ordered the whole complex of issues.

Bernoulli (in 1735) may have been the first to attempt the construction of a utility theory. He tried to determine the "moral utility" of money, which he understood to be of subjective value. He argued that the value is not proportional to the amount of money, but that its utility per unit decreases with every additional unit. He made some fundamental assumptions and derived from them a kind of marginal utility principle. His theory is normative, like all the utility theories in the next 200 years—including the Gossen marginal utility theory.[6] Only in 1950, with the work of Mosteller and Nogee,[7] inspired by the work of von Neumann and Morgenstern, was an effort made to measure utility: the theory of utility and value become an empirical science. It became evident that the multitude of human desires could not be derived from a few principles which could be considered as "generally human." There is nothing like a "minimal need" valid for all human kind, nor any agreement as to what "happiness" is. With this insight, the theory of values becomes much more complicated, but also more realistic. A "descriptive history of value systems" remains to be developed. The sketches of the necessary analytical apparatus and a few normative models already exist, at least for some simple cases.

X

The large number of gigantic planning tasks with long-term effects, such as those encountered in the military, but increasingly also in economic and technological developments, have brought the problems of goal formulation to high prominence. The subsequent well-funded research in this domain yielded a series of fundamental insights that substantially changed the focus of inquiry and understanding of goal-oriented decision-making.

Traditional maxims for action, such as "maximizing profits, national security, power build-up," are useful at most for short-term, narrowly defined decision situations. For larger decision tasks they are useless, not only because uncertainty increases with the time span of the planning interval (the prognostic ability to estimate risks diminishes rapidly) and the range of possible alternatives shrinks, but also because this kind of maxim loses its meaning. This holds particularly in times of rapid change of political conditions and technological options. Even value systems can no longer be seen as stable over longer time spans. What can be wanted and what can be achieved depends on what one wants. Goals and utility functions are not independent and autonomous orders. They stand in interaction with the decision space. And the range in which values can be changed is considerable (think of the "need generation" for consumer goods).

In view of the uncertainties of alternative "futures," constructing rigid decision models which would yield strategies over a longer time span is a hopeless task, no matter the care with which one tries to determine an "optimal action sequence," by considering a great number of variables, well-balanced goal functions and great number of alternatives. Such an optimal strategy would make all the considered actions dependent on *all* eventualities

It would be more appropriate to see the decision problem in more general terms and to consider the organization and aptitude of decision-making systems: what are the characteristics of an organization that can cope with the uncertainties brought about by the already-mentioned innovations and political changes? Here, decision theory and "systems research" become intimately intertwined. The "natural" goal functions are now replaced by such goals as "stability," "ultra-stability," "adaptability." Instead of adopting a specific decision-making system and value system, one investigates the aptitude of a system to accomplish its tasks:

- What kinds of feed-back from and to the object system are required? What kinds of data about the object system are needed, and with what precision? What kind of device is needed to process the data?
- Which value systems are consistent and non-contradictory?
- Which value systems provide a chance for "adaptation" and hence for "survival"?
- In view of unknown "futures", which "innovation policies" (i.e. policies for the expansion of the decision space) should be pursued?

Some examples for this type of problem: It would be nonsense to design today an educational system based on an estimate of the demand for electrical engineers, biochemists and so on, in the year 2000. An optimization under this point of view would, in view of shifts in demands due to an unpredictable development, soon be falsified. Instead one should seek an educational system that is capable of adapting to a changing demand.

Or: In the USA research is conducted under government contract that seeks to find out what attitudes and value systems the population should adopt to improve political and economic stability, that is, to reduce the susceptibility to disturbances. Included in these considerations are even such deep-rooted attitudes as the "attitude towards death." "Survival" alone, as a long-term motto, is useless. To this same context belongs a program to raise the "economic awareness" of the US population through, for example, carefully and professionally designed TV courses on national economy aimed at improving insights into the mechanics of the national economy and thus reducing the susceptibility to crises. The program is based on the assumption that economic crises are to a large extent the result of "false" reactions by individuals which trigger "snowball effects," and the assumption that a widely shared knowledge of these conditions and their consequences could dampen, or even dissolve, the almost law-of-nature-like course of such crises.

Another example: the political governance of a major modern state needs a high decision capacity, namely, a variety of important decisions per time unit need to be made with as little delay between the decision and its implementation. For this a great number of receptors are needed, which transmit the messages to the decision-making systems. In the USA, the continuous processing of this data stream into intelligible messages is mechanized to a large extent. The data transmission systems and the processing centers guarantee the necessary reaction speed and therefore the stability of the decision capacity. These systems must, of course, be protected against failure and destruction to diminish their susceptibility. To this end, most sophisticated measures were developed for even such events as the psychic breakdown of the president. Another set of investigations concentrates on the stabilization of the state against catastrophes brought about by mistakes of the political organization. The question is: what forms of state organization and what kinds of constitution fit some given political convictions and at the same time ensure stability?

Finally, the results of yet another consideration of this kind are particularly important because of their long-term significance. This is the domain of innovation planning.

As mentioned above, it is primarily the continuous change of technological possibilities that frustrates rigid planning for the long range. This change is primarily the result of research and development. As a consequence, all long-term planning needs to take into account the programming of such activities. One can frankly postulate that long-term planning is equivalent to innovation planning. This does not mean that inventions and discoveries can be predetermined. But the relevant activities can be carried out with different intensities and be organized differently in this or that domain. Already the fact that resources for research need to be distributed among various domains of research, that new research institutions are founded, that there is a politics of science, and research projects are commissioned, indicates that actions with long-term impacts are taken. Neither in Germany nor elsewhere is the awareness of these long-term impacts sufficiently developed. Not only what tomorrow ought to be, but also what could be wanted and what will be wanted tomorrow depends on today's innovation politics. The part of decision theory that focuses on this type of decision is called "research planning." In the last ten years, especially in the USA, a large number of results have been elaborated, dealing with questions of appropriate project selection, planning of education and training, work organization of research, budgeting of R&D, and so forth. Even then, one can enumerate many failed organizations and faulty decisions in R&D in the USA. But the awareness of the long-term impact of these activities, the influence of the organizational forms of science, as well as of the coupling of these activities with political decisions, is widely developed. It has become obvious that political decisions cannot be exhaustively derived from the proclaimed classical ideal of the history of philosophy. Every serious political strategy has to take into account the changeability of thinking possibilities. The direction and intensity of this change is the object of today's decisions on innovation planning in a competitive situation

XI

After these last remarks one could suspect that the "penultimate" traditional goals have sneaked in through the back door. What else does "adaptability" mean but that certain variables remain within "desirable" bounds and where questions of desirability are obviously answered by given and recognized value systems?

This objection can be disarmed. It presupposes that the determination and changes of value systems is arbitrary. But that is not the case. In spite of all "feasibility" (*Machbarkeit*), even if it is true that the existing systems of norms create situations that are modifiable within limits, they cannot be changed at random. The above-mentioned difficulties with interpersonal utility calculations are regulated through negotiation processes (where game theoretical considerations may become useful). In the pluralistic social structure of modern societies there is no concentrated omnipotency—and even if that was the case, for reasons mentioned before, no one could detect it. The negotiation processes guarantee that no decision has random elbowroom as a basis. Power relations, habits, rules and "fantasy capacities" reduce the arbitrariness. It is in this that rests the most important potential of decision theory. In that it establishes playing fields, formulates rules, and determines the frameworks for argumentation, it can become an aid to describe argumentation and therewith also cultivate it and make it more concise. In place of battle about ideological constructions, one turns to a discussion about the second decimal point. It strongly suggests replacing rabid fight with debates. The example is the chess player who gives up a game based on his "insight." In recognizing that a game is hopeless, one does not have to play it. It is no longer a matter of fighting the "battle for survival" with atavistic means—it would be too costly for all involved. Decision theory is an expression of the insight not to start conflicts that bring nothing. If one so desires, one could call the motivating attitude for such a behavior "rational." Among American decision theorists, the word "Peace Games" has become a common gloss. It is an English word that has been coined in analogy to the German *Kriegsspiel* (war game). *Kriegsspiel* designated the sand-box games played by military general staffs to simulate an "emergency," namely war. Peace games simulate peace. Decision research could help to make peace the "emergency."

The Theses Summarized

1. Since World War II there are an increasing number of tasks in science that offend the proclaimed principles of scientific ideology.
2. Since then there are the beginnings of "meta-sciences" that not only allow the conduct of "research on research", but also to have as their object [of study] the discrepancy between science and its applications.
3. This science is a "general science of action," the focus of which has been systems theory and decision theory
4. "Decision" as an object of science has repercussions on the concept of science.

5. Decision theory can be pursued from two points of view: that of the external observer or that of the participant.
6. The peculiarity of a conscious decision consists in its dissolution of its [own] problematic.
7. A methodological aid for the analysis of decision processes is that one proceeds "as if" the decision were to be taken by a machine. Sometimes this can even be realized.
8. The notion of goals and the value scales pose methodological difficulties.
9. The conventional maxims for action are insufficient in view of long-term and far-reaching decision tasks. Instead, goals like stability and adaptability become relevant. In this context, research and development as determinants of long-term planning play a significant role.
10. The problems around goals are solved in negotiation processes. It is the task of decision theory to cultivate these negotiations.

Notes

1 Originally published as Überlegungen zur wissenschaftlichen und politischen Bedeutung der Entscheidungstheorie (Karlsruhe: Gesellschaft für Kernforschung, 1963). Translated by Jean-Pierre Protzen.
2 Here Rittel is not concerned only with justification, but with the individual's desire to avoid liability for potential problems.
3 Rittel did not provide a citation for this quote.
4 C. W. Churchman. Precise source not identified.
5 Translated as *Lafcadio's Adventures*.
6 Hermann Heinrich Gossen 1810–1858, Prussian economist.
7 Co-authors of a 1951 work on utility functions (Mosteller and Nogee 1951; see references to Seminar 9).

Reference

Steinbuch, K. (1961) *Automat und Mensch* [Machine and Man]. Berlin: Springer-Verlag, p. 3.

Chapter 1.2

Science and Design Seminars

Introduction: Out of the Cave

Donald E. Olsen

The spring 1964 faculty seminars conducted by Professor Horst Rittel, which are represented in the present book, constituted the most noteworthy event in the history of the School of Architecture of the University of California at Berkeley. Because of the uniqueness of the occurrence and the scope of its subject, this attribution may include almost any other architecture school. It is doubtful that anything even remotely similar had ever taken place at Berkeley before this event, and I can attest that nothing approaching it has happened since. The fact that the once-a-week evening meetings were voluntarily attended throughout the term by virtually the entire faculty was remarkable in itself.

These seminars provided only a sketchy preview of Professor Rittel's 26 succeeding years of research and personal and teaching-related inquiry into design theory. His program comprised not just the latest technological exploits, but also more fundamental philosophical questions such as the history and structure of ideology, epistemology, substantive and operative technological theory, substantive scientific theory and research methodology, economic and sociological methodology, and ethics. It is important to emphasize that neither his own research nor his graduate and doctoral seminars were mere surveys. Quite the contrary, his purview included great historic theories as well as critical interpretation of contemporary scientific and philosophical positions. His own pathbreaking theories were also opened to critical discussion.

However highly I regard his views, his thinking and his writings, I shall make no attempt to interpret, review or abstract the work of Professor Rittel. Such an endeavor clearly lies beyond my competence. It also should be added that while we held substantial agreements, this is not a guarantee that he would necessarily share all the views expressed here. As an architect, most of my remarks will concern "design" in the sense that it is an integral aspect of architecture both professionally and academically. My present interest is not to describe or to criticize actual current design products or constructions as such. It is, rather, to characterize some of the current ideological positions in the leading or avant-garde constituency in architectural design, and to describe their influences on the profession, and principally on its academic component. The aim, then, is to contrast what appears to me to be much of the current subjective intellectual climate with the rationally objective contents the reader will find in Professor Rittel's Universe of Design.

As normal dictionary definitions go, the term design seems understandable enough, at least in its several main senses. The public perception of design in general, and of architecture in particular, suggests a pursuit featuring profound human sensitivity along with intellectual sophistication. In support of this, the "design" element of architecture sports a philosophically pretentious, gratuitous rhetoric intended, it would seem, for intramural mutual impression, if not for the promotion of a condescending image toward the public.

The designer mystique is supported and promoted in various ways in architecture schools as well as in the profession—frequently in the form of esoteric, obscurantist "literature," often in connection with a hero-cult epistemology, or in specious sure-thing design recipes. These self-ordained seers of the Delphic ritual engage in superficial discussion about the conceptual basis of building design while disregarding the whole complex production process that goes into it. This ritual is meaningful only to their sect.

If I may speculate, wealth and widespread higher education in the Western world may have mitigated the pragmatism that, until the last two or so generations, had underpinned much of the vocational imperative, especially in American college education. Among the benefits of the recent cultural awakening has been an enrichment of history and the social sciences, the reawakening of a noninstrumentalist understanding of science, and an expansion of the study and practice of literature, psychology, and the arts. Sensing the winds of change in the awakened yet intellectually parochial and naive field of art practice, rapidly emerging art literati were provided with a receptive audience and a new means of support. This literary blossoming in architecture paralleled certain popular, already developed idealist, often radically subjectivist, philosophical movements. These philosophies are deceptive in their self-immunization from criticism by virtue of being merely descriptive, and as such they are of virtually no explanatory value. They are, however, often rich in quotable aphorisms, which may account for much of their popularity.

While the ideologies or philosophies popular among architects comprise a fair variety, they seem to share certain common characteristics—the quest for certainty while eluding refutation and even criticism. The insulation from criticism and protection from refutation through the stratagem of incommensurability, for example, is to "paradigm" insularity what disjunction relative to logical criticism and interdisciplinary judgment is to "forms of life" exclusiveness. "Historicism," which concerns the inevitability of historical destiny, plays a strangely ambiguous but enormously popular, almost ubiquitous, role in current architectural discussion. Inasmuch as it is a deterministic doctrine, and as it stems largely from the Hegelian dialectic triad, contradiction of its statements is not something to be avoided for fear of refutation; rather, it is enthusiastically welcomed as the natural lawlike idealistic order of the world. Except for its materialistic distinction, Marxist historicism is also derived from triadic Hegelianism and is likewise protected from refuting criticism by its embrace of contradiction. And it is hard to see how emphasizing the actual Helgelianism and alleged idealist side of Marx can help to mitigate the historicist confusion. Currently some of the most fashionable ideologies stress freeing design from supposedly rational, rigidly conventional aesthetics, utility and technology by contriving a more profound revelation of essences and of unmediated knowledge of "things in themselves." Again, these philosophies are unassailable as they are virtually empty of criticizable content. Almost any interpretation is possible since they afford little more than analogic or metaphoric description or sentimentally poetic inspirational support to fads or styles with scarcely any coherently identifiable causal relation or historical evidence between design neologisms and supposed related aphorisms. These are but a sampling of the ideological "isms" affecting current architectural discussion and criticism. Meanwhile, the already inflated elitism separating much discussion in the arts from the mainstream historical, cultural, political, and scientific world remains endemic.

By and large, architects are so isolated from mainstream intellectual discourse that they tend to expect, somewhere, an indubitable source of firm, dependable, and ultimate truth. As they found science offered no such thing, they rejected it with contempt. Science has been accepted condescendingly only in instrumental form, little different from stereotypically catalogued technology. But in credulous conformity to the pathetic fallacy, the "deeper metaphysical matters" so dear to the avant-garde designers in their concern for human–artifact relations, to say nothing of so-called "artifact-to-artifact dialectic," science has been regarded as laughably irrelevant.

Inasmuch as science and objectivity are anathema to today's avant-garde architects and designers, the idea of a systematic procedure, perhaps going to such extremes as to employ logic or mathematics in the attempt to better correlate decisions and facts, tends to be scorned as superficial and, worse yet, Western. Though "absolutes" are largely doubted, it is nonetheless evident that "essences," whether Platonist or Aristotelian (though rarely named as such), are alive and well in the "serious" literature on architecture. "Place," although a subject of ancient theories of Plato and Aristotle, and even earlier the subject of one of Zeno of Elea's paradoxes, is a term (as now used) probably stemming from modern phenomenological intuition of "vision" of essences. But whatever the source, "place" appears to act as one of architecture's current popular essences. This term is often not qualified as "a place," or "a pleasant place," or "an ugly place," and so forth. So, without qualification, this vacuous, ceaselessly voiced new "essence-word" explains nothing. Yet the obscurantist writing in which this word is cryptically embedded has not only mesmerized a generation of gullible students (and many professionals and academics) susceptible to faddishly popular mysticism, but the term has even entered common speech, especially in the supercilious use of the ambiguous phrase, "sense of place."

The architectural design avant-garde is, almost by definition, isolated from intellectual evolution in any other part of the creative world, artistic or scientific. The high-prose journals, as well as the picture magazines, show little interest in anything beyond the ideological pronouncements of their greater or lesser prophets. For the avant-garde, criticism and argument primarily consist of a war of sentimentally genial aphorisms, a highly intellectual exercise in beating each other with pillows.

By sobering contrast, Professor Rittel released us from the cave to a larger world of creativity, to a world of design that transcends the categorical pigeon-holes offered in the yellow pages of the telephone directory, and the mutual admiration and condescendence offered in the popular architecture journals, that even transcends the interdisciplinary teams believed to bring syntheses to complex nonconventional design problems. Professor Rittel has, for example, raised the issue of the design approach and design method relative to problems with stated missions; new problems which in the overall are unprecedented and outside the purview of any professional category or coalition thereof. It is here that we may encounter the limits of the designer's main claim, creativity. And it is surely here that Professor Rittel's intellectual rigor would not allow matters, large or small, to remain "mysteries that make design so fascinating." His Universe of Design challenges fundamentally consequential questions and problems, the life blood of academic growth.

The question is often raised, why are there not more truly new problems or projects in architecture? The answer is, at least in part, because architects and patrons occupy a conventionally similar world. They operate relative to each other with sets of mutual expectations. Moreover, as the architecture schools follow, rather than lead the field, they give little indication of catching up, let alone overtaking the field to assume the lead, despite their convoluted intellectual efforts.

In a free pluralistic society the recognition of new problems is limited in most cases only by our inability to articulate them. New and unexpected problems often arise from the unintended consequences of conventional solutions. Unwanted repercussions are always the more conspicuous, evoking the demand for correction or redesign. In this respect, I may conjecture that the fecundity of any proposed design may be measured in terms of the degree to which it evokes new, as yet unknown and unrecognized questions demanding new problem formulations, and new problem solving methodologies. If this is granted, it may seem contrary to that understanding of design according to which it is a cyclical error-correcting cybernetic goal-seeking system. Yet it seems there can never be an exhaustive statement of the goals for the design of any artifact for human use or interaction where the human component in an artifact–human interaction is completely predetermined without reducing the human to an automaton. If this is the case, then all designed artifacts can become the source of problems large and small, complex and trivial, sometimes new and sometimes important. The study of unintended consequences of serious undertakings is surely one of our major means of discovery and advance of knowledge.

The purpose–consequence duality predicates that our most important cultural productions are the evolutionary result of human action but not of conscious design. Of these, natural language, natural numbers, and markets, from primitive barter through modern anonymous exchange, are only three of the most important. Although myth and history tell us about some of the earliest practitioners of the arts, we have no idea who invented or designed any of the arts, on the basis of which we have long been designing with articulated intention. We can never exhaust the empirical attributes and properties which may be discovered in any production. We are, however, conscious of the possibility of various consequences to the extent that some of our most extensive design efforts are imaginative hypotheses (or "designs") as to what can or might go wrong with any designed artifact. But, as I believe Horst Rittel would have been quick to add, matters by no means end at this point. No matter what is designed or produced, be it machine or institution, the results must be administered. Unforeseen economic, social, political, and technological changes over time, of which the product here considered is a contributing factor, elicit the necessity for new and further decisions. Thus, any human action manifests the necessity of ever new and subsequent decisions, a portrait, in effect, of human cultural evolution. As a parting remark, this is largely what the teaching of architecture fails to amply consider with its nearly singular interest in relatively static objects, despite its anxious advocacy of flexibility and expansion, as well as of preservation, concerning change in the name of that umbrella term "environmental design."

Professor Rittel's investigations and design of areas of inquiry are, in principle, virtually infinite in interest and fascination. The few remarks, examples, and the proposition offered here are but margin notes to Professor Rittel's Universe of Design. I have little complaint about what designers in the field are doing, be they Olympian gods or telephone yellow page entries, but if the study of architecture is to maintain a place in the university setting, it is unfortunate that so much of this study avoids most substantive theory, criticism, and concern about consequences of action, which should be the concern of university culture and which propels the growth and advance of design. With the exception of the program in the history of architecture, Professor Rittel's courses and research comprise, to my mind, the closest academic enterprise we have commensurate with true university academic status.

In addition to the initial inspiration afforded by Horst Rittel through his lectures, discussions (in seminars and personal) and writings, my major influences (explicit, and some implicit) come from the works of: Karl R. Popper, William W. Bartley, Mario Bunge, Fredrich A. Hayek, Peter Munz, Donald T. Campbell, Ernst H. Gombrich, John Weightman, and Ronald E. Engiefield.

Seminar 1: Modes of Innovation

Horst W. J. Rittel

The following considerations are directed towards the following aims:

1. To discuss the developments of theories and methodologies for design and to check their implications for environmental design.
2. To analyze the relationships between science and design in connection with possible research in design, for design, and on design.
3. To find any implications for education for design and find if knowledge and skills of this type can be a useful part of the curriculum.
4. To discuss the nature of design tasks, to analyze them and find out how they fit into the existing professions.

We will take a view of various approaches. There are several reasons for the current attempts to establish methods and theories of design, mostly effective outside the fields of conventional design—in systems engineering for example—and one of the problems is the "peaceful application" of these methods. These methods will be termed rational. Here we shall take a very weak concept of "rationality" by saying that a solution is rational if the arguments for its solutions are communicable.[1] One of the objections to such rational methods is that they seem to be anti-genius oriented. The belief in genius implies that really important changes or designs are only produced by imaginative persons with certain abilities. We are talking however about the everyday application, and if you look at, for instance, architecture as a design field, then, in fact, more than 95 percent of design is done by persons who are in the non-genius category.[2] The influence of genius on the environment is very small, but on the profession very great.

Science and Innovation; Science in Design; Science for Design

Science and design are usually taken as polar contradictions. Science is not allowed to be mentioned in the same breath as design, nevertheless, we shall have to do so. First, however, we must look for more general concepts. What do the words science and design mean and what do they have in common?

We can say that they are both:

1. activities,
2. names for the results of activities,
3. associated with social institutions having members, standards, admission procedures,
4. directed to the achievement of new realities—to changing the world, though what they understand as the world is different in both cases,[3]
5. problem-solving activities,
6. activities having unpredictable results in the sense of extrapolation. Frequently they have unique and non-routine results, otherwise they are not interesting from the scientific or design point of view.

If we are looking for an embracing concept for both of these activities, one which we might take would be that of "innovation." As a more general concept this will include science as well as design. This concept also covers the activities of management, engineering, all kinds of planning, and policy-making, and if we want to describe innovation we might define it as any act directed to a purposive and controlled change of an object system in a specific situation.

What does this mean? We shall take:

1. Innovation as an activity (and not a result of this activity).
2. The objective of innovation as being directed towards the change of an object system, which can be a scientific theory as well as a building site or a social state.
3. Innovation is controlled—we do not include discovery by chance under this heading.[4]
4. Innovation is directed towards "change." What is change? It must always be considered from a particular point of view, or determined according to a set of someone's expectations or their "image." Everything that happens and can be predicted by extrapolation and actually happens can be said to be not a change in this sense. Therefore, neither growth, nor cause and effect, is innovation. This is the only way to avoid endless discussion on this point.

The change of an object takes place in a particular situation. The objects themselves in science and design are different—in design the objects are usually artifacts; in science they are theories or a state of knowledge in a field. The scientific objects are artifacts just as the objects of design are . . .[5]

We can define a chain of expected behavior. Somewhere the expectation is limited for a certain time and a certain interval. If the designer wishes to innovate, he has to conceive a measure replacing one of the terms by something else. He has to give the chain of events a different direction. He has to establish a difference between the two and this difference is a measure of the intended innovation. We can also look at the change of the whole situation, not just that of the object. We can compare the two and this can be a measure of the success.

Figure 1.3.1

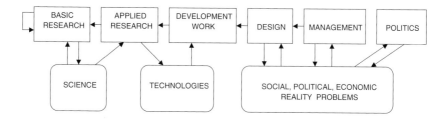

Let us now look at innovation as an institution. There are various types of innovating activities that are professionalized and which have a mutual connection by the passing on of problems and solutions.

First, we have basic research, an activity aimed at achieving scientific innovation. Then also we have applied research, development, management, and politics, all innovating activities according to our definition. Where do these institutions obtain their problems and where do they obtain and how do they pass on their solutions?

Basic research gets its problems from the kind of reality we call science. The results of the scientists are fed into science forming a self-stimulating system. Then there are the applied researchers who obtain their stimuli by browsing through the results of basic research.

Then there is the reality of technologies. (We will explain "reality" later.)[6] And from the results of the innovations in the domain of technology come their uses in development work, and from there they flow into design.

The problems of design however come from a fairly large reality: the social-economic-political reality. Politics and management are related to this reality, too. Taken as a whole this is a kind of "trickling down" process of the knowledge created by innovations, functioning independently, and working according to the demands of the situation.

We have also the sub-culture of art, not having much to do with this. There are also sieves for improvement, and behind the whole is a certain ideology, the more we go to the right, the more data are involved—more parameters which are unique for a particular situation. There is less and less critical data to the left and more generalized results are obtained there.[7]

This institutionalization and social organization is a product of the nineteenth century and is now very rigid though not very old. Previous to that time, a mathematician, for instance, dealt also with astronomy, the design of fortresses and columns, and other subjects.

There are many reasons for the system in the diagram above (Figure 1.3.1), and others against it. Amongst those for it are the:

1. Belief that there is progress in a well-determined direction. Whatever science does is progress. From investigation and flow can come only good, and design is identical to this.[8]
2. Organization of "guild-like" professional institutions with their own sub-cultures.
3. Belief that science is working on the establishment of a big framework of

knowledge and that in the future all phenomena will be understood and predictable.
4. Science has proved most successful when left alone and undisturbed.

Against these attitudes, however, there are other reasons against the validity of this mechanism:

1. There exists a kind of "uncertainty effect" which makes such a Laplacian demon of a gigantic predictable clockwork system of knowledge impossible.
2. Different tasks have now been incurred which should be solved at all levels. How do we assign the sub-tasks to all these types of innovating activity simultaneously to bring out a common result as in military design or in space programs? This happens more and more, and more and more problems are of this kind.
3. The direction of progress is subject to decision-making. One has to control and make decisions on the direction of progress, not just let it "trickle down."
4. There is therefore a necessity for innovation management by somebody. Who? A politician? A manager? A designer? Who is to do this is still an open question.
5. The current ideologies do not fit as rules for this decision-making. Marxism, Liberalism, and so forth are too primitive. One cannot define criteria for specific decisions from them. All ideologies claim a certain stable state towards which they tend in the long run, "a classless society" for instance, but they give few indications on how these are to be achieved.

Let us return to our basic question. What has design to do with science? First some common fallacies:

1. "Science is analytic; design is synthetic." Any approach to a design method must give up this distinction. They cannot be separated.
2. "Analysis is the natural enemy of creativity." This makes not much sense either for the same reasons.
3. "Design is concerned with 'hardware,' science is concerned with theory." But are designers only concerned with hardware? Every piece of hardware is a "means" and not the end by itself; the designer therefore is really designing modes of behavior. If hardware is the final result, the designer is nothing more than a basic scientist.[9]
4. "The world of thinking has nothing to do with the world of doing." Knowledge is a prerequisite of any action that tries to control its consequences. Any action is based on knowledge and an inquiring system is a necessary part of any designing system.

Design will never "become a science" as science is directed towards the consideration of unrestricted factors and changes in cause and effect. The designer, however, cannot cut off particular chains of causes and effects, he must consider all that are relevant for his problem, and that changes with the problem. The scientist can build his own sub-reality (e.g. in an experiment) by neutralizing any factors which are inappropriate. This is not possible in design problems. Also, science has strong channels of communication and rigid concepts;[10] this is not as easily possible in design.[11]

Research and Design

We can determine three interactions between research and design as follows:

1. Research *on* design . . . Observing the designer as a biologist observes an animal. How does it work, or behave, or obtain his results?
2. Research *in* design . . . Research into the specific knowledge needed for a particular design problem—methods of inquiry, inference, etc. about the particular object under design. One type is the study of the consequences of design. This is almost never attempted. Once a building is completed, unless it collapses the profession is no much longer interested in it. How it serves as a framework for human behavior is almost never investigated.
3. Research *for* design . . . Research on generalizable knowledge which the designer can use to control innovation.
   (i) research on how to achieve knowledge about the object and about the behavior of users and their attitudes in reference to their environmental conditions.
   (ii) research on the available means of changing environments and objects in certain conditions. Technological information to a primitive degree is already available, but what other means are and how they might influence behavior is not well established.
   (iii) research of the effects of the choice of certain means on the object processes. Which means provide certain consequences? Some primitive technological means have been considered but their influence on behavior remains conjectural.
   (iv) research on the objectives that have to be achieved by the object. This cannot be done once and for all. Methods of finding out the needs, objectives, and goals of a particular design problem are more interesting than finding normative solutions. We need a natural list of goals—who ordered what and when.[12]
   (v) research on how to organize the procedures of design. Much information only needs reshuffling. However, much psychological or sociological knowledge cannot be directly applied or translated into a design problem.

Notes

1 As Rittel notes, this is a weak definition of rational. This notion—that the ideas behind a decision are communicable—is similar to the notion of transparency that becomes important in Rittel's later work. In later work Rittel will speak of rationality as understanding the outcome of actions before taking them, and will speak of other versions of rationality as well. In the article "On the Planning Crisis" (presented later in this volume, pp. 151–65), Rittel writes of "paradoxes of rationality" that use a very different view of rationality than the one presented here.
2 The percentage might not be exact, but Rittel's point is that the great majority of the built environment is not built by geniuses. The buildings built by "great" architects are rare.

3   In his later teaching Rittel would say that science is directed at observation and is not intended to change the world.

4   Rittel's intention appears to be to suggest that discovery is accidental while innovation is intentional.

5   The original transcriber notes that a section of the audio recording was undecipherable at this point.

6   Unfortunately, there is no such definition of "reality" in the seminar transcripts.

7   Left and right here refer to the accompanying diagram (Figure 1.3.1)—showing science on the left and politics on the right.

8   These statements and the emphasis on progress seem to reflect an optimism that Rittel later lost, as well as still giving some indication of an idea of objective value that will later be replaced by an idea of relative value.

9   The last sentence here is questionable in the sense that science, as Rittel himself defines it, is concerned with theory, not objects. Rittel marked this paragraph with a question mark. The crucial insight, perhaps, is the notion that designers are interested in shaping behavior.

10 He is perhaps referring to the greater codification of what can be considered in scientific circles as knowledge as well as the more strict codification of language.

11 Rittel marked this sentence with a question mark, perhaps due to awkward phrasing, but in this remark about the absence of rigid concepts we can see a hint at his later notion that design problems have no exhaustive formulation.

12 If Rittel is here using the word "natural" to indicate some sort of universal truth—an objective set of values—it would contradict his later work where relativity of values is one of the primary principles. See, for example, "On the Planning Crisis" (this volume pp. 151–65).

References

Ackoff, R. L. (1962) *Scientific Method: Optimizing Applied Research Decisions*. New York: Wiley.

Churchman, C.W. (1961) *Prediction and Optimal Decision: Philosophical Issues of a Science of Values*. Englewood Cliffs, NJ: Prentice-Hall.

Kroeber, A. L. (1948) *Anthropology: Culture, Patterns & Processes*. New York: Harcourt, Brace & World.

Popper, K. R. (1959) *The Logic of Scientific Discovery*. New York: Basic Books.

Chapter 1.4

Seminar 2: Images and Messages

Horst W. J. Rittel

Some questions from last session to begin with . . .

First, the model of the innovation chain presented as a "trickle down" process was not presented as an ideal system but, on the contrary, only as a simplified image of the nineteenth-century ideal of the mechanics of progress, which does not work in this form today (and possibly has never worked), at least not with respect to today's innovation patterns. Nevertheless, the model has become a social reality because professional organizations and social systems and universes of discourse are organized according to this system. People behave as if this system was relevant, therefore it exists. Perhaps it has never worked exactly as described but the mainstream follows the prescribed path and even today the majority of innovation follows the prescribed path and "trickles down" the train as a consequence of the classification into "professionals," "artists," "theorists," practitioners and because of the corresponding division of labor also, the innovation processes cannot differ entirely.

Second, at the end of this series an overall innovating system, including an enquiring device and a direction-determining device as well, will be proposed.[1] We will now have a discussion of the components and prerequisites for the design of such an innovating system.

Third, the discrepancies between the self-images of the innovators, their universes of discourse, their tasks, and the demand for innovations leads us to a prophetical assumption of such a "box-with-a-question-mark" which deals with the management of innovation.[2] Today there is much evidence of changes for us and for organizational responses to them—especially here in America, the innovational industry of new examples such as the RAND Corporation, Systems Development Corporation, of new organizational patterns to deal with tasks which do not fit into the chain—organizations which have been designed to meet the necessity to solve new kinds of innovation problems and it is interesting to observe that almost no attempt has been made to adapt the established innovating systems to the changed tasks. No attempt has been made to reform, or even evolve the existing established institutions of research, development, and design. Instead these novel tasks are

dealt with by newly founded institutions and now after 10 or 15 years a kind of dialectic feedback may be observed where all the techniques of innovation developed
in these institutions come back to the traditional universities and are adopted there.
Nevertheless, the innovation industry will continue to exist in parallel. Innovation
itself has become a commodity that is produced, bought, and sold.

Fourth, I have tried to demonstrate the change of engineering tasks,
research tasks, and design tasks and the particular properties of the changes.[3]
Many traditional innovation processes can be understood as a result of evolutionary
innovation, and as a policy of research, development, and design which modifies
existing devices and patterns, improves them from a certain aspect but leaves the
rest unchanged. The history of the bicycle, motorcar, etc. can be seen as the result
of policies of successive improvement and it is interesting to look at the history of
technology under this heading which covers "evolution" to the present shape. In all
these cases the end of a development or design process has been of a purely technical nature and in this case the hardware aspect was overwhelming.[4] In contrast,
the changed tasks can be called "mission-orientated tasks." There is a demand for
an object that has to fulfill a certain "mission" defined in very broad and abstract
terms. The challenge of the situation must be met, no existing devices or ideas will
suffice, and the basic type of object-system may be quite unclear. Even the disarma-
ment problem is understood in these terms. In the jargon of systems engineering
the following distinction is made: any development and design task has to deliver
as a result three components of a solution:

- The hardware: Physical objects and devices and manufactured items that
  provide the framework for the behavior of all people dealing with the device.
- The software: That which is concerned with the design of modes of behavior
  of all those connected with the device—handling instructions, communication rules, and these are as important as the hardware and also subject to
  design.
- The testware: Consists of devices for controlling the fulfillment of the mission.
  It is necessary to design a device for the collection of experience as these
  mission-oriented tasks have no analogues. This is not solely a military application—any attempt at innovation in the form of a design task not relying on
  self-regulation needs this component of the results also.

These categories could also apply to architecture and industrial design, any kind of
planning or communication design, any instance where the fulfillment of the mission
cannot be read from the particular technical aspect of the solution, or if the language
of the object evaluation is different from the sub-cultural language of a professional
universe of discourse. It can be very dangerous for the designer to take himself as
a system of reference for the evaluation of the software and testware factors. If
this is true then the objective, for example, of architecture can no longer be limited
to the realization of spatial images or the building of buildings but will be directed
to the organization of frameworks for behavior, or of the design of environmental
controls for certain processes or of providing environmental conditions for certain

missions. The results of this type of consideration may no longer be buildings as we know them.

It is interesting to ask students to design a house for five dollars. They usually laugh! Why? They laugh because they have a very fixed concept of what a house is and it does not fit in with five dollars. As Sigmund Freud has said, if you bring concepts together which do not fit together according to a framework of expectations then one gets a joke![5] Therefore this reaction shows that a mission-oriented design approach allows one to liberate oneself from the restrictions of preconceptions and expectations. It is often useful to reformulate the task in the sense of a "mission" to produce solutions that are not of evolutionary character or modifications of existing solutions.[6]

A final peculiarity of the mission-oriented tasks is that the designer himself is often involved in the formulation of the mission. In this case the value system of the innovator comes into the problem as a partner of the decision maker himself; he becomes politically involved.[7]

Later we will try to establish a coordinate[8] system for the problems arising out of the reformulation of innovation tasks; its primitive nature is part of the price of generalization. We shall cross several disciplines and domains, perhaps missing some contributions, but the ultimate objective is to provide a unified frame of reference in which to embed the organizational and methodological problems intrinsic in the system.

What has this to do with architecture and design? For a critical approach to the existing innovation system we must first find a more general concept (i.e. innovation), and because the present professional structure must be considered as well, we must not specialize too early into a special traditional professional conceptual system.

A final criticism was that I forgot to mention that science has to do with nature, but design with the world of man. I deliberately avoided the concept of nature as an "aquarium" objective frame of reference containing all natural happenings because the whole concept of nature is one that is very unstable through time in its meaning. The seventh, tenth, and twentieth centuries' views of nature are entirely different, and even the attitude to nature has changed from enmity to cooperation at various times. I would say that undoubtedly nature is one of the greatest inventions of man, an artifact to replace the multitude of personalized demons, and a concept to describe those regularities which are out of control or which are so general and ahistoric that they occur everywhere. Therefore nature is a concept to combine these functions and is an artifact designed by man.[9]

In order, also, to avoid questions like "is the moon a pig?" we will say, "yes, there may be some for whom this is so, but not for us." We will say that electrons, genes, etc., did not exist in the seventeenth century in the sense that they did not appear in anyone's world. They are, however, "artifacts" that have been designed to explain a bunch of phenomena, to establish a conceptual framework, to predict the outcome of certain experiments and make them understandable. For our considerations we cannot use a concept such as nature as this suggests "natural" solutions, or values, or "natural" needs or "natural" rights as if there was an absolute measure of objectivity for all these "in nature" and that the answer derived from this absolute coordinate system of nature's would be true and valid everywhere.

We shall say that science is an attitude and a certain approach that is applicable to human objects and societal objects as well, not[10] that science is concerned with nature and design with man.

Images and Messages: Communication for Design and Design for Communication

In the nineteenth century it was traditional to take the materialistic or energetic point of view of an assemblage or distribution of matter—a kind of hardware thinking. It was accepted that if man could describe the laws of the distribution of matter everything could be predicted. Even its opponents shared this belief, which had to be abandoned with the development of modern physics when it was shown that how we observed something determined what we observed. In modern physics there is a good deal of evidence for these influences—the Heisenberg uncertainty principle or the de Broglie duality being examples. In consequence of this, many philosophical difficulties arose because if one takes the aspect of the ultimate frame of reference being matter, something must be matter, or a wave, it cannot be both. In the late 1940s a new kind of philosophy or approach has been developed disclaiming that this could ever be understood by understanding the distribution and laws of matter. This was the approach proposed by Shannon and Weaver's "Information Theory" and Wiener's "Cybernetics." We must look at certain properties of this approach.

Instead of having theoretical systems with hardware objects as entities and theoretical statements about these physical and material objects, for many purposes it has been shown to be more fruitful to have the idea that all that we can talk about, and all that we know, comes from messages that come into our sensory organs, and even all we know about material objects is by messages, and all that we can know, is knowledge about messages. Of course we are accustomed to take the message for the object and perceive things as real, as material, and behave and talk as if these objects were really materially present. However, in the social sciences where other aspects become more important, concepts like cooperation, conflict, value, and information become central and this aspect of the world as being of messages and of relations between messages is very promising and unifying and applies equally to physical and social processes. All our experiences are based on messages and all our knowledge about the effects of our actions can be understood as messages.[11]

This applies in several ways. The manager of a factory having statistics of material flows, manpower, and machinery, has a view of his factory based on talks and communications of various kinds. We will try to see what these channels are. Again, a politician's knowledge is based on agents, referees, and standards, and hardware is much less important.[12] Again, an architect's plan is a set of instructions or messages. Descartes's idea of a whole world as a grand deception here makes no difference so long as the "grand deceiver" behaves consistently and in accordance with previous behavior. It has also been shown that the physical and material sciences are inadequate to explain complex entities. The quantum theory becomes impossible to apply to more than two electrons. Cars, chairs, and other complexities can never be interesting to a physical scientist therefore.

We shall take as a basis for the following discussion the aspect of scientific communication. This aspect is not new and various approaches and attempts have been made in biology to understand the behavior of biological organisms in terms of communication. Von Uexküll in about 1910 tries to understand the behavior of animals by finding out what their world is.[13] He says there is the world of perceptions and the world of effects and describes how they are structured, commencing with the way the various zones of the environment are tuned, some have a danger "zone," others an eating "zone," etc. and he gives maps of these. This is a very early and convincing approach but it has the disadvantage that the external observer is not involved—his perceptive and effective worlds are not involved.

Another approach, semiotics, originally developed by [Charles Sanders] Pierce, a philosopher and mathematician—one of the originators of pragmatism—whose idea was that there is nothing like an objective world that can be approximated more and more but only subjective worlds structured by our perceptual judgments. He claims that the system of concepts that we have structures that which we understand as the world, just as Von Uexküll's claims for the fly—and we are living in a "conceptual cage" and we can perceive things only as our system of concepts permits us to perceive them. This is another source of modern communication theory. A further source is that of the psychology of perception, the Gestalt psychologists and later the Transactionalists who give evidence that what we perceive and which perception hypotheses we "dare" depends on what we have learned. The empirical evidence is very impressive.

We will concentrate on the sources, first, of information theory of Shannon and Weaver, and Wiener, and, second, the image theory of Kenneth Boulding, which tries to unify all these aspects.

Boulding's proposed new science "eiconics" could well be a foundation for a design theory.

Now, what is an image? At the least it is the subjective knowledge structure of an individual, what he knows, believes, expects, more or less ordered and structured. All his expectations, attitudes, and his values are part of this image, and this image consists of what the world means for him, as he understands the world. That there is such a thing as an image can be derived by the fact that people seem to behave according to their image, that we can get evidence and observe behavior according to it. The image is the world of events and Boulding makes the following statements about it:

1. All behavior depends on the image.
2. The history of the image is part of the image. We know how things came into the image and we make this knowledge part of the image.
3. The meaning of a message is a change produced by the image. If a message is sent to me and doesn't change my image it wasn't a message for me. Some messages from outside leave the image unaffected, others change it in a regular way, for instance further observations of the same phenomena

stabilize the image. If a message is significant it can restructure the image to a remarkable extent.

4. The image is resistant to change and it can be observed that favorable messages are accepted and unfavorable ones rejected. There is a kind of selective perception process; prejudices are of this type.

5. Within the images there are many scales of evaluation for certain purposes, some valid at certain times, others not, all stored or built into the image without conflict.

6. There seems to be a principle of internal strain at work, operating towards a kind of unification of the image. Split images tend to be simplified, unified, and restructured in an appropriate way.

7. Any perception is mediated through a sieve of value systems, established by the image. Facts are "made"—factum—by those who accept them into their image.

8. Images are socially shared. There is a coincidence between various persons, they are not private, and this can be checked by the success of symbolic communication between persons. This means a language, and in terms of this language we can talk about the image—even talk about the image of the image and this is an aid to the socialization of the image.

It can be observed in a particular social group, the value systems are the same for all persons and even the perceptual systems are similar. It is possible to describe madness as someone whose image is completely private.

Messages come not only from others but from outside, or "nature." The image can grow or develop by conversation or discourse and not necessarily only by direct observation itself. The question of course is, is this "image" verifiable scientifically? Boulding argues in the other direction by saying that what is described as scientifically true is a certain truth with respect to a certain sub-culture called science with its own image and if we talk about images we cannot make a sub-culture with its own image the authority for truth or untruth. An important epistemological point is involved here. He says that scientific truth is a particular kind of truth springing from a particular image and that knowledge without a "knower" is an absurdity and you have to learn about the truth question if this extra-image sense cannot be decided.

In a certain situation only a small segment of the image is activated, belonging to the one of the following zones of the image:

- the spatial image
- the temporal image
- the relational image
- the self image
- the value image
- the emotional image
- the conscious image
- the unconscious image
- the subconscious image.

There are also the images of certainty and uncertainty, of reality and unreality, and public and private images. These are all subject to the development of the various parts of *Homo sapiens* and perhaps they do not form mutually exclusive categories.

Let us see what this relatively simple concept can be used for. To begin with, expressions like the following can be found:

$I_A(O)$—A's image of "O," of something.

$I_B(I_A(O))$—This means B's image of A's image of O, or what B thinks A thinks of "O."

$I_A(I_B(I_A(O)))$—Then A's image of B's image of A's image; what A thinks of how B imagines A.

Then, A's expectation of how his message from A to B will affect the image of B. We can find rules for this grammar but we shall not discuss this in detail.[14]

A more important question is that if we assume that there is an image for everyone, then it is extremely important for the designer to know about other people's images, about his own image, and about his image of other people's image and other relationships of this kind.

It is not possible, however, to get a projection of the total image as a message to someone else. We can only obtain indicants, hints, and certain properties of the image. We cannot examine someone's image in total as one can analyze a molecule because the process of analysis will change the image. A kind of uncertainty relationship is established by the fact that any messages change images, and if we exchange messages about images of images they will be changed. Difficult to imagine—but it works! It is quite useful, however, to explain situations of knowledge and the relationships with objects, and we can say that all statements are about images.

How can we obtain information of this kind? At this point the concepts of information theory can be brought together with these image concepts to make them more rigorous. Information theory has been developed for the purposes of communication engineering and is not concerned with the content of messages but with the amount of information—to put it simply.

Let us study the process that happens when a part of the image is activated. A person is in a certain situation and he perceives this situation. He perceives certain things and categorizes them into tables, green tables, motorcars, etc. Sometimes some categories occur in the activated image because of their "noncategorization," for instance a motorcar without wheels is not a category, but it is a kind of category because of its unrepresentative nature.

For every moment in the description of a situation a certain amount of such categories are activated, according to which the necessary distinctions are made. Some quantitative information on the number of categories always present in the activated image will be given later, and some of these properties are not present but the categories are "activated" nevertheless; some are present. These are the criteria or categories according to which a certain situation is observed. Some are present, others are not. You notice things by their absence. Sometimes it is economical to replace a whole set of perceptive judgments by what is called a supersign. We recognize a cat as a whole thing—"cat"—not as a number of components. The quality of "catness" might be put on a scale between 1 and 10.[15]

If in a certain situation this set of categories is very stable it may be that the messages show that certain things change and sometimes any behavior is mapped into this frame of reference and if we talk about beetles we forget about astronomy and it is not necessary to activate this part of my image. For beetles certain combinations of zeros and ones are possible and already observed and others are excluded. This means that by experience there are certain expectations with respect to beetles, that by experience we activate these categories and we extract certain combinations of alphas to a more or less degree of probability or certainty. What we call knowledge is partly the ability to set up these categories and partly the ability to guess the zeros and the ones. Here, for the second part of knowledge, information theoretical considerations can be applied. Information theory, however, deals with a given frame of reference, and the establishment of the variety of categories of the coordinate system has not yet been included. What is given, however, is included.

Notes

1 Unfortunately, no such system is discussed during the seminars. But this goal would seem to be a largely logical outcome of the premises that Rittel takes and uses. We have a folder of notes written in German in Rittel's hand on such a system, from the summer of 1964, but the notes never developed into any published work. In Rittel's career the largest system to develop out of his work was the IBIS—a system that could be considered an enquiring device, but one that does not provide innovation or direction. The morphological system of Fritz Zwicky—mentioned in Seminar 8—is an innovation system, but not a complete design system. Indeed, it seems that Rittel's conclusions by the end of the seminar series suggest that no such complete system is possible (see Seminars 9 and 10).

2 Presumably the "box-with-a-question-mark" is what is more commonly referred to as a black box: a box with known inputs and outputs but whose internal processes cannot be known. Rittel himself marked this sentence with a question mark.

3 As Rittel himself noted in the margin of his copy of the seminar transcripts, though promised, this discussion is, "Not in this text."

4 "Overwhelming," perhaps, in the sense that the hardware aspects dominated the issues of concern, as opposed to the related modes of behavior, which, as noted in the first seminar, are the designer's real concern.

5 Arthur Koestler defines a joke this way. We are unfamiliar with any such claim by Freud. We do know that Rittel was, at the time of these seminars, already familiar with Koestler's work.

6 Rittel continues to use the contrast between "evolution" and "innovation" that he set up earlier.

7 This notion of the inescapable effect of the values of the designer (and of others in the design process) will later become one of the central issues in Rittel's definition of wicked problems. See "On the Planning Crisis" later in this volume (pp. 151–65).

8 Rittel puts a question mark by this word. Perhaps he is thinking in terms of some issues he will discuss later: the idea that problems can be represented mathematically, and therefore graphically, leading to what is called "the problem space" and the "solution space" (see Seminar 7: Design).

9   Though Rittel put a question mark by this sentence, we can see in it, possibly, the recognition that concepts like "nature" are human conceptual constructs rather than objective truths.

10 The original transcriber inserted the emphasis on "not"—presumably because in the audiotape recording of the seminar showed emphasis.

11 While the notions in the paragraph are closely related to, and perhaps may be found in, the work of Shannon and Weaver, and Wiener, these last two sentences as stated here are very close to statements that can be found in Kenneth Boulding's *The Image* (1956), which Rittel discusses at length later in this seminar.

12 Rittel put a question mark by this sentence, but it seems, again, to fit his focus on behavior not hardware.

13 Uexküll, Jakob Johann, Baron von, 1864–1944, Estonian biologist. His works are not readily available in English.

14 While Rittel almost certainly had a formulaic expression of this idea, we do not present any such formula here. The formulae given were added by Rittel to his copy of the seminar transcript.

15 In the 1960s at the University of California, Lotfi Zadeh developed the notion of fuzzy logic. Psychologist Eleanor Rosch was to demonstrate the psychological validity of graded category membership in studies published in the early 1970s. We do not know whether Rittel exchanged ideas on these subjects with Zadeh or Rosch, or whether there was any contact between Rosch and Zadeh, but clearly the idea of category membership as being a scalar (rather than bipolar) concept was present at Berkeley in the 1960s.

References

Boulding, K. E. (1956) *The Image: Knowledge in Life and Society.* Ann Arbor, MI: University of Michigan Press.

Shannon, C. E. and Weaver, W. (1963) *The Mathematical Theory of Communication.* Urbana, IL: University of Illinois Press.

Wiener, N. (1950) *The Human Use of Human Beings: Cybernetics and Society.* Boston: Houghton Mifflin.

Wiener, N. (1961, 2nd ed.; first published 1948) *Cybernetics; or, Control and Communication in the Animal and the Machine.* New York: MIT Press.

Chapter 1.5

Seminar 3: Communications

Horst W. J. Rittel

First, some additional remarks concerning the previous week's seminar. Boulding's concept of an image was introduced as a basic concept for subsequent considerations. This may sound more complicated than it actually is. Even an automaton must contain a model of the external world—there must be some long-range influence systems built in. "A's" image is "A's" model of his world. What is the reason for introducing this concept? First, it provides a language permitting discussion about science, history, politics, etc., and capable of describing and admitting logical or anti-logical structures of knowledge. It is necessary for subsequent discussion to have a language that is open for the strategic and political aspects of the language of innovation of types, which can be used not only from the standpoint of an external observer but from that of an involved person as well. There seem to be two positions that any scientist, designer, or historian may have: either as an engaged decision maker or as an external observer, and we need a language structure or coordinate system admitting both these standpoints.[1]

What does this type of consideration mean to us as designers? Boulding says that the worst criticism one can get is "What is new is bad and all the good things are not new." All these considerations can be used to reorganize existing knowledge and bring knowledge together for comparison. I have talked exaggeratedly of the world as a world of messages as against an assembly of hardware. That this is more than just a neat construct has yet to be proved. However this image fits into the present philosophical situation, as Zopf has said: "Thousands of years of externalization and of creating objects have rigidified our conceptual cage. It is difficult to escape from the cage, or from this construct to the independent world" (Zopf 1962). Nevertheless there are some advantages for this kind of world, as everything that can be talked about as relationships between material things can also be talked about in terms of messages, but *not* vice versa.[2] We cannot talk in a physical language about non-physical things and therefore a more general language is useful. The scientific image of a world would be just one among others with no a priori reason in favor of any one of the images in this way of talking about images.

One may have one of two points of view and no one can prove either to be correct: on the one hand the firm belief in an outside world independent of our schemes, on the other, the belief in the physical world as a construct. As Susanne Langer has said, "The world divides into facts because we so divide it" (Langer 1948).

Whichever position one takes makes no difference to what one can achieve. There is one heuristic argument in favor of taking the world as a world of messages: that the assumption of an independent and objective world in the old sense tends to be, or is, a permanent temptation to be taken as a frame of reference, and its proponents might say that they are closer to it than someone else and argue as if they were nearer to the final truth than others. This is a danger, and therefore it might be more appropriate heuristically to take the other point of view.

Next, certain conventions. Instead of "concepts" we will concern ourselves with "someone's concepts," instead of "facts," "someone's facts," and the same for values as well. Any hypothesis is part of someone's image and there are many ways to achieve a hypothesis, for example, a scientific one. We will also say that any design problem that is not routine demands a new conceptualization and to understand it all the images of the participants have to be examined by the designer and so a framework which is not too rigid is necessary.[3]

Let us translate this into an eiconologist's view of *Homo sapiens*.[4] Whose image do we mean? An eiconologist assumes that individuals are organized in the following way and able to receive messages:

The sensory organs such as the eyes, etc. are already selective. A stream of unstructured signals is presented and this goes into a device that seems to be an assembly of many filters, approximately 16 and not more, which act as a conceptual sieve at any prior moment. The neurological evidence for this is of a kind of switching service which allows one to recognize one object from another. This abstractor, or invariant finder, is a device to find out certain invariants—properties of the message which are invariant towards certain transformations or which are abstractions for classes of signals; straight lines, curves, etc. The filters encode signals and they are transmitted to the "black box." The image consists of two parts—activated and

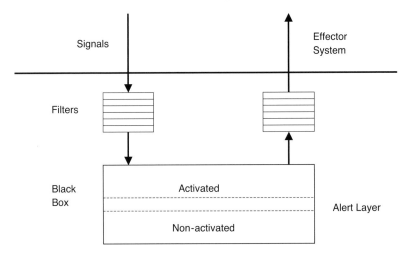

Figure 1.5.1

non-activated—possibly described as the conscious and the unconscious and perhaps a portion in between called the subconscious—an "alert" image having certain
control functions. The encoded message is interpreted here as a more or less digital
message rather than analogue and is projected into a pattern of expectations. This
"black box" is nothing mysterious, it occurs in communication theory and biology,
and is a similar thing to that called "memory" or "value." It keeps the whole thing
going, and Zopf has pointed out that we introduce such concepts as intelligence,
memory, etc., but they are not understood in total and are in fact "black boxes."

There is also an effector system with another sieve of alternative actions
which are taken as appropriate or possible at a particular moment, and from which
one is chosen.

The content of the sieves or slides is not constant but changing and this
change originates from the black box, the environment, and the even deeper layers
of the image. A sieve corresponds to a concept. The fact of these concepts depends
on the propensity for perception and if something does not fit we are extremely
confused. Our propensity to perceive is permanently changing by that which we
expect of our activated image as well as the deeper layers of the image. This system
of concepts is changed by the previous experience as well as by the expectations,
and this sub-system is an intensive action and reaction.

How is this "black box" organized and how can we find out all about
it? This is a difficult situation but not a unique one. It occurs anywhere where one
destroys what one wants to observe by the use of analytical methods. Other techniques must be used to investigate the black box, which, in fact, transforms inputs
into outputs. We can imagine this as a machine and try to define its characteristics,
build such a machine, and test it.

Our propensity to perceive is not subject to will, but are there any sieves
that are rigid? There is some evidence that a few of them are: there are some encod-
ers that seem to be rigid and to act all the time.[5] Also, if certain sieves are activated
with a simultaneous correlation, there is a mechanism that replaces all the sieves
by one and therefore one obtains more capacity for other conceptual slides and
a permanent redesign of their storage. This simultaneous correlation is termed a
"supersign" and is very useful.

Another sieve seems to exist to collect the unexpected, as a control of
normality and seems to have a direct wire to the "alert" area to replace a new set
of sieves for the new situation.

The activated part of the image seems to be the Freudian "state of consciousness" with the "audience" somewhere in the lower layers of the black box.
This audience consists of the "thoughts" that are constantly trying to disturb the
performance, as Freud has described.

What of the "black box" and evidence for its structure? It seems that a
certain environmental condition in terms of messages and images produces behavior.
For many types of behavior this is constant and we do not need to take into account
the full range of the image, but for some it is necessary to, and the definition of the
image and the model of the world is that if one has perfect knowledge of a person's
image and model of the world and the stream of messages that person receives, one

could predict behavior. The question is how to get this information of the black box and to keep in mind that the image of the designer of himself is of the same type! Does he have the self-image which allows himself to be understood in this way?

Certain parts of this model agree with communication theory, so a few remarks about this at this point. We must introduce the idea of information content—starting with a few remarks on the restrictions on its applicability!

Communication theory was developed after the war by Shannon and Weaver,[6] and brought into cybernetics by Wiener and is now commonly used in many areas of engineering, but also in science, as in the study of genetic processes. It was designed for a completely different purpose, i.e. communication engineering, and therefore its restrictive applicability is only normal.[7] The engineer is not interested in content (of a single telephone call) but in the appropriate transmission of a whole set of telephone calls. This restricts its applicability for our purposes. It is predominantly concerned with cross-statements of information flow, amounts of information, intensities, not particular semantic information. We can obtain general and abstract statements on information flows but information theory is not concerned with the semantic aspect of a message—the aspect of meaning which is so interesting for our purposes by reason of the fact that the meaning of the message is expressed in changes of the image and this is therefore extremely interesting for us. In all cases the patterns of reference are taken as given rather than the selection of the problems themselves. The starting point is always a given set of alternative messages, in which behavior can be mapped,[8] but the finding of the frame of reference is not part of information theory. Further, capacity problems are considered in information theory, what can go through a channel or not, and here this becomes interesting. We can set limiting statements about the mechanisms for this and we shall use this to find a few limitations for perception and action because we can discover statements about the statistical mechanics of messages and their effects, about flow of messages over a long time for instance. Certain necessary conditions for the transmission of any message can be discovered.

In the meantime the methods and language of information theory have proved useful for many aspects of communication—warning processes, aesthetic information, and in different problems of some complexity.

Now a few words on information content. Let us assume that the propensity to perceive allows certain things to happen. Obviously one consideration is that the more things that can possibly happen the more uncertain we are. If we expect one thing to happen we can be certain; if we expect one of many things to happen then we are uncertain. Therefore the information from a later realized event is the larger, the higher the uncertainty has been before, and if we assume that these things[9] are mutually exclusive and one only can occur and it is a complete system (one and only one of them must happen) then the worst case is when you have no idea which will occur. This is a starting point for a definition of information content of such a scheme. Here it is measured by the logarithm of the number of alternatives, the likelihood of their occurrence being equal. Why has this been defined in this way? A deck of cards represents maximum uncertainty of the outcome and other situations correspond—dice, etc. If we assume [a deck of] 32 cards and we can cheat. We can also ask someone what the next card is and he can answer yes or no. A stupid strategy would be to ask consecutively and 31 questions might be required. An optimum strategy of course would be to take halves and therefore we can cover the whole deck of cards in five questions maximum.[10]

Now let us take the argument the other way—by opening the deck and showing a card one saves five questions, therefore the information content is measured by the amount of effort of questions you have saved. Therefore the information content is five bits and if there is twice the number of cards only one more question is necessary. If one doubles the number again, once more only one other question is necessary. This is a logarithmic increase—the dual logarithm in this case. The information content of the scheme of alternatives is given as equally favorable. It took mankind some time to find this out because of the difficulty of proving a dice to be "true." Any variation could be chance![11]

We can take various meanings from this. Information can be a measure of the maximum selection effort, a measure of the necessary length of a code of a series of events, a measure of the amount of information you get from any event which is a realization of a given scheme of alternative events, a measure of the decrease of uncertainty and of decision effort. It is also a measure of the difficulty of the search problem and finally of relative order. These are seven interpretations of this function, which has been shown to be the most reasonable function to deal with such a phenomenon.

If, however, we take a loaded dice, because the possible outcomes are mutually exclusive events, it being a complete scheme, the probabilities must add up to 1. But if we assume the 6 shows up more often, it would mean that a 6 increases at the cost of the 1 on the opposite side, and the more throws we make the more the probability will accumulate for certain events. However, the more asymmetrical the distribution of probabilities is, the easier it is to predict and the information that a person who knows that the dice is loaded is less than that which a person receives who does not know and believes the dice to be true. This case where probabilities are not equal is a special case of the more general case. If we are sure of a certain event then the information content is zero.

This is one way to talk of uncertainty, flow of events and messages, and if we have any diary of behavior this algorithm can be applied, the measure of information can be defined, and if all the rules governing the behavior are known, the information content will be zero.

To express this more concisely another more important concept known as *redundancy* must be used. Redundancy is defined as:

The max. information possible under a scheme

minus

The effective information

[all] *divided* by

the max. information

$[R = (H_{max.} - H_{effective})/H_{max.}]$

For example the maximum information in a deck of cards is 5 bits and any informa-tion reduces this.[12] The more we know, the smaller is one part of the fraction. If we know nothing the effective information equals the maximum information and the result is zero. Therefore redundancy is always between 1 and 0. Total uncertainty corresponds to R=0 and full determinacy to R=1. The moon for example, fully deter-minate, would have a redundancy of 1.[13]

Redundancy will be used to describe the degree of order. Much of design is directed towards the increase of redundancy, to making things determinate with respect to an expectational pattern. One example is that language has a redundancy of about 50 percent and could be coded much more economically, but we can recog-nize printing errors and mistakes because redundancy stabilizes the meaning of a sentence. In other kinds of message the redundancy is 0. In telephone numbers if one letter is wrong, the whole is wrong. Similarly in a Stock Exchange report. It can be shown that any planning behavior is based on the presence of redundancy, and any acquisition of knowledge can be expressed in terms of increasing redundancy in two ways—one by adjusting the conceptual framework and secondly by improv-ing the knowledge of these probabilities. This means better design of the system of conceptual sieves. Laws, physical, astronomical, or ethical, increase redundancy and therefore redundancy can be taken as a measure of lawfulness. There are some counteracting effects but we cannot deal with these now.

Finally, let us consider *Homo sapiens* as a data processing system.[14] The sensory organs are capable of discriminating between a very large amount of information, for example, in the human eye the possible states that can be discrimi-nated are in the order of 10^8 bits per second (or 10^8 alternative states at the retina) but the nerves passing from the eye do not use this possible variety of images operating there. Many receptor units lead to the same nerve which may be activated or not, but in the brain where the sieves are located, at the entrance to the central nervous system, hundreds of thousands can still be distinguished. However, what enters the image, or consciousness, is only between 10 and 16 bits per second—a tremendous loss, but there are good reasons for this.

These activated concepts remain so only for approximately 10 seconds. After this they either break down or are sent to the long-term memory. This means that in our consciousness at each moment there are approximately 160 bits of information, not more. This means that one's model of a situation is capable of 2^{160} different states that could be discriminated at any moment but some are not dual nor are they equally probable and the number diminishes rapidly. We can say that one bit subjective time quantum having a length of 15 seconds [has] a possible access into consciousness. The 15 seconds is derived from the time an impulse takes from the brain to the tip of the toe and back. We can use this as a measure of the capacity of the effector and receptor systems. We can derive formulae for, for instance, mechanical learning, for the number of repetitions necessary in learning French, for instance.

Notes

1 Rittel's belief here in the possibility of a designer as an external observer does not match his later work, in which he views the designer as necessarily an involved participant. One of the crucial elements of his formulation of wicked problems is that the designer "has no right to be wrong," as he puts it (see "On the Planning Crisis," this volume, pp. 151–65, or Rittel and Webber 1973). He argues that planners are liable for their work, eliminating the possibility that the designer take a position as an external observer: "The scientific community does not blame its members for postulating hypotheses that are later refuted . . . in the world of planning and wicked problems no such immunity is tolerated" (Rittel and Webber 1973: 167).

2 By this sentence Rittel noted "imp!!"

3 When, some five years after these seminars, Rittel describes wicked problems—and argues that all design problems are wicked—he will take the position that no design problem is routine, but rather that each design problem is unique. The only routine for a real design problem is that a designer might follow a routine in developing a response to the problem: the routine thus becomes a characteristic of the designer's process, not characteristic of the problem itself.

4 Rittel notes: "Boulding has proposed the science of 'eiconics' for the science of images."

5 The underlining is Rittel's.

6 Also known as information theory.

7 I.e., to be expected.

8 Rittel's underlining.

9 Rittel's underlining—perhaps he was looking for a different word here?

10 The logic of this passage is obscure; Rittel placed a question mark by it. We presume that Rittel's point is to show that in certain situations there may be more or less elegant and efficient methods of determining, and that the measure of information content is related to the dual logarithm. This card example uses a deck of 32 presumably because 32 is a power of two, and assumes that the question regarding each card is not simply "is it card X?," answered by a yes or no, but rather the answer includes some directional information (larger/smaller) that allows the questioner to infer something about not only the one card in question but also about a whole class of cards, so that the first question can exclude 16 cards, not just one.

11 Rittel brackets these two sentences and puts an uninterpreted mark in the margin by them.

12 This is true if you continue considering a 32-card deck. With 52 cards, there is an additional "bit" of information (i.e. one binary digit) necessary.

13 Rittel puts an "X" near the end of this paragraph—probably intending to delete something—but how much he intended to delete is uncertain.

14 By the top of this paragraph Rittel notes "not quite accurate." He was likely referring to the numbers given, as the basic principles in this passage are in accord with his basic ideas about human reasoning in general.

References

Cherry, C. (1957) *On Human Communications: A Review, a Survey, and a Criticism.* Cambridge, MA: MIT Press.

Langer, S. K. K. (1948) *Philosophy in a New Key: A Study in the Symbolism of Reason, Rite and Art.* New York: Penguin. (Later editions were published by Harvard UP)

Zopf, G. W. (1962) *Principles of Self-organization: Transactions.* New York: Pergamon Press.

Seminar 4: Establishing Order

Horst W. J. Rittel

Some further basic concepts have to be developed.

We have been considering the idea of the "image" as developed by Boulding as a general concept for design. As well as the image of the structural part of the design there is the image of an individual in his environment. Last week we said that the "model" for the description of individual behavior in an environment is as below.

The difference between this and any other model in systems engineering is that we assume that the content of the coded device is controlled by the image as well as the chosen selections.

The image is organized at various levels, which at the moment we know little about. The activated image might be described as consciousness. The preconscious image is that part of the device which is controlling all the events that are unimportant for the activation of the image. There is also the unconscious mind and the subconscious about which we know little.

Many stimuli are coded in a rigid way—the eyelids, etc.—and here there seems to be a direct feed between in and out messages.

The introduction of this subject enables us to talk of receptive perception. No mechanical simulation of this has yet been tried out. We introduce this in order to understand human behavior. To try to find out from input and output, the values, regularities, and so infer what is going on in the "black box."

Much human behavior is difficult to study because between stimulus and response there can be an enormous length of time—up to years in fact. Also, the situation is not a simple additive one. The image has a very complex structure.

Earlier, some facts were discussed about the capacity of the throughput of the system—10–15 bits per second can be decoded and the same holds good for the responses. It would be useless to have more capacity in the effectors than in the receptors. In all organisms and organizations there is approximate equality between input and output (cf. e.g., the work of Shannon or Ashby).

Each bit of coded information can stay for ten seconds and there is therefore a total capacity of 10*10 pieces of information. This elapsed period of ten seconds is derived from and connected with the passage of signals within the nervous system and the time taken.

How do we know about the image? What are the dynamics? Can we understand it or change it? We shall talk about socially shared images and the process of socialization of the image.

First, however, about redundancy and order.

We have introduced redundancy expressed as a message composed of signs which will have a maximum information content if they are all equal. Relative redundancy is defined by:

$$R = (Hmax. - H\ effective)/H\ max.$$

If R = 0 there is no redundancy. The effective information would equal the maximum information, the result would be 0, that is, *chaos*. If R = 1 there is clockwork behavior. If we are sure what the next event will be then complete surety means mechanical behavior. Any expectation must be between O and 1.

Order. Order is not something that exists in an absolute manner. It varies with persons and there can be a high or low degree of order. Order has to be established again and again, too. It has to be realized in two ways; in both cases by active behavior to make something into fact. According to the dictionary "realize" is defined as: 1. To give apparent reality to something, 2. To perceive or apprehend something in depth. There is a third: To convert something into money!

The establishment of order takes a personal effort. Order is not discovered but realized. Some philosophers say it must be discovered but we will take the view that it must be realized or established. For us there is no absolute or true order based on a well-structured world—only order that is realized. What of degree of order or type of order? There are many types of order, and there can be more or less order. Order is always related to a path of expectations. The expectations are the set of further realizable alternatives. We can only speak of relative order. Order is not arbitrary because of the filters. We can detect only those patterns of order of which we are already aware. We are not able to find every order or to order every finding. We do not find any order, but we order our findings.

For instance, if we have 1, 2, 3 . . . then the expectation would be for 4.

if we have 1, 2, 3, 4 . . . then the expectation for 5 would be even higher, but if we have 2, 3, 5, . . . then uncertainty . . .

2, 3, 5, 7, 11, 13 for most people would be a very weak order. (Prime numbers)

For many people a well-defined progression is necessary.

We extrapolate. We make a hypothesis of an underlying structure to explain the untidy things offered to us. This is similar to a perception hypothesis which might be that a free-standing blackboard is black on both sides. Similarly, order is not necessarily a numerical sequence.

If we have 1, 2, 3, 4, 5, 6, 7, 8, 9, 10, 11, 12, 13, 14, 15, 16, 17, 18, 19, then the "model" of sequence has already had 19 successors or confirmations, and the expectation of 20 is extremely strong.

The more we are successful, the more we cling to our hypothesis. But why should not the sequence continue, not to 20, but to 18, 17, 16, 15 . . . etc. This could be, but the expectation would be very slight. Why 19? Nineteen is a very unimportant number and we can by no means extrapolate successfully. 1, 2, 3, 2, 1, 2, 3, 2, 1, 2, 3, 2, 1 . . . would be much easier to expect.

The sequence of natural numbers is shared by everyone. But there are personal concepts of order, such as the ordering of a desk! To the person not using the desk there might be no order apparent, but we could test the degree of order by the time the user needs to find something particular. This would provide a measure of order amidst apparent visual chaos. Therefore *visual* order is not necessary for there to be *order*—you cannot infer from a visual order an overall order and it may even, as above, suggest an absence of order.

For instance, in a computer memory, the cells which are charged electrically and their "order" is important and this is invisible. Visual order is merely one type amongst others. From the plan of a city one cannot tell the order OR the disorder of social relations. For example, consider New York City's apparent "grid order." The important types of order depend on other things.

Is there order in a message or not? One can offer a person a message and make him extrapolate it. You can by this method deduce the degree of ordering and type of ordering present for someone who extrapolates. Another possibility to find out someone's concept if order is to disturb a message: e.g. What is wrong here? 4, 6, 8, 12; [the last number] should be 20 for the number of sides in platonic solids, but who knows about platonic solids?

Easier is:

WACHINGTON[1]

or

-BS-RV-R

One characteristic of the degree of order is the amount of disturbance you can apply without it becoming meaningless. The stability against disturbance we call redundancy. The more stable anything is to disturbances the greater its degree of order. If we say "I am thinking of a sentence, What is its first letter?" etc. . . . the strategy is that it could be any of 26 letters. But most sentences begin with A or TH. We can plot vertically the number of guesses. The whole information was at the beginning—and all messages have principally the same character.

We can take redundancy as a measure of order, by having a scheme of alternatives and using different persons for the same message. Research here reduces surprise in looking for constructions amongst a certain collection of phenomena. If we know how bodies fall in a gravitational field, we are not surprised by the behavior of a stone. Similarities in design, construction, etc. increase redundancy; variety, etc. reduces redundancy. Some portion of the design process is concerned with the creation of redundancy and order.

Certain messages are meaningful, however, others are not. The sequence of dice throws of 6, 6, 6, 6, 6, 6, 6 is taken to be less probable than 1, 2, 5, 2, 4, 3, 6, though the probability is exactly the same. "Luck" here in this sequence occurs not as the result of dice throwing but as the sequence of identical items, the repetitive sequence; in addition 6 usually means the winning number and this all changes the pattern of reference and thus we expect 6 less often than the other numbers. It is more meaningful.[2]

A redundancy can be assigned to every process provided such a pattern can be defined. R = 0 means chaos, complete unpredictability. R = 1 means dullness. All actual systems are somewhere in between. If one were to look at a swinging pendulum for five hours, providing no information at all, then there would be absolute dullness and this would be unbearable. Somewhere between 0 and 1 is the optimal amount of redundancy.

Sequences through time and space have the same characteristics as numerical sequences in this connection. For instance, if a user meets only unexpected spatial experiences, he is uneasy—a trap behind almost every door, for instance! This does not mean that we cannot have innovation of course, but any innovation from the original concept has to be different from the set of expectations; but, on the other hand, if the set itself is uninteresting, then it may be very little different.

Contemporary art violates this rule—parts of the artistic sub-culture have developed so that they cannot be understood even by the members! They have a reference system of order types so far from expectation that it seems chaotic from other reference systems. Only an avant-garde person can keep up with the order types; they soon become obsolete and continuous action is necessary. One can test this by asking people, regarding a group of modern paintings, which have an ordering, e.g. a common painter, style, etc.

There are many possibilities too in that the degree of redundancy present for any person and any innovation has to be different from the learned set of order

Figure 1.6.1

types, and on the other side it may not be too much so. Information theory gives measurements for the degree of redundancy and it can thus be quantified.

One way to classify the process in our own world is to say that there are processes of type A and B.

Type A—entropic processes—those subject to the second law of thermodynamics—the entropy of a closed system tends towards a maximum. In a highly ordered system, according to our ability to perceive it, the degree of order is unlikely to increase of itself. Time, dust, rats, are always working to reduce order. Any process involving heat is of this type. Everything decays to its more probable state. Redundancy is decreased, order is decreased; any energy-producing processes are of this type. Hot and cold water tend to mix. Complicated molecules tend to decay to form less complicated atoms and the very highly ordered atoms of the periodic system decay to form the less highly ordered and only the middle ones are left.

Type B—*neg-entropic* processes. Teaching makes someone's behavior redundant. Design is a neg-entropic process. The degree of neg-entropy can be measured by the time that a certain pattern would take to occur by chance. The arrangement of rooms means the imprinting of less order than that of making bricks to produce rooms.

Order is established as a profession develops. A concise code is developed sufficient to trigger off a process, for example, the process of getting a bricklayer to build a wall is very efficient and ordered.

The law is that you can never imprint more order by type B than you thereby level out under type A somewhere else. The creation of a wall by the laying of a brick is nevertheless reducing the energy level of the universe.[3] In each process the amount of redundancy is taken from somewhere, and seems to be equal to or a counterpart to the energy conserved. This is part of the physics of matter and we shall not go into this too deeply.

There are many types of redundancy too, but again we shall not go into these in any great depth.

From any flow of events only a limited amount of order can be drawn. If one offers a subject a message, the probabilities are several, even on a very long run. The sequence is never actually determined. People tend to overestimate the probability of rare events. They underestimate frequent events. This is something more, however, than curiosity. There is a tendency too, to overestimate the degree of order in a message.

For example, if 20 observations are made of the concurrence of full moon and change of weather, then the change is commonly suspected to occur in 10 instances, some people would say it occurs in 15 cases. The exact occurrence is about 0.1???[4] This is commonly called superstition and superstition is prevalent everywhere!

Most of our judgments are on statistically unsound bases.[5] Our willingness to enter into any discussion as an "expert" is due to this fact. We take a few cases of evidence as being sufficient to establish a general rule. A lot of social psychology deals with this phenomenon.

When Skinner fed pigeons at random intervals, peculiar dances were developed due to accidental movement, which, once or twice were coupled with the appearance of food. They imprinted order into their environment, as an unordered environment cannot be borne. In anthropology too, savage races dance to get rain. If rain does not come, the dance was "wrong" for some reason. Superstition cannot be falsified!

By overestimating, the perceived order of the world is increased, and the mechanism that does this can be very well described.

Also another similar superstition is that "everyone with a high forehead is intelligent" or "intelligent people have intelligent faces." There is a self-fulfilling prophecy in this—such people probably, as a result of such prejudices, get a better education and thus the superstition is reinforced. This holds good for any stereotyped judgments.

Of course we have a lot of well-justified beliefs too—that the sun will rise tomorrow, etc., but the tendency to overestimate is always present. This can be shown if we imagine we have to engage a member of staff from eight persons. There is an immediate uncertainty. We want persons who are intelligent and diligent. There is an uncertainty of two for each person.[6]

However, one might say that Negroes are idle, and that intelligent people are diligent, so the uncertainty is reduced immediately. We do not always have statistical information and we have to advance hypotheses, which are ill-balanced but very effective methods of reducing the decision process. People with a lot of hypotheses have a very positive view of the world. Such a person never hires a Negro, so he is never proved wrong.

Another facet of the dynamics of the image is that of the learning process. The learning process means sharing the image. This is much more difficult. We can distinguish between eight types of learning; the process of learning by:

1. an unconditioned reflex;
2. a conditioned reflex (Pavlov);
3. "Skinner" conditioning—success, reward or punishment;
4. imprinting;
5. trial and error;
6. training—repetitive doing;
7. instruction;
8. insight;
    (i) irreversible—concept formation—the name, structure etc. built into the conceptual image;
    (ii) conscious—by thinking what is the right or wrong way

In any culture, the relation of variation of judgment is widely shared, and there is an acceptable or permissible range of judgment. If you go beyond the range you are a communist, crank, etc.

There is a regulator mechanism for such a system, the narrower the range, the greater the chance of heretics. The wider the range, the greater the chance of the system to fly to pieces. This mechanics of the range of judgment has been found out.

How do you find optimum redundancy? For example, how often do you have to repeat a sentence to a child learning French before he knows it? Say you wish to stabilize a message against noise—a written or spoken message. One can derive the amount of redundancy destroyed by noise—even at a cocktail party language can be understood, personal differences, environmental disturbances, etc. have had order imposed. How much redundancy you can take out depends on the noise level, and intensity can be expressed in terms of entropy as well.

Notes

1 Misspelling intentional—Rittel's intention being to show how it is possible to understand a message even if there is some variation from the expected, or "correct," message.

2 Rittel marked this paragraph as "imprecise," but his reasoning here is basically in agreement with the conclusions of the work of Daniel Kahneman, Amos Tversky and their colleagues that shows the importance of framing effects on judgments of probability (see, e.g. Kahneman 2002; Kahneman and Tversky 1984; Tversky and Kahneman 1974).

3 Presumably Rittel's intention here is to suggest that while local order is increased to create a wall, the overall process still tends to serve the second law of thermodynamics by destruction of other forms of order.

4 Rittel's precise mathematical intention here is not entirely clear. The general principle seems to be that which he has been discussing: the gap between the mathematical probabilities, i.e. the 'rational' answer, and the estimated probability made by most people.

5 As previously noted, a large body of research has shown this to be true.

6 The uncertainty of two is because there are two traits in question. But Rittel does not examine the mathematical details; the explanation that follows is non-mathematical.

References

Bendix, R. and Lipset, S. M. (eds) (1953) *Class, Status, and Power: Social Stratification in Comparative Perspective*. Glencoe, IL: Free Press.

Lazarsfeld, P. F. (ed.) (1955) *The Language of Social Research*. Glencoe, IL: Free Press.

Osgood, C. E., Suci, G. J., and Tannenbaum, P. H. (1957) *The Measurement of Meaning*. Urbana, IL: University of Illinois Press.

Chapter 1.7

Seminar 5: Measuring Values and Images

Horst W. J. Rittel

Previously we have talked about the capacities of man as a data processing system, the methods we have for organizing the image, the dynamics of the image and socially shared images, and the economics of judgment on perception. No other construct seems to be as appropriate as a unifying concept as "the image" and this seems to offer an appropriate access to social science research, historical research, and so forth. The concept is as good as any other one using terms such as "memory subconscious" etc.—equally justified, but also in this language the designer is a participant as well as his client and the users of his results; he doesn't play a special role. He doesn't have an outside standpoint. For all design participants, it is possible that one's memory says, "I did this," while one's pride says "I cannot have done this," and eventually the mind surrenders.

Last week we discussed the degree of order, trends, etc., but we did not discuss the actual content of images. Information theory is useful here as we saw, on amounts of information in images or messages, but content we have not dealt with—and it cannot be dealt with by laws because of the strong historical content and the great inertia—images may be inherited from generation to generation. In talking about images there is a conflict between personal and archetypical images. In literature, by comparison, the emphasis is put on personal or shared parts of the image. We have to take both these parts; we cannot take only one.

There are certain ways by which we can obtain evidence of someone's image. We have no possibility of exploring anyone's whole image as any attempt to investigate an image will influence it strongly. The kind of image we study therefore has to be partial and refer only to particular situations. Also any kind of anything, i.e. another person's image, for instance, is structured or filtered by the observer, too. The basic ways of obtaining evidence consist of:

1. Introspection: One's own images are assumed to be sufficiently similar to someone else's. By analogy my own construct is similar to that of someone else. Most of what we do is based on the fact that "what is good for me is

good for someone else." We can predict other people's behavior by assuming that they are similar to us, but this is not always true.

2. Analogy: We observe someone behaving like our subject and we imagine or presume the subject will behave in the same way. This process needs:
   - Indicants—people with these properties have such characteristics and your subject will behave accordingly; and
   - Intimacy—you have long-term personal knowledge of behavior.

3. Observation of behavior . . . manifest behavior: How people spend their money, time, Sundays, the houses they buy, etc. We observe, define, and draw conclusions about their image. This is dangerous. The evidence does not say much about the image as often people have no choice in matters—they may not have enough money, or no knowledge of the opportunities. We can only observe behavior in response to an existing environment and how they would like to behave in a different environment may be quite different. These observations therefore should be restricted.

4. Experimental observation of behavior: We set up a controlled situation and observe the controlled behavior or changes in behavior. External influences must be reduced as much as possible. Only a few of the parameters change and we can therefore formulate general rules of behavior, and/or get an idea of a person's image.

5. Conclusions from general theories, i.e. conclusions based on the tendencies towards biased estimates of probabilities: General theories are applied to a particular situation and can be used to explain particular types of behavior.

6. Symbolic communication: Talks, books, etc.
   - (i) Direct communication: e.g. talking—as in psychoanalysis
   - (ii) Indirect communication: from documents or transcripts.

These are the main sources of information about images. Why do we want this knowledge? Shouldn't ability to predict behavior be enough? No. We have seen that manifest behavior for instance might spring from quite remote influences.

Another question is that many attitudes might never become manifest. Some people are never satisfied throughout their lives: is this significant or interesting or not? The science dealing with these questions is social psychology, which has certain techniques, dealing especially with methods 3–6.[1]

A whole list of methods has been developed under the heading of content analysis, especially in linguistic communication developed by Harold D. Lasswell in the late 1920s. Also work by Berelson was much used in the last war to detect subversive groups, Russia's next move, etc. Techniques have been refined and computerized procedures worked out. Given a certain body of text, the message is categorized according to an imposed set of certain concepts to try to categorize the content as such a text. These techniques are often used in advertising to analyze foreign news bulletins, etc.:

1. These categories are applied to the text and the occurrence or nonoccurrence of certain words is measured.

2. Rates can be charted for various categories.
3. First single words, then the whole concept, can be assessed.
4. The evaluative concepts that are used can be assessed.
5. Statistical evaluations are assessed. The categories can be adapted so far as necessary to find certain evidence or not, and are mostly used for the:
    (i)   design of techniques of persuasion, and in advertising. The techniques can also be used to analyze vocabularies and find out what is important enough to be named, and what is considered self-evident and so not named.
    (ii) also what are people's evaluation vocabularies? What are the attitudes of the sender compared to universes of discourse?
    (iii) also evaluating the effectiveness of messages.
    (iv) also we can investigate stylistic qualities in Shakespeare, the Bible, etc.

The most interesting studies are those in which conclusions are drawn about the producer of the message. An assumption is made in that corroboration in texts means corroboration in intent. These techniques have become important in predicting certain actions or developments—for example, Germany's V-weapons predicted from an analysis of propaganda texts. The split between Germany and Italy was predicted from fitting together German and Italian texts and finding that they didn't fit. Hundreds of persons are now analyzing Russian and Chinese texts to see if and how they corroborate.

It is even possible to give the zeitgeist of a period a precise meaning in terms of its vocabulary. The goal is always to quantify the frequency of certain content units.

A further technique of analysis is that of semantic profiles. A person is offered a stimulus, word, or object, a situation, and is asked to take a series of decisions against a set of scales with seven intervals in it of direct polarities. You then get a line called a profile made up of a series of decisions on where the individual person would place certain words. Most profiles produced are very similar but not identical.[2] The categories of types of person used in social psychology become relevant as they will produce significantly different profiles. The profiles are difficult to interpret alone, but by comparison with others they become interesting.

"Lonesomeness" in American English means or implies weak, bad, unclear; in German it means great, good, and healthy. There is a good deal of work on standardized lists of polarities, but with different interpretations.

There are several other techniques in Osgood (Osgood *et al.* 1957). Also, Attneave, *Applications of Information Theory to Psychology* (1959).

These techniques have been applied to the American fashion industry. This becomes interesting where fashion is a worldwide organization and the old mechanisms of production and decay do not work any longer. From the fourteenth century to the 1900s, there was a high regularity of change of fashion. A cycle of 95 years occurs five times in the shape and length of women's skirts of three types over 500 years. The change in the cycle's pattern occurred in about 1900 when fashion

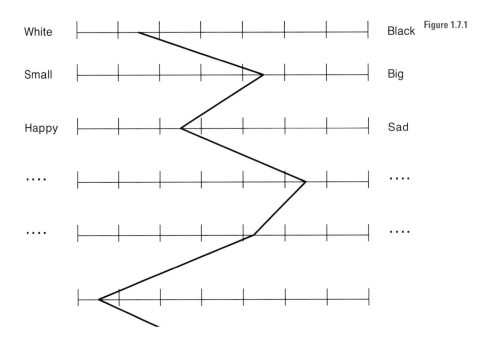

Figure 1.7.1

ceased to be a self-regulating process, but a highly organized process, and the old periodicity no longer occurred. Kroeber has a correlation of the length of a skirt and the average wealth. This was very apt through the first 45 years of the century, but now other kinds of regularity occur. Some effective research was undertaken when it became necessary to try to predict next year's fashions. These certain regularities were found out.

Barber and Lobel in the late 1940s and early 1950s compared fashion, women's clothing, and the American social system. They tried to correlate fashion with environment and discovered that fashion change has three purposes: 1) utilitarian, 2) aesthetic, and 3) symbolic (to indicate a social role). These processes for the dispersion of fashion are different for different countries, but in America, role 3 is particularly important.

Barber and Lobel assumed a well-established social stratification. This oddly enough is the result of sociological effort to develop a stratification system for society in the 1920s. The classification of the American people on this system was tried and social status was matched to it, together with other variables such as consumer behavior, etc., and it was found that there was not a very good correlation.

However, this stratification system was applied as IF they existed and such was the imprinting power of concepts that in fact they now not only exist but are recognized to exist by the population—a pretty awful result of sociology. It has now become a reality after three decades.

Barber and Lobel had to assume the system as significant, and in terms of the methods in the section above they made a content analysis of the existing documents: the fashion magazines—who reads which magazine, etc. They decided there must be a kind of mutual adaptation to what the magazines write and what

the readers want to read, otherwise they wouldn't read them. From this they got an impression of the image of fashion of the readers—by descriptions in the texts, etc.
It appeared that:

1. Women have the task of practicing consumption to demonstrate status. Buying and wearing dresses is an effective way to do this. Also a higher status can be symbolized by wearing clothes of an upper level.
2. Women have the tendency to maximize status on a given budget; "Clothes for climbing, etc."[3]
3. On the other hand, fashion is available to all—all can climb the ladder and this contradiction is the motor of the fashion industry.

At first glance there are not many major differences in clothes, but many minor ones, and the silhouettes trickle down from the "haute couture" to the ready-to-wear with tiny alterations at each stage. The whole industry relies on this "trickle down" process.
We could carry out this process with the language of architects and their critics. How the concepts are related to their designs could be studied, together with the use of advanced computer techniques carried out automatically by machine, or by interviewing techniques, etc.

Discussion

If we presented persons with 60 photographs of houses we can, or could, characterize their architectural preferences.
Warner's (Warner, Meeker and Eells 1949) social class scales were used to characterize the Americans.
We can also get scales of the residual nature of the image—a person willing his behavior against the environment.
We can also scale people according to psychological types—permissive, authoritarian, political types, etc.

Notes

1 Rittel marks this passage with an "X"—did he intend to delete it? Perhaps his answer to his own question was that it was not significant or interesting.
2 Rittel crossed out this sentence. His reasons for doing so are unclear; perhaps he thought it inaccurate or had no evidence to support the claim. It is an intriguing possibility that this similarity does exist. It also seems like the kind of thing on which we would presume similarity, despite evidence.
3 Rittel's intention here is unclear. He seems to intend to suggest differential behavior patterns: e.g. some women are concerned with making resources go a long way while others are more concerned with using resources to achieve higher social class.

References

Attneave, F. (1959) *Applications of Information Theory to Psychology: A Summary of Basic Concepts, Methods and Results*. New York: Henry Holt.
Barber, B. and L. S. Lobel. (1952) "Fashion in Women's Clothes and The American Social System." *Social Forces*, 31: 124–31.

Foundations

Berelson, B. (1953) *Content Analysis in Communication Research.* Glencoe, IL: Free Press.

Osgood, C. E., Suci, G. J. and Percy Tannenbaum, P. H. (1957) *The Measurement of Meaning.* Urbana, IL: University of Illinois Press.

Warner, W. L., Meeker, M., and Eells, K. (1949). *Social Class in America: A Manual of Procedure for the Measurement of Social Status.* Chicago: Science Research Associates, Inc.

Seminar 6: Environments

Horst W. J. Rittel

It is necessary to start once again by making things perhaps more difficult than they seem to be. However, if we want to use the concept of environment—and we do, it is a useful one—we have to fit it into the system of concepts already developed.

First, the notion of environments can only be used in respect to someone. One can abbreviate this to:

$E_A(t)$: *A*'s environment at time *t*

We know that this has to be a part of A's image, and in particular part of his situational image, part of his image of the external world. Second, we have to distinguish between A's environment and the image that someone has of A's environment. These are not identical. One can abbreviate this to:

$I_D E_A(t)$ The image of a designer (*D*) of *A*'s environment at time *t*

This is made up of both the designer's knowledge of particular circumstances and his expectations concerning them. The environment is part of his image, which is externalized—the outside world. This is objectified, or ordered, or made redundant by the brain system we have previously discussed. We can define the environment as the totality of sources, messages and the foci of attention to which the actions of A are directed. The environment is the "here and now" in which the eye plays its part. In this "stage" the messages get their meaning, the "stage" is set so that messages get their meaning by being placed on the "set."

As the environment cannot be determined by the exterior situation alone, e.g. by specifying the physical surroundings of A, at least as important is the interior state of A described by the activated image; any prediction of A's behavior has to contain information about the interior state as well—and there are interesting statements about this too. The outside messages are received by A, and the actions of A are fed back by messages from outside, and thus we have a closed circuit between action and perception via the environment. These are correlated with incoming messages by controlling the success or failure of A's actions to find the most appropriate courses of action.

That the environment is not so easily determined by external objects has been best described by an American psychologist in 1915 who took senior students and presented them with an apple.[1] They were asked to consider it, to think about it and then were asked to sit in front of a screen and imagine the image of the apple upon it. The image was actually projected on to the screen with low intensity but all observers considered it to be their own.

We have therefore to deal with the internal state and expectancy and the external stimuli. What of the usage of this concept of environment in other disciplines, i.e. sociology, psychology, and biology? We can only point out here a few contrasting standpoints. There is, or was, a schism in the behavioral sciences between those who believe in "heritage" or hereditary forces as the main ones affecting our behavior and those who believe in the "imprinting" forces of environment as being dominant in molding behavior. Both these views have now been further studied and relativized and a dynamic compromise has made this dualism now seem to be obsolete. Both aspects of environmental influences are effective, and which one dominates depends on the nature of the phenomena considered.[2]

PASTORE. The investigations of the psychologist Nicholas Pastore in 1949 dealt with the literature of the quantification of the dominance of both inherited and environmentally influenced characteristics. He investigated the relationships between the political attitudes of the researchers and their standpoints. The assumption of the heredity standpoint he found is inherently associated with conservative views, the environmental influences being most stressed by radicals, socialists and liberals. They take the other side of the milieu standpoint and reject heredity.

For all participants the environment is taken as given and as objectively described by the observer. In all cases the scientists claim they have better access to knowledge about the subject's environment than the subject himself. The naiveté and limitations of this view of the arrogant assumption by an observer that he was able to recognize a "true" environment were not at the same time forgotten, however.[3]

Let us take further examples of the study of environment, how it is defined and dealt with.

WATSON. John B. Watson was the founder and inventor of behaviorism. He defines environment as "our world of stimuli." He takes the sources of information about the environment to be restricted to observable facts and their interpretation. He emphasizes the fact that the stimuli that act on the individual not only act on the body in general but on particular parts of the body, which may be of great interest. Hunger contractions of the stomach for instance, and pain originating in any part of the body are both part of the environment. They form, therefore, an external environment and an internal environment—a child for instance is under permanent stimulus from the outside and inside and adjusts by reflex action and habit formation.

Watson maintains that the environment may be shared by others but the image is not shared. This is a peculiar view as the inner boundary is lost, as any part of the body can be the source of stimuli. There is no inner boundary and thus any local stimulization is lost; it is in the environment in general and so this point of view is an implicit description of an "immaterial essential" of the individual.

LEWIN. Kurt Lewin describes an interesting concept of "fields"[4] and topological considerations—psychical situations and their relationships to behavior. The environment is understood sometimes as a momentary and manifest situation and at other times as "the milieu" of the chief characteristics of the permanent situation. The "present" is taken as an actual and manifest situation and distinguished from those concepts common to a whole sequence of operations operating over a longer period of time—the "milieu." This has certain important implications. He says it is impossible to single out one part attributed to the individual and one part attributed to the environment. We cannot have one part ordered from outside and one from inside. Both heredity and environment must work together in the same sense in order to affect certain modes of behavior. It is impossible for these to be in conflict and he maintains that you cannot make a clear distinction of dominance of one over the other; however, a certain predisposition must be accepted. The sensitivity varies with the individual—psychopaths are more sensitive to their environment than normal individuals for instance. He says that the dynamics of environmental differences can be investigated only simultaneously with the study of individual differences and general psychological laws. This means the complete renunciation of the environment as a separate entity; the two factors, he says, are connected in an inseparable way. Some parts of the environment have a challenging character and stimulate active behavior; some have an activating function on the "field" concept.

Lewin goes on to define the circumferential "field" as structured significantly by the individual situation, by experience, personal needs, personality, etc. This concept makes sense to the psychoanalyst who is interested in personal characteristics, not general ones, and so a concept individualizing the environment is very useful. He establishes an "incomparable" individual world but nevertheless says that these worlds can be compared.

VON UEXKÜLL. Von Uexküll, the Estonian biologist, takes a counter position. He is interested in environment related specifically to a particular species. He takes an arrogant view of the human species as a superior one with a richer and more complex view and knowledge of its environment. He is able to define man as able to describe the environment of a bird as different from the environment of himself and the human is someone who can "embed" the environment of a bird in his own concept of environment. The human can visualize then that his own environment is more complicated and he can understand the bird's environment better.

Each organism, he says, has a sensory apparatus and an effecting apparatus. The first permits an appreciation or "tapping" of information from the environment and the second permits a transformation of this into active behavior. The environment is considered as a source of food, danger, pleasure, etc., and each individual organism has its own proper world which is almost synonymous with the environment: what the individual organism realizes is the "world outside." This is the assumption of an object world in order to understand animal behavior. It is a peculiar mixture of a subjectivist point of view by assigning a subjective world to any organism and objectivistic by claiming such a reference system.

CYBERNETICS. The cybernetic point of view of environment is especially useful. We shall discuss the views of Ashby.[5] He is interested in using this concept to describe the behavior of a "machine" under various circumstances. He describes a machine as an entity having an output and an input. He could have used the word "system" in place of "machine" and sometimes does, perhaps deliberately, in a provocative way. For him, the environment is the set of those variables that change, or are changed by the behavior of an individual. These are the source of inputs, origins, and destinations, and these variables are his "environment." He considers only such cases as described by a finite set of parameters—but this is not a serious restriction. The emphasis is that he defines his concept of environment in a purely functional and non-materialistic sense—in terms of relationships between inputs and outputs—not of physical objects or pieces of hardware. He says the environment begins with stimuli, not with objects causing stimuli. He assumes that the environment can be represented by "dials" or variables, presumed to be explorable by the observer and intrinsically statically determined. A "state" as being understood by an observer makes it predictable by an observer. He says the organism and its environment form a single state-determined system, and there is feedback between the organism and its environment. They form a whole and must be viewed as such. Ashby maintains that an environment is in no sense an isolated concept, as Lewin does, the environment and the "machine" have to be considered as linked to make sense. The fact that physiologists and biologists can speak of a separate environment is because they design their experiments so that feedback is cut off. Reflex investigations and perceptual experiments are designed so that feedback to the causing stimulus is blocked. Feedback is often prevented since in many cases the object is acting against the stimuli. There is a closed circuit of cause and effect, not an open one. However, it is good and useful in psychology to cut the closed circuit, but for the cybernetician the concern is with both the organism and the environment and the dividing line is partly merely conceptual and arbitrary between the two. All these considerations are in accordance with our original specification.

What are the boundaries and structures of an environment if we accept this new proposal? If we want to detach A's environment from A and A's perceptions, where "A" is human, this is a very difficult task. There is a complicated structure of human images and also man's ability for symbolic communication, i.e. what we see, and an ever-changing pattern of goals and values. We cannot take the view of an objective external viewer. The observer and the observed are in the same order of magnitude with respect to their capacities and complexities. To demonstrate their complication, it might be useful to consider the meaning of the statement that environment is the "here and now" of an individual.

What does "here" mean? This depends on our image of what "here" is, the Cork Room, the Berkeley Campus, the University of California, one side of the table, the earth, the USA, or the solar system, and so forth. What is understood here as the locus depends on the context, or any situational image, even of certain aspects of the actual environment which might be disturbing. We can put ourselves into contexts of various—even continental—dimensions and the radius of environment changes constantly with the context or "state" of the situational image.

What does "now" mean? This again is not well established—especially compared with animals who seem to have a stable, and well-ordered "now." Human "now" can be 13 April, or spring, or the 1960s, or the twentieth century, under the presidency of Johnson, after World War II. There are many meanings and again a complete list is impossible and depends on the temporal part of the situational image.

To each part of any temporal or spatial localization, the "here and now", belongs an ego, and the choice of the "here" and the "now" seems to be related to the role we are playing at the time. In any situation, we "play" certain parts according to whether we are speaking, or behaving as a citizen of the United States, or as a taxpayer, one of an audience, an architect, etc., and to each and every role seem to belong different notions of what the "here and now" mean. There then seems to be a link with the sociological concepts of role differentiation.

These few remarks show how the environment is very flexible. The question is—is it determined by external stimuli? Not entirely, because of the internal component in the sense of Watson. But not only are the feelings of pain and hunger of Watson significant but we can choose our situational image and concentrate and pretend to be in a particular situation. It is not entirely determined by macroscopic stimuli in the behavioristic sense. As we know, the actual environment is also determined by a selection of external stimuli, filtered receptive signals from our conceptual devices, and therefore our environment is partially determined by this choice of concepts.

Also, stimuli in this establishment or realization of a certain environment may be involved, as we have seen, with perception over a very long period. Present stimuli are not the only ones influencing A's environment in time. The time slice is not a rigid one. The environment, too, is flexible in connection with symbolic communication. One can influence a person's image of his present situation by talking, and this is a very powerful influence indeed upon the situational image.

The choice of environment is subject to internal communication, too. One can train oneself to choose the environment one likes and become independent of stimuli in the physical sense, and also choose the stimuli one prefers. The practitioners of yoga, and the Stoics, have "internalized" their environment and admit only internal stimuli to the "stage" of performance. They reject all adverse stimuli and take as their environment something entirely differently determined.

The determined stimuli come from not only the internal organs as Watson suggests, but the individual image is the source of relevant stimuli as well as manifest, observable stimuli from outside. On the other hand, there are also strong environments that can force the individual to adopt a different reality to that which he would prefer. Extreme pain or astonishment can force the individual to revise the "stage of performance" in a situation which does not fit the pattern of expectation—and adopt another moveable "scene." All those situations for which the expectational pattern is falsified beyond the threshold of tolerance produce this occurrence, and these are the strong environments.

For environmental designers the following questions are fundamental and have to be raised. For whose environment has the object to be laid out, and in which situation? How is this to be done for several, or hundreds, of different users? How can the influence of an environmental change, as perceived by the designer, on the set network of the user, be calculated? What influence will it have on the situational image of the user?

To sum up, neither the internal nor external boundaries of an actual environment, nor the fine structuring are easily determined. The environments of the professionals are not coincidental with those realized by the users. There are also sub-cultural environments, such as architecture and the fine arts, which define a certain kind of standard description, but it is still an open question if other persons see them in this way.

Perhaps there are different strategies to bring these into coincidence. One is to adapt the professional language, the other is to train the users and beholders to see the way in which the professionals see the environment. Two extreme strategies are therefore to put the learning effort on the side of the user, or on the side of the designer.

It would be wrong to assume that the "set" of the conscious environment under the same external condition has a kind of invariant "onion" structure, with a person on the inside and an outside shell, thinning out to the more distant parts. There can be many meanings of "here and now" which cannot be arranged in a serial order as if each member were contained in the former member. To say a concept like "1964" is part of "the "'60s" is not true—it involves an entirely different structure. There is no system of sets containing each other.

Similarly the idea that an environment "thins out" towards the periphery is also false. In some instances the boundaries are most detailed—for instance all boundaries relating to circumstances of unknown danger, in which case the emphasis of environment is put on the boundaries, not the center.

Again, A's environment is to a constant degree determined not only by present stimuli. The freedom of the Schiller type exists:[6] "Man is free even though he is born in chains." This German idealism is just freedom from social and physical conditions. This is, however, only true in a dialectical sense. The above-mentioned strong environments of the extremes of pain, etc. stimulate the internal exile in non-fitting and uncomfortable environments.

Information Content. One invariant for all these situations seems to be the capacity of the situational image—the capacity of consciousness. The simultaneously present amount of information cannot exceed 150 bits. This is the upper limit of complexity of an environment according to the capacity of the short-term memory, but this is really never reached. The environment is never seen to be so complex. Only if all one's capacity is used to understand a situation can one say that the maximum is reached.

The capacity of the short-term memory is shared between the attention of the individual to the environment and other things, for example, if one thinks, the environment becomes simpler because the sum of the variables or information contents has an upper threshold. Also, the redundancy of an environment can be 0 or 1. In a completely chaotic environment where $R = 0$, or in a completely ordered environment where R = 1, we feel nothing, the environment is completely deter-mined, dull, sends no messages. All actual environments are somewhere between these two extremes—a tautology according to our vocabulary.

Parts of our environment are very complex and much of environmental design is an attempt to make environments redundant. The "best" part of an environment might therefore be considered as that which sends no messages. But this is only so from one point of view; perhaps it should send messages, but not too many or one would do nothing but participate in the messages! Most of our environment is very, very redundant, and those parts that we are happy with are fully determined. These parts send no messages and are comfortable,[7] those envi-ronments sending messages again and again are uncomfortable. Each environment must have a balance.

The more messages we receive the less we can perform on the stage of the situational image, and we can take as a working rule that environmental design is directed towards making environments redundant, and establishing an environment that does not send messages. This has certain implications on the situation of the designer. He has to have a more complicated image of the user's environment than the user has himself. He has to consider many things which, one hopes, the user will never consider—for instance, the collapse of the building. He has to complicate the environment. He generates the messages of the future environment in order to reduce their information content by deriving appropriate measures or regulation. His image of A's environment must be more complex than the image A himself has of his own environment. Both deal, however, with 150 bits at one time—but this is not a contradiction, as there are various strategies to deal with this problem that the designer may employ.

For instance, the designer can look at the environment piecemeal. Secondly, he has a good deal of time to consider the environment. Third, he can deal with the 150 items of the environment exclusively, whereas the user must, we hope, do something else as well.

These various strategies to bridge this gap of inflexible capacities can be used to define different types of design that deal with this question of capacity. We can describe types of design by the ways of handling this lack of capacity.

The explicit view of Ashby is of the designer as a regulator; he destroys sources of information. For any regulator, the information content to be regulated cannot exceed the information capacity of the regulator. (This is from Shannon, as discussed earlier in connection with the situational image.)

In addition, there are many automated stimulus-response reactions between the individual and the environment—such as the heat production and constant-temperature regulation mechanisms of the body.

Then, also, we have in recent times, in connection with research into man's behavior in space, much research into completely redundant situations. Usually termed "sensory deprivation"—nothing happens and madness results. A minimum of "noise" in the environment is necessary, but, of course, as we have seen both extremes must be avoided for any actual environment.

The behavior of any organism has a regular pattern against environmental disturbances. When the expectational pattern is not in congruence with the observed messages then a correction is required in order to act against the source of disturbance, and most of animal and human behavior can be understood in this way.

Then, there are certain components. The environment is not an unstructured thing and there are several ways of breaking down or classifying environments:

1. Classification by von Uexküll into affective and receptive environments. Usually the receptive environment must include the affective environment if you want to control what you are doing. If your range of action goes beyond the limits of what you can perceive, then action beyond the affective limit is out of control, and most organisms are organized in such a way that their receptive environment is larger, in a set-theoretical way, than their affective environment, in order to be able to appreciate the consequences of their actions, behavior, or decisions. There is no complete symmetry between receptors and affectors, but there must be an overlap or it would be impossible to make sense of the world. This is one decomposition.

2. One of the difficulties of human environments is that they are not determined by the range of the sensory and affector organs alone. There are the push-button systems. The affector environment may go far beyond the range of direct perception. On the other hand, too, one can hear the spoken word by radio, and images via television and these can become part of your environment even though the natural organs do not have this range. Again, it is extremely difficult to detect the environment of a particular person.

3. These claims can extend over great distances involving cause and effect but nevertheless there may be a feedback by another crutch of perception—telephone, TV, radio, etc. On the other hand, in addition, it is not always necessary to observe directly. An indicant is often sufficient, as a cloud indicates an approaching thunderstorm. Even when beyond the horizon and although it is not perceived directly, it is already within the environment by change of temperature, or atmosphere, and we must be very careful in determining these parts of the environment.

4. Another component is the focus of attention. This is that which gives the environment its true meaning. If one asks a person what he is doing and he replies "writing a letter" for instance, by this, the focus of attention is determined and the remainder constitutes "the surroundings." The more one is engaged in focusing on the activity, the less one can perceive from the surroundings.

5. Another distinction is that between the actual environment and the potential environment. The "actual" environmental field is what is actually perceived or realized at a time "t." The potential environmental field consists of the set of choices of available environments from which one is activated. The latter type is usually more interesting to a designer than a particular one, as he designs for a set, or sequence of environments, not particular situations, and over longer periods of time.

6. Another distinction is that between the active and passive environment. The active environment is that which produces effects or events. The passive

environment exists only for the designer who has invested his efforts in making the environment passive, unrealizable by the user. We can take this concept and apply it to several persons. We can make a topology of environments by describing the situation of a lion and a cow, and describe what their respective environments would have to be, if the cows were to survive. For example, the effective radius of the environment of the lion must not be greater than the receptive environment of the cow, and many rules for this can be devised topographically.

7. Shared environments, another distinction, involving the part of the successive communication process means the mutual tuning of environments. If one talks, or cooperates, with someone, it is necessary to establish a congruence of common environment and structure. The environments, though congruent and shared are not so very much more so than necessary. If this stress or cooperation is not given, environments diverge. For instance, if one takes several persons' descriptions of a film, this is not a stressed situation, and they will vary widely. Also the description of traffic accidents—the temporal order, persons involved, and other factors. There seems to be no objective description of an accident or crime. This fact shows the effect of the personal individual situational image on that which they each call reality.

To sum up:

1. The environment is only meaningful for an individual A at a time "t."
2. The environment of A is part of A's situational image. It is the realized set of observable sources and stimuli, and foci of action.
3. The maximum information content of an environment is not higher than the 150 bits of the short-term memory.
4. The environment is the "here" and "now" in which one person—an "I"—plays its role as a letter writer.
5. Many environments are socially shared. This means that a high degree of unanimity between different persons can be observed.
6. Environmental design is concerned with the establishment of such conditions that make the environment redundant.
7. The boundaries between the individual A and his environment, and between the environment and the non-environment, i.e. the outside zones, cannot easily be described by a radius, nor can the constituents of the environment, the objects which sum up to the environment and the world between them, be determined once and for all, or be determined by looking at that which is physically given.
8. A and his environment are inseparable from each other and only together do they constitute a meaningful unit of behavior.

Notes

1 Source unknown.
2 This argument has since been explored by many, see, for example, *The Triple Helix* (2000) by Richard Lewontin.

3 We have been unable to decide, in reviewing the seminar transcript, whether Rittel is here simply paraphrasing Pastore, or if he is critiquing him.

4 Commonly translated as "force fields" in English.

5 William Ross Ashby. Specific citations at end of seminar.

6 Friedrich Schiller (1759–1805) *Die Worte des Glaubens (The Word of the Faithful)*, st. 2 (1797).

7 This notion that the comfortable parts of the environment send no message is consistent with the communications theory idea of messages, but not with Boulding's idea of messages: by being redundant and static, comfortable parts of the environment send precisely the message of comfort: the message that things are stable and unchanging. Given the prevalence of change in the natural environment it is only natural that we be alert to both change and to stasis.

8 Specially recommended where he deals with more quantified sequences of events—descriptions of homeostats and mechanisms showing adaptive behavior.

References

Ashby, W. R. (1956) *Introduction to Cybernetics*. New York: Wiley.[8]

Ashby, W. R. (1952) *Design for a Brain*. New York: Wiley.

Lewin, K. (1935) *A Dynamic Theory of Personality*. New York: McGraw Hill.

Lewin, K. (1936) *Principles of Topological Psychology*. New York: McGraw Hill.

Pastore, N. (1949) *The Nature-Nurture Controversy*. New York: King's Crown Press.

Seminar 7: Design

Horst W. J. Rittel

From this point we will talk only about design. In the first lecture we began with a definition of innovation and we tried to describe innovation as a social activity, and in particular an institutionalized activity. Now we shall examine a particular feature of the innovation process and its concepts and characteristics.

We have said that innovation is an activity directed towards the controlled change of a particular object system with respect to a given pattern expectation and a predetermined purpose. Innovation has been used as a concept which includes other concepts such as design, research, planning, etc., and all of them are particular types of innovation. This definition of particular types of innovation is not, however, very easy. It is not really satisfactory to use innovation as an "umbrella" concept—a more general concept with all the subconcepts beneath it and all equivalent, for three reasons—that we can "plan" for design, we can carry out research for planning, there is policymaking for design—and so this distinction cannot lead to a mutually exclusive definition of those activities on the same logical level in a kind of hierarchy, i.e. a "tree" cannot be used and we have to distinguish those variables and various activities by their temporal range, the type of objects and events they are dealing with, the nature of the problems, the results and the purposes they are fulfilling, and by their social context.

Today, however, we are not going to talk about the conceptual distinctions between these activities but about environmental design alone, and it might be sufficient to give an assertive description of positive *properties* of design rather than a rigorous definition.

We have already shown that the idea of "physical" design, as compared with other types of design or research, is not a very powerful categorization, and the question of whether a design problem results in physical entities or not is one of the temporal range of the project and not something of fundamental difference.[1] The longer the planning interval of a project is, the less "physical" in a primitive sense is the result.

For other properties of design we can say that:

1. Design is directed towards a particular situation which is historically unique, rather than towards a class of situations as research is.[2]

2. Design is concerned with the alteration of an expectational pattern, or the making of things different from the expectations.
3. The object of design is a deliberate falsification of prediction, while research is directed towards the improvement of the expectational pattern.[3]
4. Design proceeds from the abstract to the concrete.
5. Design results are highly improbable events, therefore they provide a high degree of information. Synonymously this means that design results cannot be predicted by extrapolation.[4]
6. Design is orientated towards the creation of redundancy—but with a high degree of order. This may seem contradictory to the previous statement but the scheme by which redundancy is measured is a different one from that used previously to describe a design problem.[5]
7. Design is an intentional activity—design by chance should be excluded.[6]

The final lecture will describe the relationships between these various innovating activities.

What is environmental design as a particular part of designing? We can say that environmental design is concerned with, and directed towards, a change in someone's environment, but this has not necessarily anything to do with physical objects. Any objective entity which is related to others can be subjected to design.[7]

Strictly and rigorously, environmental design is a pleonasm—a redundant formulation. As a situation exists only for someone and contains his environment within it, then if the situation is changed—for instance, by environmental design, then the environment is changed automatically. We will not, however, go much further into this linguistic problem.

Using our concept of environmental design, however, it could include therefore enabling someone to appreciate his environment differently, without actually changing it—but merely by changing his image. In other words, education is a type of environmental design for the pupil. Teaching and learning concepts affect the behavior; they involve therefore design of behavior and thus environmental design.

It could be said, however, that we do not want to change the user, only the environment, but in fact any environmental design process changes the user in some way because he has to adapt to the change in his surroundings. Therefore learning and adaptation processes have to be the concern of the designer—even his own, which we hope are not static!

We can symbolize the situation by using the following as a "first model" which the designer has of his problem:

The designer establishes a more complicated situation by taking the larger environment into account—the part which does not send messages to "A". The designer's problem is to choose the characteristics of the object, and a good designer will design objects, the major part of which do not overlap the experienced environment. Therefore a good part of design is regulation, or the making of objects unobtrusive, if not to disappear!

None of the above boundaries is very sharp but we shall revise this figure later on.

Figure 1.9.1

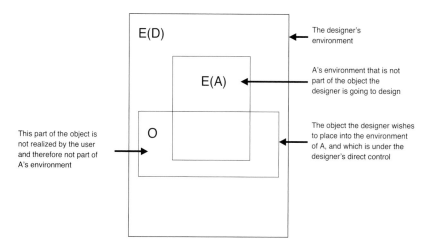

We said that design is purposeful. Usually this is multipurpose not simple, as the objects to be designed are involved in a class of situations, not a single one. The whole class of situations means that the experienced environment is constantly changing but nevertheless the object must always be just as good a solution, or fit, to the situation. In order that A's purposes may be achieved the object may be merely a tool, or a framework, but then again A's actual purposes may change too.

The environmental design problem, however, depends upon the definition of the purposes to be fulfilled. The problem is multipurpose in another way, according to the many persons involved in the problem. The designer, the user, the producer, the investor, for instance are a few, and usually these roles are not played by the same person, and all have different purposes with the object. These are usually incompatible and conflicting—the investor may want the greatest profit from the design solution, but the user may desire the least rent. It can be said therefore that the best solution is that which best fits the pattern of conflicting requirements.

Some philosophers of design assert that a genuine designer acts as a representative of the consumer or user alone, but if one represents only one party, other requirements cannot be fulfilled and the concepts are not as simple as that.

Design problems and their life cycle: Any problem has to be generated, picked up, formulated, dealt with, solved or forgotten, or passed on. The problem needs a permanent conscious effort—it must be kept alive or it disappears.

What is the origin of a problem? First, there must be a person who feels that his essential variables, his purse, mode of living, etc., are outside the pleasant range. There are characteristics of situations which people tend to keep within certain limits and if a situation shows changes beyond these limits or even tendencies, which if they go on would tend to an undesirable state, then a general problem exists.

The shortest description—"a perplexing situation."

What are these essential variables? Ashby, a biologist, mentions the volume of blood in the body, or body temperature, for mammalia, and biologists know of many essential variables of an organism that are designed to keep them within limits by regulatory, or ultra-stabilization processes. We cannot use this bio-logical concept, however, as it implies that we can find from outside sources what the essential variables are. Instead we shall have to say that the essential variables are those characteristics of A's image in the terms of which he evaluates a situation. But there are changes here too. The state of the stomach is an important character-istic sometimes (but not after dinner) and these changes mean that the whole value system is reorganized.

We have to take a situation that takes into account the momentary state of the image of the person in the situation, but as everyone knows these essential variables are not very consistent. There is, however, a high degree of unanimity and tolerance as a result of permanent communication with others. We all know how pleasant it is to meet someone with a consistent value system. This has led to a mutually agreed value system within a certain culture. Its by-product is a rigidifica-tion of the value system and the system of the essential variables, and one of the pedagogical objects of education is to rigidify the essential variables.

Another characteristic of the problem situation is that the solution is not apparent. It is necessary to be at a loss to know what to do. If a standard-solution technique exists there is no problem. Here again problems can be generated by symbolic communication without changing the situation as described by the physical surroundings. By symbolic communication alone we can produce satis-faction and dissatisfaction, this being the reason for advertising and teaching, and vice versa. Problems can also be "dissolved" by this means—e.g. by providing reassurance, etc.

What is a solution? We can say a solution exists when the essential vari-ables are in an acceptable state again.[8] This can be obtained by actually changing the essential variables, and/or altering the range of desirability—making people take other things as desirable, or by changing the environmental situation. The prob-lem in environmental design is that several persons are involved in the biography of a problem in one of the ways mentioned above, and therefore for the solution of an environmental design problem in a temporal way we can take the following temporal pattern:

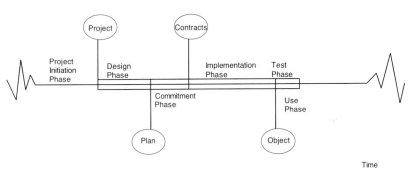

Figure 1.9.2

For a sculptor the temporal pattern is quite different:

Figure 1.9.3

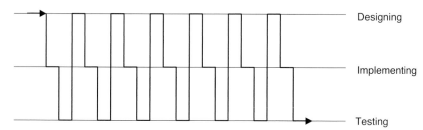

Designing

Implementing

Testing

We said that design is purposeful and controlled. This implies that the designer must have an image over the whole length of the problem—he has to imagine what will happen over all phases and this aspect of his work is particular to the design phase. The other phases are not concerned with all the dimensions of the problem in quite the same way.

The design phase therefore consists of the sharpening and refining of the image of the lifetime of the problem and instead of talking of particular "stages" of analysis, synthesis, etc., we shall say that all systematic design and model building is concerned with the business of progressing outwards and constantly refining in order to obtain an appropriate and sufficiently detailed reference model of what happens in the later phase.

In the beginning the designer has to have an image of the design process itself. We have to plan, utilize resources, time, manpower, etc. The first part of this image formation might therefore be a plan for the design phase itself and how it should be utilized, as in most cases time and resources are limited. We shall look at the design process as a continuous effort to refine and develop an image of what is going to happen later. The designer is in a very unfavorable situation—he has to use his knowledge and that of others to imagine the outcome of his design, to build up a system of "vicarious perception." He has to design devices to prove his ability to perceive vicariously what will eventually happen. The result of the first phase is a *plan* or a set of instructions—*not* hardware—instructions for the implementation and prosecution of the object.

A convincing model for the design phase is that developed by Ashby in which he considers designers in the same way as he considers any behavioral system, as "machines."

The designer, Ω, designs a machine or system M. How are the characteristics of such a system different from others? He considers all the following as design processes:

1. The genes determining the formation of a heart.
2. The parts of the brain determining the internal connections of a nerve net.
3. A works manager laying out a factory.
4. A mathematician programming a computer.
5. A politician devising a law.
6. A general devising a strategy.

The question for the cybernetician is what is the final model, what determines it, and how does it, and not any other, come to be selected. We cannot of course use these general concepts—we must maintain humans in the role of "A" but nevertheless the whole thing is very useful. The concepts involved in building a machine or an object system share a common property of the variables contained in the process, and Ashby looks at design from the variables from which the result was chosen, not by looking at the result itself. He describes design as "a realization of a set of other possible realizations." He says the act of designing or making a machine is essentially an act of communication from the maker to the made, an activity of the transmission of information and of selection from a set. Therefore communication theory applies and the number of bits of information involved is important. Briefly, design is the reduction of several messages to one. He examines the question of whether designing can be done by a machine, and finds the laws conditioning their possibility. In fact, obviously the client treats the architect as a machine into which he feeds the problem and pays for the solution without worrying too much about the mechanism involved. Thus the idea of a machine designing another machine can be stated in exact and general terms, and he does it. Next we must consider the quality of selection as related to the act or communication, not the result. The only meaningful question is how much design is contained in such an object, as a representative of a whole set of other possible alternative objects.

To continue, selection can be done in stages. For example, shape, then material, then color; this is a general technique. In addition there can be supplementary selection by a color consultant, and all the selections come together in one solution. The capacity for selection is limited by the information capacity of man as a data-processing system. For instance, when ordering a dinner in a restaurant, the available items on the menu are reduced to one which is realized. This reduction is a measure of the design effort and much of design is of this kind selection from a catalog, for instance. This could be taken as a first model of the design process but it is not sufficient for our purpose.

Ashby takes the view of the variety which has to be reduced or destroyed as given—the catalog or menu already exist. He says variety means nothing. We could codify all the design variables and treat them as a random number set, and use a die as a source of variety. A certain coding system is applied to determine the outcome of the origin in terms of the whole problem and the system offers design solutions to make the mechanism work. It is only necessary to choose a solution. This is a tempting point of view but we know that variety must be generated yet we have no idea of the alternatives. We do not have appropriate concepts that can be coded—what alternatives are there for doors, etc.? What is offered is naked variety without meaning.

We have to make the offered variety meaningful by coding it into useful concepts as appropriate to the problem. If we are to take this model of design it is obvious that the generation of variety is just as troublesome as the reduction.

Let us take however, as a first model, the designer as a data-processing system or a machine that can design as follows:

First, someone sets a task, one element of a set of possible tasks. The

Figure 1.9.4

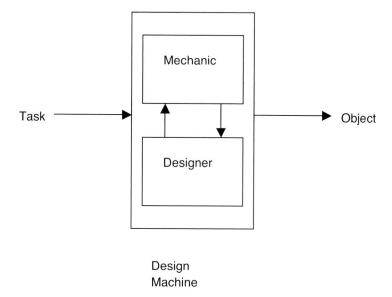

Design
Machine

designer telephones his message to the mechanic. The mechanic can perform certain operations; he has shelves of parts, and skills. What the designer needs is a catalog of what the mechanic can do. Another necessity is the message. A message can be taken as a primitive but practical measure of the design effort. The message or design effort necessary to make a transformer when the mechanic has only coils of wire and sheet metal can be compared with the message required if the mechanic already has parts of transformers in stock.

In other words, any standardization reduces the number of messages and makes them shorter. The content of the catalog and the length of the message together express the amount of information involved in a design task. This would work well enough if the designer knew the effect of his instruction. He must know the consequence of his choices and how they fit together in order to make this simple model work—or it will not. He must know the qualities of the items and their fit and this type of knowledge is essential. We shall now improve this primitive model and look at descriptions of the design process, comparing the various approaches by means of simple models.

One important question remains as to whether two works of art are, or can be identical, i.e. if the *Venus de Milo* were reproduced by a transfer milling machine in exactly the same material, would it be identical? We shall take it that it would be and substitution of an exact copy would not make the slightest difference. However, it will be shown that this point is not as unimportant as it might seem.

Let us consider various types of design. One particular problem is that of writing the catalog, formulating a coding system in order to reduce the variety. Let us deal with a schematic description of various methods.

If we take for instance a painter executing a picture, there must be a starting point. He may commence by choosing his brushes, i.e. a set of alternatives

Figure 1.9.5

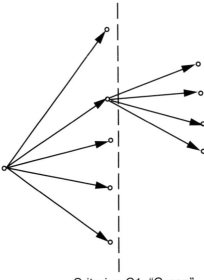

Criterion C1: "Green"

is imagined in his situational image. He then applies a criterion, formulated or not, communicable or not, stable over time or not, or just the product of mood. If he takes the wrong criteria, no solution gets through. In this case he can give up, look for further alternatives, or change the criterion. If there is only one alternative, he is very happy. There is no design involved here, it is merely *routine*. Routine is distinguished from design by the fact that no design is involved.[9] But any experienced designer routinizes what he does. He has certain general and selected problems solved forever, like the use of his favorite doorknobs. This is one method and a very common one of problem solving.

There is still another method, however, and it is even more common. A problem situation exists. The search for alternatives is begun and suddenly a solution comes to mind which is adopted. The first solution is realized and one does not look for a second. No criteria are involved. Sometimes, however, the right choice is not made and it is necessary to go back, or one may come to a dead end. It is necessary to make a loop and start again, and these loops are expensive. In an expensive design problem, these erasures are very undesirable.

It might be worthwhile considering therefore if any methods exist to insure the process against such occurrences. One method is to organize the system in the following way. Variety is continuously generated until each path leads to a solution, and this group of manifold paths we call the solution space. There are in fact billions of alternatives, the difficulty is to find the tree! Finally, several sieves are applied at once and it is hoped that one solution will emerge. If it does not we can give up, increase the variety, or change the criteria.

In the first example, the solutions were alternatives, here they are done cumulatively. In this example there are "n" bits of information for "n" paths, and

Figure 1.9.6

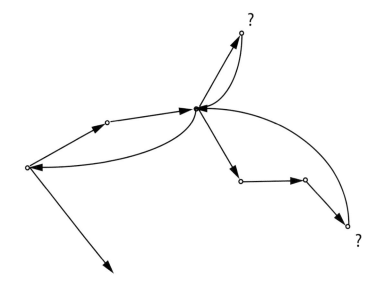

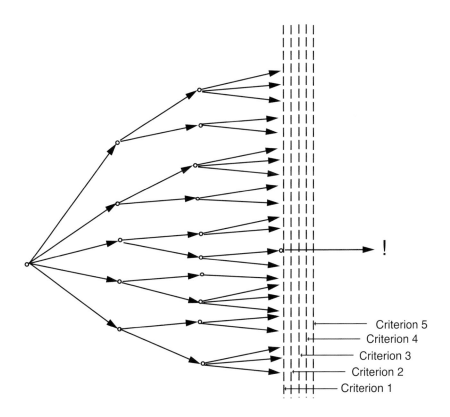

Criterion 5
Criterion 4
Criterion 3
Criterion 2
Criterion 1

Figure 1.9.7

this means an enormous number of possibilities. But if we had to guess numbers the total would be the dual logarithm of "n" – (ld sub n).[10]

The difficulty is to find the tree and reduce the area by guesswork, reducing it by half for instance would be enormously useful, but in most cases you cannot do this—you have to check each solution individually—a possible decision effort for each bit of information. Therefore we try to order the solution space according to certain parameters—where little change of the parameters orders a similar situation. Previously the properties of adjacent solutions could be entirely different, but by parametrization it is at least possible to introduce some order. In other words, "the better the catalog is ordered, the easier it is to find something." In fact most of the techniques we are dealing with are devoted to the organization of the solution space, so that it is possible to browse through the solution space without checking all the alternatives.

Notes

1   This hints at Rittel's later definition of design where design is an activity aimed at creation of a plan, expressly denying such activities as engage immediately with the final product: "Design is an activity aiming at the production of a plan, which plan—if implemented—is intended to bring about a situation having specific desired characteristics without creating unforeseen and undesired side and aftereffects."

2   One of the characteristics of wicked problems. See property number 10 in "On the Planning Crisis" in this volume, pp. 151–65.

3   Rittel's choice of the word falsification is likely due to the influence of Karl Popper. "Alteration of prediction" might have better expressed the apparent intention.

4   Design results are highly improbable in the sense that they would not occur by random chance.

5   This redundancy is associated with the high degree of order and information mentioned in the previous point. The redundancy is the same sort of redundancy mentioned in Seminar 4 which allows one to infer a pattern even when some information is missing; this abstract order and redundancy manifest as the characteristic regularity of designed artifacts.

6   Although point number 5 says that design is not predictable by extrapolation, this is not inconsistent with that point. In 5, Rittel is arguing that because one is making changes in the world, previous predictive patterns will be limited. In this point Rittel is arguing that in order to consider an activity design, it must be intentional, and perhaps even hinting at the designer's responsibility for the project: a designer should be acting in accordance with the best possible predictions, not simply trying at random to create a good result.

7   For example, one might seek to design the image held by an individual—this is, to a large extent, the intention of advertising and education—rather than designing physical objects, education and advertising seek to shape beliefs and actions.

8   This is an unusual perspective of solution—one completely determined by the individual. It is appropriate to recognizing problems as completely dependent on the individual to perceive the problem. Later in his life, Rittel shifted from talking about problem solution to problem resolution (see the Introduction to Part Two in this book).

9   Rittel's point is to refer back to the importance of innovation; routine by virtue of repetition is not design—even if the routine was designed originally.

10 This math works if you presume, as he did in guessing cards in his example in Seminar 3, that each choice is able to eliminate half of the remaining options.

References

Archer, L. B. (1965) "Systematic Methods for Designers." Reprinted in N. Cross (ed.), *Developments in Design Methodology*. Wiley, UK, 1984, pp. 57–82.

Starr, M. K. (1963) *Product Design and Decision Theory*. Englewood Cliffs, NJ: Prentice-Hall.

Seminar 8: Models of and for Design (Part 1)

Horst W. J. Rittel

Last week we considered certain particular features of the design process and in particular we distinguished between two kinds of activities, using a modified model from Ashby:

1. the generation of variety
2. the reduction of variety.[1]

We discussed various different approaches to a design problem in terms of these characteristics and their alternation, and we designed a scale of approaches with routine at one end and the complete model approach at the other—with variety generated at the beginning and the criteria applied together last. In addition we agreed that the design phase is only a part of the biography of a design problem and we must keep the whole biography in mind if we wish to make a meaningful analysis of the design process. There is the birth of the problem. Then the design phase produces a set of instructions for the implementation and execution phase, and, as a result of these, the object is embedded into an environment and the phase of functioning begins. Also in parallel is the testing phase. The functioning of the building ends the "problem." The phases are organized in different temporal patterns and for various types of design there are various patterns but they are always made up of the same components.

We said that the design phase is one of model-making as the designer has to make a "model" of the whole lifetime of the problem—and this fits into the dictionary definition of design: "to devise a mental plan." Design is therefore a teleological activity which ends in a plan or programmed instruction.[2] The design phase therefore can be understood as a preliminary stage in the lifetime of the problem—an image formation period—the designer develops an image of what the object is to be and also the whole of the lifetime of the problem, and the phase ends with a set of instructions, a communicable presentation and this programs the implementation and execution phase. In many cases the output of the design phase is used as a control message for the problem generator too—a message for the client to make up his mind—as a control message. The whole may be taken as a communications process with the input a test, and the output a test result.

Such a means of programming is known as a "model." What kinds of models are there, which parts are used, when, and to what extent are they used? The model allows "vicarious perception". It allows the outcome of the decisions to be imagined, and there is no design process without image formation.

The question is therefore what kinds of models there are, which parts should be used and to what extent. When should they be rational, i.e. consciously and explicitly formulated, and when should they be communicated to others? What techniques are available to facilitate model formation and what language should be used? All recent efforts to develop methods for systematic design can be understood as directed to the provision of models as tools and methods for communicable model formulation:

1. A model can be defined as a suitable abstraction of reality, presenting the essential structure of a problem, a representation of a subject of enquiry into objects, processes, or systems, for prediction and control. It can be used for the manipulation of the represented entity if the manipulation of the entity itself is too expensive or impossible.
2. A model is always of something.
3. Models have certain relationships to what they represent—for example homo-morphism, in which every element of the object has its counterpart in the model and any relationships in fact are represented by corresponding relationships in the model. This does not mean that all entities in the model correspond. To different parts of the subject usually the mapping in a model is one to one, but, for example, a photograph may be taken as a two-dimensional model of a three-dimensional object. Each point in the subject has an image in the photo-graph and all parts are in equally corresponding relationships. But one part in the model (the photograph) can correspond to several in the subject (the object modeled) which lie on the same straight line through the camera lens.
4. Each distinguishing element of "S" has its counterpart in "M" and if a particular relationship holds between two elements in "S", the corresponding relationship holds in "M".

Therefore from the same entity "S" we can derive many models, related to each other. For instance, if we take an object "house," we can distinguish various models, e.g.:

1. a three-dimensional iconic model in cardboard—geometrical;
2. a camera and color film producing a colored photograph, a more primitive model of the cardboard model;[3]
3. a black and white photograph—a more primitive model still;[4]
4. a set of plans and sections;
5. a circulation drawing of the heating system.

These "models" become more and more similar to each other and more and more simple, and the system of possible models is structured in size and shape so that even ultimately some individual quality persists. This is called a LATTICE and for each entity, at least conceptually if not very simply, we can construct a lattice of models, characteristic of a certain entity.

The concept of a lattice is:

1. That if we take any two of its members there is a common superior model from which both can be derived;
2. That from any two models can be derived a simpler model, a least common model.

All models form a lattice of a certain entity, and for different entities the lattices are different.

The designer's models are analogues, not analogies. An analogue is a model representing as completely and as satisfactorily as possible what is represented. An analogy is a model having similarities only under certain aspects.

What is a *structure*? If we have a model describing an object in the lattice of possible models, in this model are certain concepts. If we forget all about the meaning of the elements and take their relationships only, all that is left is the structure, the grammar and syntax of the model, the "meaning-free connectedness." Of course many models may have the same structure, but in one the elements may be electro-chemical parts, or in another a nerve system and we can have, therefore, identical structures of different entities. This is known as structural isomorphism.

To sum up, a model is a compilation of knowledge and experience derived from particular experience, analogous cases, the penetration of the problem and gathered data, embodied in a simplifying and unifying system to find alternative courses of action and derive estimates for their consequences.

It is very interesting to look at the various types of models that exist, but unfortunately the classification systems we have are by no means perfect. Here, however, is one:

Type 1—Iconic Models: The attributes and properties of the object under a given aspect are represented by the same attributes and the same properties but to a different scale and with a different—greater or lesser—degree of distinction. An older, more primitive but illustrative definition would be to say that the object "looks like" what it represents. This is a little too narrow for us as it is restricted to the visual aspect. Examples are drawings, wind-tunnel models, all toys, globes of the earth, photographs, cardboard models, etc.

Type 2—Analogue Models:[5] Here one property is used in the model to represent a different property or quality—for example in a flow diagram, or as an abscissa where length represents time. These analogue models are such as colors on a map to represent different geological epochs, or electrical circuits to represent hydraulic phenomena and vice versa, or hydraulic devices to represent traffic flow. It is assumed that a translation rule can be formulated from one to the other, a translation rule therefore applies to any analogue model to explain now the properties of the model represent properties or the object.

Type 3—Symbolic Models: Here the entity is represented by symbols and a set of rules about how to deal with the symbols. The elements are the theoretical constructs of physics, chemistry, accountancy, etc., rather than graphical ones. All these types have advantages and disadvantages and the question of which to apply depends on the requirements of the problem. The higher the degree of theoretical penetration into the field, the more useful is Type 3.

Further characteristics are:

Type 1: Cost specific, simple to produce, concrete rather than abstract and little interpretation effort required. But difficult to manipulate and change, and it is very difficult to investigate the consequences of change through time—except by using film. Also one limitation of iconic size is described by Haldane in "On Being the Right Size."[6] He describes the limitations of iconic models without mentioning them! Some properties are changed directly in proportion to the scale, others to a different scale, and the balance is disturbed when the dimensions of the model are too different as compared with the balanced state. Similarly, with mechanical devices, such as toys, etc., and also every architect knows that the small model has its limitations, even visual ones.

Type 2: More abstract and therefore more general. They are [more] easily modified and the influences of changing parameters can be studied by changing the device.[7]

Type 3: Easiest to manipulate and most general, but the most difficult to interpret and understand. The parametrization of the object or the list of variables must be as complete as possible; there must be a sufficient list explaining the state of the object. We can say that the amount of analysis needed to construct a model is inversely related to the ease of manipulating it, and to its usefulness. The more abstract a model, the more general its range or usefulness and applicability, and the more useful it will be for prediction.

Can one use an iconic model for prediction or as an aid to prediction? Certainly. We can use floor plans, etc. to predict future behavior but for this it is necessary for the analyst to imagine the behavior of the object. He projects himself and his expectations and predicts behavior by introspection; by "walking through" rooms on a plan and from a few cross-sections he can be taught to be able to imagine a complex spatial system, or appearance, but for this to be possible the model must be highly conventional, because one cannot simulate behavior with an iconic model if the experience of the observer does not permit it.

Of course, many models are composite mixtures of these types—a floor plan is not strictly iconic but incorporates many features of an analogic model. All models begin as iconic, the more symbolic they become, the higher-degree of control and the better the prediction. There is also perhaps a fourth type:

> Type 4—Conceptual Models: These are models that are expressed in words, verbal descriptions of objects and events, which we assume are sufficiently sharp and meaningful. Most social science models are of this type, and also models in philosophy, etc. Each symbolic model can be translated into a conceptual verbal model and the formula is "read" by a common language.

Conceptual models are used for all descriptions of styles, and often have metaphorical elements—"as if", "looks like" and this seems to be a kind of parallel to the analogue in the scale of models—a metaphor being a "name" or descriptive term applied when it is not literally applicable but only in a figurative sense.

Static and Dynamic Models

Dynamic models, a further type, describe the behavior of an object through time. They can be continuous or discontinuous. Continuous models are easier to handle; quantized data are embedded in a continuum, and therefore calculus, etc., can be used to evaluate them. Usually, however, each observed process is discrete.

Static models: Models that do not consider the time dimension.

Models of and for Design

If we wish to understand the design phase as a sequence of model formation or refinement, then the procedures can be said to lead to an iconic model which the designer delivers as his instructions—instead, for instance, of a list of instructions.

We must distinguish between models of and for the design phase. So far we have considered design as a biologist considers an organism and in order to discriminate design from other processes and to develop processes and theories. There are also models used *for* design, those used by the designer when designing. Of course both types are related to each other and in order to develop model types we must have an idea and a philosophy, or image of the model structure of the design process—a "model" of the activity as a whole.

One of the reasons for the relatively poor state of design methodology may be the neglect of this aspect—models *for* the design process are poor because models OF the design process are even poorer, and it is a peculiarity that the role of design and its connection with other activities are not very well investigated.

The model of the design process that the designer has depends on his self-image to a large extent, and vice versa; the situational image and the model condition each other. His models for design depend on his self-image and therefore his choice of models of design. Not only the type but the content will be affected, e.g. a designer who despises rational processes will not use symbolic models and he may even deny the existence of tasks requiring communication and justification of his actions. Furthermore, if a designer has a model which says that externalization endangers creativity he will not use any practice which forces him to externalize his ideas.

We will assume that the designer is trying to achieve a controlled solution, trying to rid himself of mood etc. and is trying to base his solutions on the best available data according to their source. He wishes to achieve a solution rationally, which is as satisfying and excellent as is rationally possible.

Consequently, the question for us is not systematic design, or unsystematic design, but the degree or extent to which a systematic approach is appropriate, the type and degree of communication which is appropriate and advisable during the design problem, the formulation of the model used and the way it is to be organized to generate ideas. We are looking for means to facilitate these activities.

To Boulding, whatever is not chaos is system; wherever there is system there can be knowledge, and wherever there is knowledge there can be expectations (of results)—and which designer will admit therefore that he is working chaotically? It is by system therefore that we live and we can show there is a third alternative and that "system versus intuition" is not the question.

Models for Design

The question is: Is it better for the designer to have a comprehensive model describing all four phases or is it sufficient to have a separate model for each of the phases? Further, should the designer see himself as part of the model, as for example in military games, where the general who is playing the game is represented symbolically in the game? This has a peculiar paradoxical consequence: as noted above, the designer projects his expectations into an externalized model and there he sees himself! Where should this model of himself be placed?

In this is the basic difference between object models—which represent only those things which are subject to design, floor plans for example, from which action models and decision models, have to be derived—and complete models, which should not only contain the entities they represent, but also the points of view from which they have been formulated and are applied.[8] This raises a serious objection to the possibility of complete models: it is impossible for a model to contain itself.

There now follows a paradigm which is suggested for all design models, which it is hoped will comprise all existing approaches to the question of design procedures which have been proposed so far under the general heading of systematic design. In other words, a general level containing all existing approaches.

We will take this paradigm for design—the system of parametric design—and commence by making a simple-sounding yet very difficult assumption that everything that is to be considered can be named. We can make this a weaker question by saying that everything which can be distinguished can be named. In this case we can set up a list of descriptions, of actions and results, and, having this list, we can say that each item stands for a variable—not necessarily numerical data, some variables may be non-quantifiable, but modern measurement theory has developed a whole series of measurement types in scales instead of by polarities. We might have porch or no-porch—P or not P—and by various methods therefore any building will fit into one or other of these categories.

Which concepts are fed into the list of descriptions is important. The description of a "porch" as "a device to trap outside air" would provide a much wider range of considerations. A useful policy therefore is to list as variables even things which are "known" to be constant—such as air pressure to show the effect of eventual variation. We distinguish between different types of variables:

1. Performance parameters. Those in terms of which the problem is formulated, the language of the client, and the language of the ultimate test. The price, the set of costs, beauty, etc. In many cases there may be merely a purpose or mission and from these the necessary parameters have to be derived. They are of two main kinds—implicit and explicit. Unfortunately, most of them are usually implicit; there is usually a high measure of agreement on many questions and in order to innovate it is worthwhile to check for tacit assumptions or tacit agreements. For instance, no problem mentions the necessity of a door, but by making the question explicit, the possibility of a different solution is immediately produced. By questioning or doubting—the Cartesian question—innovation can be generated. Each parameter is formulated with respect to inputs—such as costs—and outputs—such as those the testing phase considers.

2. Design parameters. The list of these determines the vocabulary in which the designer expresses his solution: size, materials, specifications of operations. The designer receives his problem in terms of performance parameters and delivers his solution in terms of design parameters. The question is, should he have a kind of intermediate workshop language between the two which helps to bridge this gap? There is in fact such an aid consisting of the variables that are controlled by the designer, called object parameters.

3. Object parameters. The object parameters describe the behavior of the object system that is to be influenced by the designer. These are the parameters sufficient to describe the behavioral characteristics of the object. Here we have to distinguish between two types of groups of variables, first those influenced by the designer in choosing the design parameters, and second those that are [not] influenced by the designer—the "disturbances" such as snow, wind, noise, etc.[9] This latter group is responsible for the difference between the designer's expectations and the actual results—assuming he has made no other mistakes, of course. Let us assume that all variables are quantified simply for purposes of easier representation—this is not, however, a serious restriction. Groups of variables define certain spaces because each variable can assume any of its values and each combination of variables can be understood as a point in the system:

1. The evaluation space is defined by the evaluation parameters. We might have 70 evaluation parameters making up a 70-dimension coordinate system and

each solution can be plotted as a point in the evaluation space endeavoring always to find a solution nearer the center.[10]

2. The decision space is defined by all the parameters that the designer has under his control. For each parameter we have an axis and an abscissa and each choice of dimension for example is a requirement of the designer.

3. The object space or "phase" space—a term borrowed from thermodynamics. Here the behavior of an object is projected as a trajectory, over time, for example, and each behavioral characteristic will be a curve.

We can assign symbols to the various parameters, which are used in the diagrams above as follows: P—Performance parameters; x—Design parameters; y—Object parameters; z—Disturbances. These can be used to formulate a very complex function of the behavior of the object which is determined as a function of what the designer does and the disturbances of which he has to make an estimate.

$$P = F(yx)$$ The performance is determined by the behavior of the object system.

$$y = X(xz)$$ The object is determined by the circumstances set by the designer and those existing.

The "X" above is awhat is called knowledge and all our knowledge of objects is of this type. The performance depends on what the designer does and what the object does—that is knowledge about the effect of "X" the design parameters—on the objectives and this is a kind of classification principle for the knowledge the designer needs when designing. This kind of knowledge is provided by science, though not very exhaustively, and it may not exist in [its] entirety—it is the professional knowledge, or "know-how" and the designer must use both scientific and professional knowledge in order to find the point in the decision space that, together with the corresponding point in the phase space, produces a sufficient point in the evaluation space.

In addition, this knowledge can be plotted into the decision space. Because of certain behavioral characteristics, certain values of the decision variables or design variables are excluded. These are called the *constraints*. All the knowledge the designer has, of a scientific or professional character, can be plotted into the decision space as constraints, for example a "maximum weight 5 tons" constraint would cut off all solutions above that figure.

Each relationship can be plotted onto a graph and it is hoped and assumed that they do not eliminate all possible solutions! In very rare cases a single solution will remain but in many cases no solution space will be defined and here we can try to move over the constraint lines on their "soft" side so as to open up a field of possible solutions.

These constraints are derived from the two kinds of knowledge and if the list of parameters is complete then any will do, but, in addition, in many cases we can look for additional evaluation principles—such as the "minimum price." We can assign an actual price, for example, and browse through the solution space until an adequate solution is found. In most cases it will not be an absolute solution according to this system. "Optimum" does not mean "absolute" here.

In this model the performance variables are influenced via the object variables, and also directly from the design variables as design costs money. The design variables are, or can be, used as a tool for goal-seeking and may not be influenced by the outcome—but the designer needs to know about the outcome too, and much of design is concerned with this flow of information via a "feed-back" which must be introduced.

Any design process can be parameterized if only in the primitive sense of "yes" and "no" variables, and, again, in a way, anything that is itemized or named is parameterized. The simplest evaluation space would be of only two "values," good, or bad, but this does not work very well because the knowledge we need is of when these values relate to others. Also the actual functions, F, are not very well known and we have to make assumptions or alternatively we can put this complication into a more complex performance space by formulating a list of the performance variables.

Usually, however, instead of setting up a grand system that includes all the variables from the site to the doorknobs, partial systems are combined and schematically dealt with. It is possible—though not very likely—that certain objects may suffer by this. In other words, by optimizing the doorknobs you may influence the choice of the site, but this is unlikely, and usually it is possible to have a hierarchy of variables and build models of this type schematically. The whole design process may be understood as a development of these models.

Existing Models for Design

The attempts to talk about design in this way date from the early 1940s in operations research, where a certain set of standard models was developed. In the case where the equations are of the first order, we have linear programming methods. Usually, however, the parameters are non-linear and extremely difficult to represent in the decision space. From these first operations research models came the first attempts to formulate symbolic models applicable to city and regional planning.

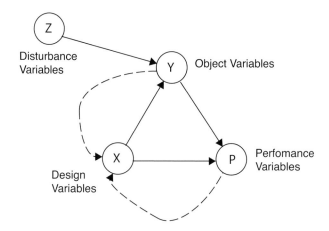

Figure 1.10.1

The next step in systems engineering was the use of computers in military and administrative systems and in the next six or eight years these were looked at in a more general sense and more general design concepts adopted.

The shortcomings of all existing models are as follows:

- Usually in these highly formalized models, the conceptualization of the problem is too rigid and is difficult to modify.
- It also has a suggestive power, and the image's effects on the recognition of problems are not dealt with.[11]
- They also all tend to start with a given problem, which is unsatisfactory.[12]
- The degree of complexity of even the most advanced operations research techniques is very limited—a spoon is about the most complex object manageable.
- The "hardware" aspect is exaggerated, especially in systems design.
- The problem of intermediate concepts is open. For example, there is a good deal of evidence concerning the refinement of the model through various phases, or concepts of A.[13] Topology, group theory, and logic can be very useful and serve as an internal means for the translation process of the evaluation parameters and the decision parameters. This is a kind of successful translation of performance statements into design statements but this internal workshop language is not well developed.

The following standard types of operations research models have been determined:

- linear programming models
- dynamic models
- scanning models
- queuing models
- allocation models
- assignment models
- inventory models.

The application can be as for instance where a door is considered as a bottleneck and therefore a potential queuing situation. Subsequently a large part of operations research has become independent and called "traditional" decision theory (discussed in the next seminar). Sometimes, but not often, mathematical operations, calculus of variation, and logic can be applied also.

A second source of models for design has been systems research, systems theory, in engineering especially this has been useful for all types of processes depending on parameters and where parameterization is easy. Processes through time and capacity problems can be solved or designed in terms of the language of systems. The formal language here consists of block diagrams, Gantt charts, etc., and equations.

An older system, but springing from the same source, is that of the Swiss astronomer Fritz Zwicky, who invented the concept of morphology. This is useful for the generation of variety but not for its reduction. Tremendous variety can be generated by parameterization. An enormous list results, making a finite and discrete model, and each combination is a feasible solution! There are innumerable solutions naturally,[14] but Zwicky unfortunately gives no method of browsing. Each idea is a recombination of existing ideas and the number depends on the extent to which the super-signs which are used as items in the image are decomposed. The more elementary they are, the larger becomes the search space, but only "rule of thumb" or trivial methods of browsing are given.

Operations research, however, has specialized in the reduction of variety, e.g. linear programming, but the rules for setting up the system, or formulating the model are very poor.

A further group consists of J. C. Jones and Bruce Archer.[15] They are concerned with the organization of the decision space. They use simple methods of organization of data, of the pattern of knowledge, of thought organization, and work patterns. They adopt very primitive methods but these are useful for better organization, for a disciplined and effective approach and to give an insight and provide a communications system about what the designer is actually doing. They also give a better basis for learning about design by enabling the designer to collect experience so as to better organize his actions.

A further group of systems designers have derived a matrix analysis system, SAIM,[16] at Stanford, which is quite useful if the list of components is known and is limited; for instance to electronic or mechanical components. The principle is to formulate a purpose or mission for the object system and derive properties from it. A distinction is made between determinants, components, and processes; a list is made for each and a matrix built to find their relationships and the object model. For each decision a different model results. Here the components are already well defined.

The method of Christopher Alexander is to decompose the same problem by taking a different point of view.[17] He has developed a matrix method and takes for his starting point a list of needs and requirements, which he considers synonymous. He checks whether there are relationships between any pair of these needs and builds a large matrix, checks to find clusters of needs and for the very intimately connected items designs a corresponding component sub-system. He has developed some methods to identify these clusters, and these form a semi-lattice— not to be confused with a full lattice of models, which is mathematically different. The emphasis is on the decomposition into connected clusters.

The above are the general types available today.

Simulation Techniques

How can the designer meet the handicap of lack of knowledge and theory about design? To a certain extent, by simulation. Simulation here being a procedure designed for vicarious experience, to simulate a serious case. There are many ways of simulation—of traffic by computers, by an analogue, etc. Another well-developed theory is that of management games, well developed at the Systems Development Corporation, and from which a few attempts at design games have resulted.

One way to collect vicarious experience proceeds as follows: each aspect is represented by a sheet of paper, there is an observation screen or scope, and a switch. Events are fed in, the observers react and discuss their reactions and so study how the system works. The game is made more iconic by taking cardboard boxes, playing with them as if they were real and so deriving the consequences of design.

Notes

1 This basic division of design into two tasks—generation and reduction of variety—remained central to Rittel's teaching throughout his career.

2 This is a clear first step towards the definition of design that Rittel would put forward and use in later years—"an activity aimed at the production of a plan, which, when implemented, leads to a desired situation without undesired or unintended side- and aftereffects."

3 More primitive, at least with respect to the amount of information contained in the model. The color photograph might have better representation of some aspects of the house—color in particular—than the cardboard model.

4 When compared to the cardboard model or the color photograph.

5 These models are clearly not analogues with respect to completely representing all aspects of the object modeled, but they are analogues in the sense that the property being modeled is being modeled completely, and therefore these models are analogues, as Rittel defined above, and not analogies. This discussion is based on the discussion of models in Churchman, Ackoff and Arnoff (1957: 157–161).

6 Haldane's point—based on studies of biology—is that structures and forms that work at one physical size, do not work on a different scale—e.g. flying creatures are limited in size because the surface area to volume ratio changes as size changes. These issues translate directly to some architectural issues, e.g. a beam of a given material cannot exceed a certain size or length, as weight, which is dependent on volume, outstrips the bearing strength, which is dependent on cross-section (Haldane 1985).

7 An important aspect of these models that Rittel would later emphasize in his teaching is that these models are also not as easily understood as the iconic models. For example in maps the spacing of contour lines is used to represent gradients (see Churchman, Ackoff, and Arnoff 1957: 160).

8 From this arises Rittel's fourth Paradox of Rationality: that the model must contain itself (see "On the Planning Crisis" in this volume, pp. 151–65).

9 This is not a statement that includes the previously mentioned design parameters among the object parameters, it is rather trying to clarify the distinction between the design parameters and the object parameters. In his later work, Rittel followed a model by W. Ross Ashby that distinguished between design variable and context variables, the distinction being that the designer chooses which variables to affect (the design variables) and which to accept (the context variables).

10 Assuming that the "center" represents the optimal/preferable result.

11 Rittel here sees how the model influences the model; this will lead to one of the later paradoxes of rationality: that the model must include the model. After all, if the model we use influences how we think about the problem, then whenever we attempt to use a model to work with a problem, the model is incomplete if it does not include itself.

12 This hints at the later claim that understanding the problem is the problem, and that there is no single description of a wicked problem.

13 I.e. the ideas and perspective—the image—of A, the intended user.

14 Working from a transcript of an audio recording of a non-native speaker of English, one wonders whether Rittel said "enumerable" or "innumerable." Logically speaking the number of solutions generated by the morphological approach is not only enumerable, but quite easily calculated.

The number is large, but neither infinite nor innumerable. But "innumerable" seems to create the appropriate contrast with the lack of a method of browsing the large (but enumerable) set of solutions generated.

15 An example of Jones's work that fits Rittel's description here, though written some years later, can be found in *Design Methods: Seeds of Human Futures* (1970). Jones was the editor of the seminal 1962 Conference on Design methods book and was one of the speakers at that conference (Jones and Thornley 1962).

16   We have not been able to identify SAIM.

17 Alexander's *Notes on the Synthesis of Form* (1964) was published the same year as this seminar; and Rittel had attended the 1962 London Conference on Design Methods where Alexander presented a version of his theories concerning the decomposition of projects.

Reference

Jones, J. C. and Thornley, D. G. (eds) (1962) *Conference on Design Methods*. Oxford: Pergamon Press.

Chapter 1.11

Seminar 9: Models of and for Design (Part 2)

Horst W. J. Rittel

Last week we discussed and compared certain types of models and tried to describe the state of a discipline by the type of models used according to the hierarchy of models and comparative systems developed by Kenneth Boulding. He uses nine levels or nine types of systems in order to classify levels of theoretical discourse according to their level of complexity and of predictive power:

1. The level of frameworks: only the geography and anatomy of the object is described and analyzed. A kind of system of static relations.
2. The level of clockwork: machines which are determined.
3. The level of thermostats: level of control in mechanical and cybernetical systems.
4. The level of the cell: the level of the cell as an open and self-maintaining system having a throughput transforming unpredicted inputs into outputs.
5. The genetic and societal level: the level of plants and accumulated cells.
6. The animal level: specialized receptors, a nervous system, and an "image."
7. The human level: the level of 6 above plus self-consciousness. The system at this level knows and knows that it knows, and knows that it dies.
8. The level of social organism: the unit at this level is a role rather than a state; messages with content and meaning exist and value systems are developed.
9. The level of transcendental systems: at this level are the "ultimates" and "absolutes" and the inescapables with systematic structure.

Today's theoretical models are equated with those up to the 4th level, and most of cybernetic and systematic research is concerned with systems of level 4. Boulding asks how it is possible to deal with systems of any level without understanding them and explains that as we are the system this enables us to utilize systems that we do not really understand. "Know-how" is possible without "know-why."[1]

   Applying this classification to the level of design activities we can say that the level of understanding corresponds to the level of systems that can be designed. Nowadays we can design up to the 4th level. This is because the level of theoretical penetration determines the degree of predictive precision and therefore the degree of control and responsibility for the consequences of design. Even today we cannot design a tree and a tree is on only the 5th level.

In design at levels 1–4, the level of theoretical understanding of the object is at the level of static relationships. The normal case is of frameworks at the 1st level—that of static relationships. Most of the processes at higher levels are out of control and the reason that there are so many systems which function satisfactorily—including architectural ones, is that:

1. Most of the solutions are of the adaptive, or modifying type. Successful solutions to design problems are adopted without knowing why they are likely to be successful, but the designer is confident that they will work in analogous situations.
2. Systems are open-ended. Facts are established by design sufficient for a solution which is offered for "digestion," for a reaction of users and cultural institutions. One sees how the system offered is used. These users and institutions "swallow the solutions whole" by adoption, or they reject and eliminate them.
3. The consequences of design at this level are taken as less important and of less interest as regards the essential aspects, and this is why design at the first level works for the behavior of systems at the higher levels.

These additional remarks define another scale of models which can determine the state of an art. We will now repeat here the idea of model formation during the design phase. This is identical to the formation of the image of the problem and the image of possible solutions and we can distinguish the following steps:

1. We develop a model of the problematic situation, conceived in terms of verbal statements or iconic models, sketches and drawings, etc.
2. A specification of the "shall be" situation is produced by a search for similar and analogous situations and by starting and target situations.
3. We try to find comparable solutions to comparable problems.
4. The models used become more and more abstract, or of more general validity to an extent varying with different professions, for example in architecture the vehicle of communication accompanying this process of abstraction is usually iconic.
5. The process ends with a specification of the design parameters. The type of messages depends on the organization and efforts of the prosecution system. It can be a sequence of verbal instructions or a plan—the construction industry habitually uses plans, not lists of instructions.

The whole process may be considered as one of generalization, or of abstraction and concretization back to a very particular statement.

The Creative Leap

In connection with such models of the design process one question seems common to all: Where is "creativity" located and provided for in these formal systems?

In many systems the creative leap occurs as something indescribable and beyond reason, but nevertheless indispensable and important. It is a kind of "divine spark" which is considered to be the central event of any creative process, the lack of which makes all organizational and systematic methods vain and futile. What does this mean?

A great deal of this veneration is a product of the nineteenth-century genius cult, and this product and justification of liberalism, proclaiming a kind of super instinct, is endowed with the capacity for producing meaningful outcomes from unforeseeable and unconditioned events—a kind of mutation—which fits into the pattern of progress thus affirming and justifying the idea. Because this belongs to a very deeply founded and established part of the occidental self and world-image, it causes much trouble to anyone who dares to secularize this concept and who does not share in the associated and necessary ideas.

The ability to produce events of this type is considered as a personal quality, unequally distributed over different persons. The ability to be creative has become a sub-state distributed in varied proportions and considered as determined by inherited factors and not determined by environmental influences. Creativity as a basic personality factor has become a criterion for personality and for a person's aptitude in particular.

Formerly other words were used to describe this type of ability, such as energy, fantasy, discipline, combinational ability, and these were taken as sufficient. Now we have a cumulative noun: creativity.

It takes some courage to deny this form. It is an island of mystery on a sea of irrationality, even for devoted navigators on the waters. Unfortunately, anyone engaged in analysis of the design process is bound to abandon citizenship of the island if he is trying to consider the design process as a conditioned and influenceable one, subject to planning and control. From him the following statements are inevitable:

1. Having ideas is only one part of the problem. In the words of the German proverb "Any traveling wine salesman can produce ideas of sufficient number and quality." Selecting the right idea, testing it, communicating it, and providing for its execution are at least as important as the developing of the idea.
2. Ideas are recombinations of items at a lower level of the superstructure or super-signs.
3. There are various processes leading to ideas with respect to an existing system. For example:
    (i)   one can find modifiable characteristics and modify them;
    (ii) one can define common features of various items and define or counter-position in a dialectic way.

These are only two of the possible methods of generating ideas in a systematic way. Another possibility is:

(iii)   one can question systematically the specifically implicit principles which are usually taken to be self-evident and unquestionable. Much of the history of thought can be understood as this approach of systematic doubt.

The situation or circumstances can be more or less stable for these processes. Persons can be trained to a greater or lesser degree to perform them, and it is meaningful to search for amplification techniques to improve the probability of having ideas.

Finally, any idea has to be understood with respect to a reference image that embodies the current expectations and ordering structure. These images are very inert, and highly socialized. The "distance" between the established image structure and the innovation may not be so large as to make the idea incomprehensible and unadoptable or it will be thought to be "crazy."

Creative ideas are highly improbable with respect to an existing image as the super-signs are so well fixed and the "unquestionable" questions are therefore not questioned. They become plausible by the arrangement of abstractions and a reduction to a common basis, but most of the creative ideas produced do not survive; they become socially irrelevant.

Bionics

A few words on this new field of exploration which looks at existing biological systems in order to exploit them on a different scale for engineering operations. For example the jaws of a beetle are studied as the source of a possible principle for the design of earth-moving equipment. The approach in terms of model theory is to take an existing system as an iconic or at most analogue model of an unknown, future system. The model is the starting point and is searched systematically for translation into a different order of magnitude. Many of the results of this technique have been spectacular.

Goals and Objectives of Design

The notes presented here come from a tremendous body of both knowledge and ignorance, from a large number of sources, some quite random, and some questions may be presented as being simpler than they actually are! This is a difficult topic too because of the extreme corruption of language. The words "values," "goals," and "objectives" are often used inaccurately and the conceptual "jungle" is very thick. Again some statements are exaggerated to be deliberately provocative.

First, what is the nature of objective goals and values? Let us begin with the problem of the problem. Why do we talk about goals for design? Design has been defined as a purposeful and goal-seeking activity, as directed towards the achievement of a target situation with defined characteristics. Recently it has become fashionable to put an emphasis on the goals for design and we now know how difficult this is. The knowledge of design goals is very poor.

However, why should we bother about these constraints? Why do we not design in an open-ended manner as we have always done, where the designer offers his results to whom they may concern for acceptance or rejection and where a natural mechanism of ultimately balancing supply and demand produces a sufficient power of regulation to guarantee a steady progression in the world of designed things?

In this case the designer's objective would be to produce solutions that are accepted and not rejected. This is a well-defined goal; it is primitive and not far-sighted, but it works. Much, if not most of all design is carried out according to this simple system. The designer here has a very clear and immediate measure of his success. He may, however, consider himself as a split personality. He may play a double role, on the one hand having an independent professional value system and, on the other, a private system of dear and complicated, inconsistent and mostly unformulated but conscious values that he uses outside his professional activity. A malevolent view of this would be to label it "opportunistic," at least in extreme cases, and if one is satisfied with such a role all that follows is unnecessary.

All such a designer needs is merely some instrumental knowledge on how to produce solutions that give rise to no complaints from the client, the user, or the profession. Sufficient indicants of his performance are his bank account, his professional reputation, the low number of complaints, and the increasing number of contracts—nothing is more successful than success. However, if a whole profession takes this view and shares this system the internal professional standards will be adapted to it, and the profession will develop its own standards of quality and excellence, not necessarily having anything to do with other peoples' views—the client's, for instance. This is the natural tendency that can be observed in the history of any medieval guild and in any "in-group" system. A tendency develops towards rigid deification and further adulation, justified by the statement that "only practicing experts can judge the work of other practicing experts." This is a closed system with respect to evaluation and the throughput of tasks from outside to outside is merely an indicant of the soundness and validity of the closed system. Architects obtain more contracts and this "proves" the system. External success exemplified by the employment of the "guild" reaffirms the internal value system. The whole has become a piece of culture, a sub-culture. Nothing is against it—it works!

Nevertheless, both in general and in certain circumstances, there are good reasons for taking a broader view and a more general framework. What are the shortcomings of the described system of values above?

1. It works only in the case of uncomplicated and relatively simple tasks.
2. It works only with tasks sufficiently similar to many tasks already successfully solved.
3. It does not work if the long-range view to be taken is beyond the immediate insight of the partners in the task—the client, the user, other professionals, etc.
4. It does not work if higher, cumulative effects or by-products occur, having a strong influence or impact on someone, or everyone, which are not wanted and for which no one is directly responsible. These side effects are the result

of many micro-processes of local design efforts, and of larger scale processes of self-regulation, unfortunately, in the wrong direction. This is a well-known by-product and price of laissez-faire liberalism and a good counter-example to the hopeful confidence of the automatic Darwinistic principle of evolution towards the "better."

5. It is also insufficient

   (i) if the overall consequences of such an innovating system considered as a social institution are under investigation;

  (ii) if the role of the profession, its effects, further development and education are under discussion;

 (iii) because it is necessary to step out of the system in talking about the design of a culture. This is not merely a slogan. The design of a culture occurs in the developing countries for instance, in the war against poverty, and the planning of a city, and these cannot be handled at this level of goal structure.

Unfortunately, the vocabulary of value structure is very confused. In philosophy, moral theology, and economics, many independent conceptual systems exist but there is no general terminology agreed upon by different authors. We will therefore take a broad view of proposals for a vocabulary to be employed in the following considerations. We can say therefore that any controlled action has one of several expected outcomes.

An *outcome* is a situation or state of a system which can be expressed in terms of performance parameters. Note, not design parameters! An outcome may be for instance a satisfied client, a guaranteed profit, a building which does not collapse or an original, but not necessarily well-received, result! Some outcomes are desired, others are not. The desired outcomes are called *objectives*.

The word *value* is usually employed for two different meanings:

(a) something *has* a value, which may be high or low.
(b) something is a value: freedom, health, democracy.

Here we shall say something *has* a value, and having a value or not is the most primitive scale of value! Beauty or ugliness, freedom or slavery is a value scale; we replace those properties which are called values by a scale. This is only a syntactical rule but it makes it possible to unify the discussion. Of course we can talk about values, but in our case this means talking about value scales. When talking about democracy we talk inevitably at least about the question of democracy or no democracy, its importance and appropriateness, and we shall say that something has a value according to a scale. This mere terminological question is at least as complicated as the problem of whether there is an objective world or not and both statements are strictly correlated.

The absolutist talks about values, others say that things have value for someone or they do not. This is a related controversy to those who assume that there is an absolute and objectively existing world—the absolutist—and those who take the world as a construct which enables individual behavior and which is a model of past experience in order to form a frame of reference for future expectations and behavior. These are the relativists or nominalists.

To illustrate the seriousness of this controversy, here are a few quotations:

Nicolaus Hartmann, the German neo-Kantian philosopher:

According to their mode of existence, values are platonic ideas; they have their own type of existence. Values are not mere functions of valuations, they have not been established, they exist independently from evaluation, they have an ideal existence.

Max Scheler:

Even if it had never been judged evil, murder would be evil. Even if the good had never been taken as good it would be good nevertheless. It is not the task of ethics to find out what is good or bad and the social recognition of good and evil.

On the other extreme it has been said that:

Value is the arithmetical form of utility.[2]

The factual part of the value of phenomena is the experience of values—they are only abstractions of evaluative processes. [3]

Peculiarly enough, the actual judgments of the proponents do not show much difference if they believe in the absolute character of values and personal items changing through time and subject to characterization by experience only. At least on the short ranges of decisions the patterns of behavior and basic philosophy of a person as derived from his or her evaluation processes alone cannot be evaluated. You cannot evaluate a person's basic philosophy from his behavior in a supermarket, for example. The differences of philosophy become apparent by symbolic communication alone—one has to talk to a person about them, but as we know, the imprinting power of symbolic communication is a very strong influence on the basic philosophy itself and on long-range behavior. The absolutist tends to take a conservative view and others are tempted to revise or abandon existing value structures. In any questions of long-range decisions for development the distinction between basic philosophies becomes relative and externally observable.

I tend of course to the second attitude for its simplicity as a kind of ultimate value, and it seems better to accord with empirical evidence. The world seems more interesting and the future more challenging if values are variable and even subject to design. However, further concepts must now be introduced.

A *goal* we can say is a future situation with desired characteristics.

Efficiency we can say is a measure to the extent of which a certain value is reached in an outcome according to a certain value scale, an outcome which exists with respect to a specific value scale.

Effectiveness we can say is a measure that comprises the values of an outcome according to the weighted sum of a set of evaluation criteria—maintenance cost, beauty, etc. These are applied to the object and according to the evaluation of each of these—here we have the value scales set up—the object is more or less efficient. As effectiveness we take the weighted sum of all these relative value judgments. Effectiveness is the incorporation of particular value judgments into an overall judgment.

Means and *ends*. We can also introduce this conceptual pair. They compose a mutual relationship only definable with respect to a certain problem formulation. The longer the range of the task, the more abstractly the problem must be formulated; the longer the chain of means, the more general and abstract the ends. What ends and means are depends on the problem formulation alone, and one can solve problems and make them very very simple by defining the short-range problem.

One particular difficulty of the design process is the appropriate statement of the ends—most problems become trivial and a mere matter of skill and routine if the goal is very short. Problems become unsolvable, however, if the range of ends is too far-reaching and they converge into the debate of the ultimate goals of human existence if one has to find the limits of the range of the problem.

Some Properties of Value Systems and Structures

First, those which seem to apply generally:

1. If stated in general terms, value systems are very stable through time in different cultures. At all times, everywhere, and in all languages good is more highly valued than evil, health is preferred to illness, democracy and freedom, even in ancient Greece, to slavery and suppression. Value systems that are expressed without reference to a particular situation are very stable; for instance, "Man should be good" is valid eternally.
2. There are almost no value categories that apply universally. They are formulated according to a certain class of problem situations and not to all situations. In war, for example, different courses may be good or admissible according to a value system and the same general value statements do not apply in peacetime. Many things admitted in peace are not admitted in war, also.

Business has its own rules, too, of good and evil, and also the nature of beauty varies with the object. Although the overall vocabularies for primitive evaluation—the overall values scales, beauty and ugliness, good and bad, etc.—remain the same in the vocabularies of war, of the seventeenth century, and of business, etc., the meaning of the determining factors of the judgment varies with the field of application. The meaning of the evaluative vocabulary varies permanently and significantly.

This is a similar statement to that in the article by Bruce Archer where he describes how each value judgment influences the center of gravity of the domain of validity and the borderlines of value judgments for a certain value. The exercising of the values, in other words, changes the value system in a way that is not very well controlled.

If stated in terms of classes of situations, value systems are very dynamic through time, and different for different persons. The particular is stated, not the general, with the result formulated and used with respect to particular situations. Beauty varies with different epochs, fashion, etc. and the John Birch Society's definition of democracy may be quite different from that of others. To describe such differences in terms of different notions of "admissible means" alone has been tried—they mean the same but what they take as "admissible means" is the difference. This, however, is not true. The John Birch Society would take the meaning of the word democracy differently and they would assign it to a different situation. The meaning of words and their range of application is constantly changing. Freedom is tending to mean freedom of choice, but for an ancient Greek this would mean slavery under the people who determine the choice, and "freedom to produce a choice" would be better for him and therefore the meaning varies significantly.

The attempt to establish a normative value system valid for everyone and claimed to be underlying any ethical system is futile. Two thousand years of frustration in occidental philosophy have shown this. It is meaningful to try to establish a science of values but it must be based on empirical findings—on the description of which values, where, and when, have been valid for whom—but this "Natural History of Human Values" has yet to be written.

An added difficulty is that the world of facts taken as a kind of reference system to observe and describe the evaluation of the people of this world of facts, is a product of evaluations as well. Conceiving things and naming them means taking them to be sufficiently important to be conceived and named, otherwise they would not be so conceived. Therefore, perceiving is a very fundamental and primitive but powerful type of evaluation. It is not, therefore, possible to take people with value structures on the one hand, and the world of objects on the other, and make people evaluate particular "constellations" of this world. The objectification is already the evaluation and application of values. It is impossible to establish a clear-cut separation between the situational image and the evaluative image.

This again has deep implications for the structure of the science of values, the possibility of which has just been postulated. The categories and terminology of such a science are subject to these processes as well as its object and it must give up several of the basic principles postulated for science. This is astonishing. For example, a science of science, epistemology, could be developed, the principle of which could be applied to this science itself without much logical difficulty. On the other hand, the implications of a science of values have an impact on epistemology which tend to transform it to a science of action rather than a science of knowledge.

If science goes this way the price will be high. As Churchman has formulated, a science treading such a path will lose its claim for objectivity and general validity. The results of such a science will depend on the value structure of the researcher in a very sensitive way, an experience known to historians for some time. On the other hand, it is surprising that these apparently simple statements are new.

That the answer to these efforts depends on the respective self-image of men and their history is fascinating. The first attempts, however, to actually measure human preferences and employ value structures for behavior preferences were not made before 1950 when Mosteller and Nogee collected empirical evidence for the utility theory postulated by Von Neumann and Morgenstern.[4]

These thoughts have arisen not just because of the time but in the face of a multi-dimensional pluralism where normative solutions to problems make no sense. Indeed, the efforts have become very valuable in making and talking about politics and the well-established balance of world power is to a large extent the result of this kind of thing. However, although much effort has been invested into this field, the results are not very advanced, but at least some empirical procedures for the determination of values have been developed and a useful terminology has been defined for the possible comparison of formulated ethical systems and to find rules for the consistency of such systems. We cannot discuss here the fascinating results of modern value and decision theory; some results relating to the dynamics of value systems will, however, be mentioned. There are two kinds of objectives:

1. To state the objective with respect to a psychological state—happiness, freedom, etc.
2. To state an objective in terms of object states—an average income of such a figure, no more cancer, a refrigerator for all, or my refrigerator for all!

The objectives in the second category seem to be of shorter and more immediate range and can be understood as "means" relating to the "objectives" in category one. We can construct a tree of objectives with many levels terminating in the nebulous systems of the upper levels of the final objectives. The lower levels at least can be constructed and we should take the upper, not the lower, primitive levels of this tree of objectives. The permanent question of any decision-making process is which objectives in (2) are appropriate to fulfill the objectives in (1). The answer to this is change[able] and cannot be given normatively. It is an approach on a different series of levels.

One example would be "What is good for me is good for everyone" (or "What is good for General Motors is good for America"). Another might be "Making someone healthy, happy, and wise." This brings a further complication and much more difficult than making yourself healthy, happy and wise, and it is even more difficult to know how to make yourself so—knowledge as well as action is required.

I will propose a kind of ethical rule that everyone who participates in social processes directed towards the achievement of goals affecting others has to express these in terms of objectives of type 2 and has to make implicit what the expected influences on the higher levels are—to make them evident and communicable. This is not as easy as it sounds because of their implications on a higher level, and it is not sufficient merely to propose and realize the low-level objectives.

The difficulties are the cumulative effects mentioned and the question of by-products.

Most public and private decision-making procedures are not designed for this but to conceal the influence of operation on the higher levels of the objectives. The disadvantage of the proposed rule above would be that decision-making would be even more difficult. It is difficult enough to know what we ourselves want; now we have to investigate the consequences of our actions upon others. A third difficulty is how to weigh the controversies and conflicts in the systems. This has been analyzed carefully in decision theory, and it has been found that it is impossible to add up individual happinesses to make a "total" happiness.[5] The difficulty is how to organize a system providing such a tracing of the first consequences of low-level objectives.

A fourth difficulty is that we cannot assume that everyone knows what he wants or that anyone knows how his satisfactions are influenced. How is anyone influenced by a freeway project for instance?

We shall consider the private case—the opportunistic previously described—as a special case of the public case. Another possibility is to look at the states of a system with respect to their influences on those states which can be reached from the starting point onwards.

We can also show that the value structure and knowledge structure are intertwined even more thoroughly because the probability that some states can be successors of certain other states influences the value of those states. States of any object system that cannot be reached are of no value and therefore the expectation structure of the realizability enters into the evaluation of any object system. Therefore the knowledge structure and value structure cannot be separated.

This works in the opposite direction as well. We try to achieve knowledge that will lead to better prediction of states which we want. One collects knowledge and does research in such directions where one expects to produce promising states of the object system.

In another way our value expectation influences our research for knowledge. We say that research is going on there and valuable knowledge is to be expected and the effects in both directions have a stabilizing effect on each other, and prophesy is working towards a self-fulfillment where a transition from one state to another is possible. We already start shaping the future by creating facts that influence it, and there is no clear separation between design and prediction in the double meaning of "determining." There are also no values of things—they must be considered in a context and in a certain situation, though there is always a tendency to make subjective awards where things are cumulative, additive, and subtractable, where they have intrinsic values in their own right. This process can be observed in art, for example. An object may be considered as a kind of Sputnik in empty space which is then evaluated. In economics a certain successful object system has been designed enabling the addition and subtraction of commodities and their comparison in different situations to be carried out. This has become one of the reasons for the present theory. A glass of beer has a different value in the desert than in a brewery. The natural approach here is reversed. One works at a thing in situ, and compares its value in other situations.

Another influence on value systems is that all identifiable ones are transient. All systems die; they are mortal—even planetary ones. Furthermore, a system orientated as a system towards mortality alone is incapable of formulating objectives at a low level because of the diffusion of the prediction structure over a short period of time. Because predictive structures diffuse through the course of time, the connection between present events and ultimate states cannot be derived and the values are indefinable.

Rational behavior exists only in a small island of time and space and is not possible beyond the immediate ranges of prediction. However, a system having its main value as "survival" cannot continue either. These problems of the structuring of goal systems, their viability and compatibility, and their likelihood of raising conflicts are only now being studied.

Finally some notes on particular ideologies of design. Design for what? First, the opportunistic mechanism of a value system has been previously described, but this is not satisfactory for many designers. They have a kind of superstructure by which they justify their actions as a social institution in a broader context. Many ideologies of design have nothing to do with what the designer does, but there are two main ones in all design:

1. The Individualistic. A person takes his own value structure and makes it a sufficient ideology. The normal practical man who wishes to behave normally and simply make his living. To quote Engels in his criticism of the social democratic program of 1891, this is described as "honest opportunism." He says that this "forgets the main issues in favor of momentary issues of the day. Longing for the success of the moment, the abandonment of the future for the sake of the present may be meant honestly but is opportunism, stays opportunism and honest opportunism may be the most dangerous." In this first category comes self-expression. "The world has to be subject to my molding efforts." "I am asked to shape the world according to my image, fast and visibly." There are many grades of this attitude.

2. The Socially Orientated. The task is taken to be the improvement of the world, to make it more beautiful and better, but for whom? The designer is the judge and his judgment is right. "Let us produce monuments of beauty and greatness to put delight and beauty into this joyless world."—symbols of greatness to which the poor can look up. This kind of ideology is not yet extinguished. There is also the attitude "let us produce the greatest possible happiness for the greatest number of people." The assumption is that there is an additive social utility function, and generations of social scientists have failed to define a reasonable social utility function as a measure of their accumulated happiness but without success. Even with democratic procedures there are many paradoxes making an absolute system of ascertaining the preferences of a group almost impossible. This springs from the utilitarian ideas of Bentham and Mill which are, at least, not formulated only in terms of the visual aspects of the world. Again one might take "Let us adopt the fulfillment of minimum needs." There are unfortunately no minimum human needs—some people even give up breathing voluntarily, and this concept is not as globally valid as its proponents would like to think. Another ideology is to say that "today's luxuries are tomorrow's basics"—a kind of World's Fair attitude.

Then there are some more primitive philosophies:

- "Organic design is correct!"
- "Advertising is enlightenment." It should not placate people but ultimately convince people that the particular products are right.
- "Simple things are beautiful."
- "Geometry is beautiful, especially the square."
- "Scientific appeal guarantees quality." Employ a scientist in the sales department.
- "Things should look like their purpose." The Jeep would be the culmination of good design despite its poor petrol consumption! And perhaps then military design would be best.

The reason for these remarks is that perhaps you can order these groups schematically—however, this is their theoretical level. The "design for minimum needs" approach found a big supporter in Henry Ford, who made a whole generation believe in the concept and made the motor car one of the "needs," an attitude that no other country has yet adopted. His autobiography is interesting not only for the fact that he was anti-Semitic, anti-Wall Street, and a friend of Hitler, but for the very primitive and poor theoretical level displayed.

For some of these difficulties which have been mentioned at least promising approaches already exist. One is that the designer should confess that he is a politician and that this is not in itself disgusting. Also, one of the present features of the socially shared value system is that it is so poor and we do not engage in it. Next week the implications of these things on the design of innovating systems will be considered.

Notes

1 Rittel here is referring to something like Michael Polanyi's notion of "tacit knowledge" (1958): the ability to do something without extensive knowledge of aspects of the procedure—just as a bicyclist does not need to know anything about the gyroscopic properties of wheels.
2 Source uncertain.
3 Source uncertain.
4 Cf. Mosteller and Nogee 1951.
5 Rittel noted "Arrow" in the margin here, a reference to economist Kenneth Arrow.

References

Arrow, K. (1951) *Social Choice and Individual Values*. New York: Wiley.

Boulding, K. (1962) *Conflict and Defense: A General Theory*. New York: Harper.

Churchman, C. W., Ackoff, R. L., and Arnoff, E. L. (1957) *Introduction to Operations Research*. New York: Wiley.

Goode, H. H. and Machol, R. E. (1957) *System Engineering: An Introduction to the Design of Large-scale Systems*. New York: McGraw-Hill.

Luce, R. D. and Raiffa, H. (1957) *Games and Decisions: Introduction and Critical Survey*. New York: Wiley.

Mosteller, C. F. and Nogee, P. (1951) "An Experimental Measurement of Utility." *Journal of Political Economy*, 59: 371–404.

Smith, N. M. (1956) "A Calculus for Ethics: A Theory for the Structure of Values, Part 1." *Behavioral Science*, 1(2): 111–42.

Smith, N. M. (1956) "A Calculus for Ethics: A Theory for the Structure of Values, Part 2." *Behavioral Science*, 1(3): 186–211.

Reports of the Stanford Research Institute by Schaeffer and Schapiro 1961. "The Structuring and Analysis of Complex Systems Programmes." and a following long list of publications dealing with such reports of which the last is: "The Knowledgable Analyst." SRI Project IMU 3546.

Skinner, B. F. (1961) "The Design of Cultures." *Daedalus*, 90: 534–46.

Starr, M. K. (1963) *Product Design and Decision Theory*. Englewood Cliffs, NJ: Prentice-Hall.

Chapter 1.12

Seminar 10: Conclusion

Horst W. J. Rittel

It is now intended not only to summarize and draw conclusions from previous considerations but to make evident all the connections to the starting point.

We began with a look at the existing innovating activities, their self-images, and their present organization. We have shown the mutual dependence of these activities and this mutual dependence was demonstrated according to the ideal concept of the nineteenth century where a self-sufficient science is taken as necessary to obtain knowledge about a physical or material world which is considered as a fundamental reference system for all happenings. The better the understanding of this world, the better for the world! Scientific knowledge is, according to this image, taken as desirable for its own sake, unconditioned and the primary source of all innovation. This scientific knowledge is data which is specialized, applied, transformed, and exploited by a chain of other, lower, innovating activities trickling down from the universal reality to everyday usefulness, and providing a more enlightened, better, and more reasonable kind of progress.

Although much evidence seems to contradict this, it still seems to determine the common gross image of innovation and its mechanics. Statistics, for example, are organized according to this pattern, and the image is still taken as valid.

In this seminar we have tried to cast some doubt on this model, especially as it suggests a determined or natural course of progress with parallel development of reasonable and universal value structures. But science itself is an historical phenomenon with its own restricted and conventionalized value systems. By definition each science is only concerned with a particular class of phenomena, described by standardized parameter systems which the lower members of the innovation chain cannot do—they do not have such systems. Also, by definition science is directed towards the achievement of knowledge and not concerned with the direct and immediate change of the world—though, as we know already, knowledge about the world will change it as well—but these changes are taken as beyond the scope of science. Nevertheless, there are relationships between all the stages of the innovation chain and these are much closer and more complicated than the nineteenth-century model permits. Instead of a one-way flow of results from science to reality there is a much more intensive mutual influence of problem generation and result flow. Furthermore, all parts or components of this innovation system are inseparable components of the grand system of culture and they are those components which provide for ultra-stability and adaptivity of this grand system of culture. They provide the change and persistence of these cultural systems. If we look for an invariant of our occidental cultural system it is very difficult to find one, but one of the few one can discover seems to be permanent and consistent change and the image that this change is necessary. This may be a dialectic, or modifying change or the like, but other processes do not seem to contain this idea or these processes in their self image.

The main question for this evening is whether this cultural change is and has to be subjected to self-regulation alone. Is it something that happens everywhere and always and which results in some kind of development or cross-change? Is it the result of many local and individual endeavors which determine the resultant direction of progression? Or is it subject to design, that is, is it accomplished by a controlled and goal-directed activity? Is there such a thing as planning for a culture or for future states of a culture? I dare to say that such cultural design is indispensable and unavoidable nowadays. The mechanism of self-regulation does not produce desirable overall states at least in the long run, and only occasionally and in certain places. Of course at least during the next decades there will be much innovation, and even more than today, better houses, faster cars, more products of art, and further debates on questions of architecture and other sub-cultures, all as previously but the sum of such activities does not produce a "super-system" or a culture having good chances for survival or even for future developments which are bearable or even optimal from the sub-cultural aspect.

The conclusion of all this is that the sum of the sub-cultural innovations which might be improving does not necessarily produce an overall state that is desirable. It may be even worse. The reason for this is that the sub-cultures are not separable components of the overall system although their self-image seems to postulate this. These sub-cultures such as architecture, art, and science consider themselves as separate systems. There are many examples for this: one is that a development plan, a set of buildings, some rules and a population does not add up to a self-sustaining community. The result is "subtopia," a mixture of the utopian image of private life and suburbs. No one wants the accumulated by-products which we can observe everywhere, nobody wanted that something which results from many sub-cultural optimizations, no one designed it, no one is responsible for it and no one can be blamed for it.

Another example is that the war against poverty, for instance, cannot be fought under the flag of free enterprise and competition. Furthermore, a developing country cannot be developed by the transplantation of one's own cultural patterns into it. Centuries have to be skipped in these regions in the face of entirely different value systems. The conclusion is that there are many design problems which are within no designer's competence if the competence is organized according to the sub-cultural organization. A city poses neither an architectural problem alone, nor a city planning problem, nor a traffic problem. Maybe the architects, city planners, traffic engineers, etc. can share the design, but the problem is inseparable.

Then again the population problem is under no one's professional responsibility. Of course some existing organizations such as the U.N. and a few of the new innovating industries are dealing with these problems, but there is no education for this kind of problem, it does not fit into any of the professions; nevertheless, it is a typical environmental design problem.

All of these problems are threatening and urgent, making all detailed design problems of secondary importance in the light of them. Many of the design problems of the present professions are inessential and in the long run, in view of these problems, may be considered a waste of capacities and facilities. There is much evidence that this kind of local and small-scale design, this sub-optimization, leads to states in the long run that are unwanted and unintended.[1] This is quite a new fact or observation, and if we look at the reasons further, we find that the reason for the burden of overall planning and cultural design—and it is a burden—is the price of 2,500 years of the occidental habit of talking about everything of systematic doubt and questioning. One can name this process "irrationalization," but the price is that each goddess or ghost or poltergeist that is expelled out of reality has to be replaced by permanent innovation efforts. Therefore each "witch-doctor" has to be replaced by medicines, psychiatrists, or other types of value engineers. Each taboo or prejudice has to be replaced by a law or rule and therefore this is the process that generates more and more, larger and larger, and more complex systems, and the domain of design is extending beyond the scope of individual experience, professional competence, and capacity. To quote Steinbuch, a communication engineer, "Rational methods are like a contagious disease, once contracted you cannot shake them off and they will continue spreading themselves" (Steinbuch 1961).

The burden of cultural design is not a hardware problem of physical design alone. Images have to be formed, social techniques have to be developed, organizations have to be founded and value systems have to be modified, and the whole mechanism of the innovation system is subject to design. This is a global problem since every country and almost every part of the world has accepted this occidental approach. There are reactionaries and conservatives everywhere, but the gross result is that they have lost the battle. It is very likely that the traditional professional boundaries do not fit into the pattern of problems, and the appropriate division of design labor of this kind is an open problem. As a consequence of last week's meeting we can say that the less restrictive the system of technological possibilities is the more solutions are feasible, the lesser is the influence of technical processes and therefore the problem of formulated values and long range considerations becomes more important.[2]

From all these things follows the necessity for innovation planning, at all stages as a sub-system of the cultural system. Any innovation planning is long-range planning because it has long-range effects, but in talking about innovation planning, planning for design, or research and so on, we easily come under suspicion of being a left-wing person because this seems to be an argument against individual freedom, free-enterprise and an "open" world. I shall not pursue this interesting argument, only quoting Skinner, "Mankind has won its battles because individuals have lost theirs" (Skinner 1961).

Long-range planning of any kind is planning beyond the horizon of calculable risk, but this horizon is coming constantly nearer. To quote Whitehead, "The time-span of important change was considerably longer than that of a human life, therefore mankind was trained to adapt itself to fixed conditions, but today the time-span is considerably shorter than human life and therefore we must train individuals to face the novelty of changing conditions." But this change makes prediction and care for the future very difficult. Long-range planning today means planning over ten years, in some fields over five or eight years and in some cases there is long-range planning against the will of the planners. They are doing long-range planning without knowing it. Any measure extending over a few years is long-range planning. For instance, in education any student starting a high school curriculum will be beyond the scope of short-range planning in a few years and we are now training students beyond the range of calculable risks. This is a typical case of long-range planning without knowing it or desiring it.

On the other hand, this increasing innovation flow is not an inescapable blind fate but the result of an expensive effort subject to decision-making about the direction of innovation and allocation of brainwork and resources. If we think of the fields of important military and space development projects, these extend over a decade and they are very well planned and we can predict very well what is likely to happen after ten years. These are the pacemakers and they determine the radius of the horizons for other fields, not by extending but by reducing them. The rate of innovation in various fields is very different. In certain fields, the more they are pushed forward in a sub-optimizing way, the more the horizon of foreseeability will change in the other fields which do not participate in this rapid innovation. For example in pushing forward certain military technologies that do not consider the side effects on other fields, the more the uncertainty is increased in these fields and some fields or directions of innovation are very far behind in their innovation rate—social design, environmental design, and value engineering, and it is peculiar to observe that it is easier to predict space development than social or economic development.

If we assume that cultural design is unavoidable, it cannot be based on extrapolative assumptions of how things will develop and then choosing the appropriate action that will match these developments in accordance with that which somebody wants. Prediction without specifying what somebody wants does not work because that which we do today will influence and determine that of tomorrow on all levels. Skinner, for example, describes certain mechanisms of cultural design by the reinforcement of changes introduced. Innovations are introduced and many survive if they are initially accepted, and these accepted innovations will determine, to a greater or lesser degree, the future development of our society. We can look at the history of innovation as of many innovations being offered, some accepted and when accepted thus begin to redirect the whole cultural structure. Skinner says that the behavior of individuals and societies is selected and shaped by these reinforcing consequences. In short, the world of tomorrow is a formulation of today's actions. As Marx says in his theses on Feuerbach (the last one, No. 11), "It is not the task of philosophy to describe the world but to shape it."

But once you adopt this model—that innovation policy cannot be based on a prediction and adaptation of today's measures to this prediction—then the question is, what kind of change? It does not seem to make sense to make "change for the sake of change." The conclusion I would like to draw from this is that any innovator—the researcher, the designer, and planner—has to be a politician.

What does this mean? One possibility of describing the role of the designer is to take him as a "need fulfiller." The designer is presented with the problem of fulfilling someone's needs and he does this as well as he can. In this case the designer would not need to be a politician in the sense I will describe in a moment, he could be a neutral and disengaged type of being. To use one of the metaphors of Christopher Alexander, the designer could act as a kind of "reaction jar" into which the needs are poured as a kind of liquid and are crystallized into a design solution. That is a passive designer. The only thing he has to do is to recognize the needs of the client and fulfill them as well as possible. The first type of goal system we discussed last week refers to this. However, as shown, there might be consequences of the solution beyond the scope of a particular task. Many cumulative effects may occur, such as subtopia, which are beyond the "needs" as the designer knew them, as the problem was stated, as the designer could foresee them, and as he was interested in them. There are side effects and aftereffects as well and the question is, to what extent does the designer take all these cumulative side, and aftereffects into consideration. If he does so, he must act politically. I would even go further and say that the "need-fulfiller' produces no essential innovation. Essential innovations are not products of existing needs. Of course they are innovations according to our first definition that innovation falsifies the expectational pattern, but they do it at a very low level. They are modifying rather than innovating. The reasons for this are that needs can be expressed with respect only to the imaginable and to that which can be conceptually realized. For example, there was no need for an automobile, but once invented and produced it was accepted, and once accepted it belongs to accepted cultural innovations and became subject to the reinforcement mechanism. None of the inventors of the automobile had any idea of the degree of reinforcement their particular invention would produce—it was beyond the horizon of their expectations. I could give a more precise definition for the various degrees of innovation, but it is very trying. There were no "needs" for this kind of client/designer relationship and most of this is true for scientific innovation.

There is seldom a need for a certain scientific innovation. If there is a need that can be formulated then you can almost be sure that this need can be fulfilled, and therefore the expectation is very high that this need will be fulfilled and therefore the degree of innovation is very low according to this definition. But if we assume that design beyond the manifest needs exists, then it is required that the designer's objectives enter into the problem. He is no longer a "reaction jar" but a partner with his own interest, and if you want to express this rigorously he must behave politically, because his own preferences and values enter into the solution and this should be a deliberate process. Of course, this always happens; but the question is does he know? Does he do this deliberately or does he do it because he cannot but, or because he cannot help himself? But if I talk about politicians I must be very careful because the word politician is a deprecating one in common language. If I talk about a politician then I mean someone who is interested in, or engaged in, politics—the original meaning—although the common meaning is tending more and more towards someone who makes a trade of politics and this is the meaning if it is used in a deprecating manner.

According to the *Oxford Dictionary* "politics" means "prudent conduct, and sagacity." The Greek origin means nothing but citizenship, and the Greek opposite to a politician—a non-politician—is an "idiot." (*Idiotes* meaning "own and private.") If I talk about politicians—I have no better word here—I mean it in the Aristotelian sense, taking man as a political animal. The reason for the deprecating effect of the word politician is largely that politics itself has become a sub-culture, and a kind of dirty trade, necessary, but a permanent madness and nuisance, and politicians are considered as doing the job for its own sake. But we shall talk about politics and politicians in its original sense.

We can say that any essential innovation is politically relevant because it shapes the cultural system. On one hand, because it changes the expectations and images of the members of the culture, it changes the possibilities and makes things possible that were not possible before; it creates facts and switches developments, it changes the needs systems and objectives of people. We can say a designer acts politically if he tries to take into consideration these kinds of changes and in addition the formation of the public or social goals—those that are commonly shared, is subject to design. A proof that this statement is accepted by at least part of the population lies in the fact that all of us are trying to do something called education. Education means that goal systems are subject to design and we can express this not only with respect to children but to adults as well. The same kind of assumption that goal systems can be shaped, which underlies this educational philosophy, should be extended, and a mutual dependence can be shown. On the one hand, we can design according to goals, on the other hand, goals are subject to design! Where does the fixed point lie in this complete relativism?

Of course this does not occur in its full seriousness in any design problem; it depends on the scope of the problem; but, *in nucleo*, it is in every problem somewhere. Therefore in order to avoid being forced to surrender in the face of this relativism it is useful to have a classification for design tasks, and I would like to use the system formulated by Joseph Esherick.[3]

Esherick says that there are two kinds of design approach—the minimal and the programmatic:

1. The motto of the minimal approach is "Do as little as possible." And there are two sub-classes:
    (i) The indifferent approach. "Environment does not matter." There is some evidence that for many types of behavior particular features of the physical environment within a very wide range of variation do not influence very much what happens in the environment.
    (ii) The frozen approach. "We have had all the ideas we are ever going to have and it is not necessary to develop new ones." It is not necessary to

invest innovation effort into new schools as we have so many to choose from already. Design is only a matter of fitting existing schemes into a particular situation.

These are the minimal approaches—apolitical or anti-political as you wish.

2. The programmatic approach. The common feature is that you formulate a problem and then you design for it. This can be subdivided into two categories:

    (i)   The "image-matching" approach. The designer attempts to produce an image that he thinks matches the image he thinks is held by his client. In this case he tries to develop an image of the image the client might have. Here he might be said to be acting as a kind of "reaction jar," because he is trying to match an image, but on a different level. This approach is very practical as the goals disappear—they no longer exist in these need-fulfilling approaches except as very primitive ones such as economics, feasibility, etc. The specific image is taken for the goal itself. Correspondingly, no new goals can come from such an approach and no innovations can develop.

    (ii) The systematic design approach. This is an approach that tries to achieve the political implications systematically. It tries to crystallize the goals and separate them from all those requirements and necessities rather than mixing them up. Many of the systematic design approaches can be understood as systems that are used in making clear where to feed whose goals and which into the system. In addition, this approach tries to formulate the goals in an unconditioned way so that different objectives may be fed into the network of necessities. This kind of approach does not try to identify goals with existing images. It attempts a separation between politics and technical necessities. However, a further complication is that a system is a teleological entity towards the achievement of a certain purpose and others come into the task. Churchman's interpretation of Leibniz is the following: "The theory of system design is meaningless unless it incorporates a definition of the most general system, a system which incorporates all other systems" (Churchman 1971). This means that at some level one should treat all systems equally—and he shows this. It means that no partial system nor element can be designed except with respect to the total system. He says "the" but I would like to weaken it to "a" total system because I assume there is no agreement in this world—and it is good that there isn't—about the central, total, and perfect system. I would say that here the problem starts again, but Churchman ends with this. I would ask which total system should we take, what do we understand by culture for example and which general system should we chose. Churchman would say of Leibniz that he would assert that a harmony of the world is indispensable, or all goal seeking is meaningless. I do not think that all people would agree about this grand system but I wish to maintain that everyone has to develop at least an idea of a grand system which he takes as a frame of reference, and this grand system is nowadays the object of design decision-making and vice versa. The innovation policy of today depends on a person's view of the grand system.

Let us reformulate what policy means. A policy decision creates a precedent and affects more than one alternative. It follows from the image of the grand system and any innovation is a precedent for further innovations. This is extremely difficult to formulate verbally, in other words. However, the approach to deal with these relativisms should be a philosophical one if one understands by philosophical that definition of William James that, "Philosophical study means the habit of always seeing an alternative, of not taking the usual for granted, of making conventional alternatives fluid again, of imagining foreign states of mind." I would say that as an independent attitude, if one wants to act politically in the face of the necessities for innovation I have tried to describe, then a political philosophy of innovation must be produced by each designer. Something must be developed by each designer as a political philosophy of innovation by producing alternatives of the grand system. Where are they? Where are the great utopian prospects of the twentieth century? If there are any, they are very pessimistic. Taking the particular task as a preced- ent for future events with all the consequences I have tried to trace, then trying to embed particular problems into a larger class that is not a sub-cultural class, and then taking foreign states of mind into account and how to negotiate with them, still there remains the question: How to produce alternatives for every action? This is the question of generation of variety we have talked about, otherwise no essen- tial innovation is possible that is controlled—that means where the designer has an image of the longer-range consequences of what he does. Needless to say, all those design ideologies mentioned last week are of little use in this connection, and though most designers like to have an ideology, in many cases it can be shown that this bears little relation to that which they are actually doing.

As I have said, the images of the grand system, if there are any, will be conflicting with each other. But whose system is the right system? How can I make other people accept my system? How can I convince or persuade them? They are actually in many cases unknown, and unformulated and not explicit but in order to socialize such a system it is necessary to provide mechanisms for this kind of conflict and debate, resulting from different goals. Much has been said about the pluralistic society; there are many forces and powers at various levels all conflict- ing with each other or partially cooperating and so on, but how can a designer or a client find out which proposals he should take? One suggestion would be to take science as an umpire. This has been tried, and is still being tried in such cases where policy-making committees invite scientists in as experts to make extrapola- tions, images, and other predictions. But this cannot be recommended in general. Science can be used to show up certain constraints, trends, and consequences in its own domain, but I do not trust scientists in questions concerning the grand sys- tem as a whole as it is not easy to transpose scientific statements out of science. In many cases where scientists are asked to give political advice, their own political opinion enters into their advice in an uncontrolled way, and in many cases it is a very naive one.

Nevertheless the conflict has to be dealt with again and again. The question is, should the conflict between different images of the grand system be resolved once and for all? I think not. It should, on the contrary, be cultivated, tamed,[4] civilized, organized, etc., but not resolved once and for all, either by law or by eliminating those with opposing views! There are good reasons for keeping it alive because any resolution of this conflict means a "freezing" of concepts, of ideas, of theories, of expectations; and if the central idea of the whole system freezes, the whole thing will stagnate. Why shouldn't it stagnate? One reason is that it would be no longer adaptable to varying conditions. Conflict is useful, if tamed and cultivated; it is useful as a permanent shaking-up effort of the whole system, it provides a permanent test of stability and adaptivity. Conflict as a means to produce ultra-stability or dynamic equilibrium is essential and should be cultivated.

Instead of proposing the result of a design or planning problem in physical terms, or as a cardboard model, or as a drawing, a device should be offered which shows the participants the various alternatives and which tries to find out their consequences. This can be done by scientific means and should simulate the future possibilities resulting from the particular problem as tactics are simulated in military games. The attempt to trace the possible consequences and have the various involved interests and different goal systems negotiate, debate outcomes, and find a common solution may be by this process of "concretization" described last week.[5] It may be that goal systems can be processed in such a way that a common and more abstract goal system will result, and many very old techniques to develop such goal systems already exist. However, these goal systems would refer to a particular design problem as a political measure. Therefore the designer together with the scientist could be concerned with building the "sandboxes" in which all the knowledge of possible consequences could finally lie, and all fantasy as well! This can be done on a very sophisticated level and to a large extent is a communication problem. A difficult communication problem exists where a client does not understand the consequences of a solution and has not the intellectual power to try to learn them.

I should here give a few alternatives in the form of block diagrams for the classification of innovation chains. If you remember the flow from pure science to "dirty" applications first presented, there are several alternatives for organizing these innovating systems. In general we can say that any innovating system should contain a strong enquiring system such as is provided by science and the philosophy of the enquiring system can link it very closely to the goal innovating system and only some dusty and unnecessary primary assumptions and prerequisites of epistemology have to be replaced to provide this language systematically. I cannot, however, do this in detail here.

Another question is, how should this innovating system be linked with the educational system? There are again several block diagram models of ways of doing this.

Let me now draw a few conclusions. There are promising approaches and bodies of knowledge which might provide a theory and methodology for innovation, and part of this might form a theory and methodology for design. These approaches are well developed and need only an effort of translation—though this is difficult enough! They are already teachable, and factual knowledge of man and his environment already exists, which could be taken as similar for all branches of design. To pose the alternative between research-orientated and intuitive and imaginative design, between rational and irrational, is the wrong alternative. The question is the degree to which the problem-solving processes are, and should be, controlled, whether the processes should be organized in a controlled way and the degree to which they should be communicated to others. The degree, of course, increases with the increasing necessity of sharing the problem. Simultaneously, because the professional structure is a reality, the adaptation to the requirements of a certain problem can only be done by putting together various people because single people having this education do not exist.

Any theory of innovation including a theory of design must be based on a theory of action, not on a theory of knowledge (epistemology) alone. Such a theory of action should contain a theory of knowledge. Here the image concept of Boulding can serve as a useful starting point. Such a theory has to consider the connection between perception and action in the complicated way following from the fact that what we perceive depends on what we expect to perceive, and what we expect to perceive depends on what we have experienced.

The professional boundaries do not necessarily coincide with the classes of the tasks, but the existing professions cannot be replaced very easily, only modified.

The innovator, or designer, or planner acts politically in all cases where he is producing essential innovation—even though he may not know it—though he should!

The goal question cannot be solved normatively or dogmatically, or scientifically, and the only way of dealing with it seems to be organized debate.

Finally, there is a need for the production of utopian images because utopian images are programs—they always have been and that is their main purpose as I understand them.

This seminar has been something of a *tour de force* but not, I hope, a *force de frappe*. Amongst the subjects that had to be omitted are:

1. The concept of structure in detail, and types of order and innovation on the structure and order type level.
2. Aesthetics of innovation and dynamics of styles.
3. Processes and their properties. (A useful concept. What the designer does is to canalize processes, facilitate them and make them possible, and we can understand design as a lot of processes of regulation.)
4. Systematic methods developed so far, and their comparison.
5. Ideologies.

The whole thing presented seems to have been difficult for the reason that it is the first time that I have attempted the linkage together of a whole range of problems commencing with philosophical assumptions and ending with political problems. The different terminology often varying from one seminar to the next has been a further difficulty, and also many hypotheses are in their early stages.

The fact that the subject becomes more complicated by intended simplifications points to its novelty. Heisenberg's thesis for his Ph.D. consisted of two pages leading to many things. In this field we are far from this simple axiomatic system, though it might be no doubt possible![6] Finally, almost every second sentence ended with a question mark and one of the next tasks might be to take these questions and find those that are deliberate questions. But that will do, I thank you for your patience.

[The transcript has here the notation: "(Prolonged applause.)"]

Notes

1　Another hint at Rittel's future definition of design.
2　Rittel noted "Freedom from necessity."
3　The specific source of this material is uncertain, but Esherick, who had recruited Rittel to Berkeley, was certainly known to all the attendees of the seminar, and was likely among the audience.
4　Rittel's notion of wicked problems was still in the future at the time of the seminars, but his use of the word "tamed" is consistent in spirit, if not in all theoretical details, with the use he would make of the word in defining wicked problems.
5　The optimism Rittel shows here will not be matched with later work which will feel/express greater pessimism about the limits of science and rationality—e.g. especially the paradoxes of rationality—which, by the time of "On the Planning Crisis", have become central to Rittel's reasoning.
6　Again, the optimism here—that such an axiomatic system can be created—is not matched in later work. See, for example, property 1 of wicked problems: no definitve formulation, in "On the Planning Crisis." Rittel's own emendation from "is" to "might be" shows this growing caution.

References

Churchman, C. W. (1971) *The Design of Inquiring Systems: Basic Concepts of Systems and Organizations*. New York: Basic Books.

Skinner, B. F. (1961) "The Design of Cultures." *Daedalus*, 90: 534–46.

Steinbuch, K. (1961) *Automat und Mensch*. Berlin: Springer-Verlag.

Part Two

Wicked Problems

The Science and Design Seminar was infused with ideas transferred from Ulm and a confidence, albeit guarded, in the powers of scientific thinking and methods. Yet one can also find a certain skepticism and incipient new ideas. For example, near the conclusion of the tenth seminar, Rittel says: "In this field we are far from this simple axiomatic system though it is no doubt possible." We can see a flash of great optimism in the statement that such a system is "no doubt possible," albeit he was less guarded in speaking to a seminar than he would have been in a written work. The optimism is not simply in the turn of phrase. He is searching for

> promising approaches and bodies of knowledge which might provide a theory and methodology for innovation, and part of this might form a theory and methodology for design. These approaches are well developed and need only translation effort—though this is difficult enough. They are already teachable, and factual knowledge of man and his environment already exists which could be taken as similar for all branches of design.[1]

This confidence in the knowledge that already exists, and in the possibility that a theory of innovation is possible, reveal his essentially optimistic vision.

But he is also struggling with the limitations that he sees. During the seminars he says, "the innovation policy of today depends on a grand view of the system," and, "I do not trust scientists in questions concerning the grand system as a whole as it is not easy to transpose scientific statements out of science." And when he reviewed the transcript of the seminars, he edited the phrase "it is no doubt possible", striking out the confident "is" and overwriting a cautious "might be." We can even find, in the final seminar, a hint at the language and ideas that will later become central: "should the conflict between different images of the grand system be resolved once and for all? I think not. It should, on the contrary, be cultivated, tamed." Though the formal definition of wicked problems, and their foil—tame problems—would not be developed for another few years after the seminars, we can see Rittel formulating his basic principles in the seminars; he sees even at this point that the problematic nature will not be dispelled, that there will be no definitive grand system.

The skepticism and doubts found an explicit expression in the Churchman Seminar held at the University of California in Berkeley in 1967. In this seminar,

> Horst Rittel suggested . . . that the term 'wicked problem' refers to a class of social system problems which are ill-formulated, where the information is confusing, where there are many clients and decision makers with conflicting values, and where the ramifications in the whole system are thoroughly confusing. The adjective 'wicked' is supposed to describe the mischievous and even evil quality of these problems, where proposed 'solutions' often turn out to be worse than the symptoms.
>
> (Churchman 1967: B-141)

The notion that design and planning problems have characteristics that set them apart from all other kinds of problems was fully developed for a joint presentation by Horst Rittel and Melvin Webber before the Panel on Policy Sciences of the American Association for the Advancement of Science in 1969. The title of that presentation was "Dilemmas of a General Theory of Planning." The text of this presentation did not reach the general audience until four years later, when it was published in the *Policy Sciences* journal.

With this article, Rittel and Webber shattered the foundations upon which the discipline had been built, the model of the "First Generation Systems Approach", as Rittel called it, and which, 13 years later, Donald Schön would call "Technical Rationality" (Schön 1983).[2] This model, which "most powerfully shaped both our thinking about the professions and the institutional relations of research, education and practice," held that "professional activity consists in instrumental problem solving made rigorous by the application of scientific theory and technique" (Schön 1983: 21). However, before "instrumental problem solving" techniques can be applied, the problem has to be clearly identified. Herein lies the difficulty: as Rittel has shown, defining the problem is the problem.

Once he conceived of the notion of "wicked problems," Rittel did not await the publication of "Dilemmas of a General Theory of Planning." He went on to ponder the consequences of "wicked problems" for a theory of design and planning. If design and planning problems are not technical, but political, and if their characteristics put them outside the realm of scientific theory, and beyond the reach of systematic procedures, even rationality, how then are planners to deal with such problems, and how is one to account for and justify planning actions? Rittel explored and developed these themes in a lecture held at the Systems Analysis Seminar in Karlsruhe in 1971. This seminar was organized jointly by the European Association of Productivity Centres and the Studiengruppe für Systemforschung. The lecture was subsequently published as "On the Planning Crisis: Systems Analysis of the First and Second Generations" in 1972 and is reprinted here.

In this article, in addition to describing his "wicked problems," Rittel spells out for the first time some of the key concepts that guide a "Second Generation Systems Approach," among them "the symmetry of ignorance," "transparency," "objectification," and "design as argumentation," which then became topics for further development.

Some questions arise in comparing Rittel's "On the Planning Crisis" with Herbert Simon's work. How do Rittel's concepts of the paradox of rationality and of wicked problems compare with Simon's bounded rationality and ill-structured problems? Simon's notion of rationality is a very demanding one; it asks an actor to consider *all* possible courses of action and *all* the consequences of each action, and then to choose the *optimal* action. Rittel's concept of rationality is a much weaker one; it is defined simply as thinking before acting. If this weaker notion of rationality leads to a paradox, then the stronger one, which implies the weaker one, must lead to the same paradox. Simon did not see it that way, although he recognized that, because of the limitations of the human mind to grasp the world, rationality, as he defined it, was necessarily "bounded"—that is, it could only partially be achieved.[3]

For Simon a problem was ill-structured (ISP) if it lacked one or more conditions of a well-structured problem (WSP)—that is, a problem that can be solved by some "mechanizable process." The ill-structuredness did not reside in the nature of the problem, but again in the human limitations. Simon believed, "there is no real boundary between WSPs and ISPs"; a problem could be more or less ill-structured or well-structured (Simon 1984: 145).

By contrast, Rittel drew a strong line between wicked problems and tame problems. A wicked problem can be "tamed," or at least handled as if it were tame, by defining and describing it and a set of possible responses, but it is in this handling as if tame that lies the danger of, say, deciding too early what the solution is, of forgetting an important aspect, ignoring other views, etc. Taming a problem by treating it as if it were tame does not remove its inherent wickedness; the description of the problem that is used is not, as Rittel argued, a definitive formulation, but rather simply one possible formulation among many. Where Simon sees the ISP ultimately resolving into one correct WSP, Rittel sees a lurking wickedness in the possibility that any definition of the problem can be completely discarded. Problems are wicked, not so much because of human limitations, but rather because of the epistemic freedom of the designer: "*[n]othing has to be or to remain as it is or as it appears to be*; there are no limits to the conceivable."[4] The formulation of the problem depends on who formulates it; however satisfied one might be with a chosen problem formulation, there is no guarantee that another person will formulate it in the same way. The wickedness lies in this uncertainty. A "tame" formulation may be chosen, but at any time, for any number of reasons, a new formulation of the problem may present itself. For example, the game of chess is a classic "tame" problem, with clearly defined rules, and a clearly defined goal. But there is a lurking wickedness once an actual chess game between two players begins: the problem can be redefined. An element of gamesmanship might enter, with one player using stalling tactics to make the opponent impatient, or trying to create distractions. Or some other goal might appear: a parent might allow the child to win; the game might be secondary to the socializing it engenders, etc.

Notes

1 From Seminar 10 of the Science and Design seminars in this volume.

2 It is one of the fates of history that Rittel and Schön, who had very similar ideas, did not know of each other's work and did not meet until 1987.

3 Simon also speaks of a paradox of rationality, but his is within the context of game theory, in particular regarding the so-called "Prisoner's Dilemma" (Simon 1969: 46).

4 Rittel, "The Reasoning of Designers," included in this volume, pp. 187-95 (original emphases).

On the Planning Crisis

Systems Analysis of the First and Second Generations

Horst W. J. Rittel

At the very beginning I would like to present some hypotheses about various systems approaches as they have been developed over the last two decades. The term "systems analysis" means *attacking problems of planning in a rational, straightforward, systematic way, characterized by a number of attitudes, which a systems analyst and designer should have.*

Characteristics of the Systems Analyst and Designer

First, his attitude should be somewhat detached from the problem at hand: he should try to be rational, objective, and scientific in attacking his problems. Secondly, he is characterized by the attempt to grasp the whole of the system rather than being someone who undertakes piecemeal improvement. And because the whole system has many facets and because the problems of planning are not the responsibility of any single discipline, the approach of the systems analyst and designer must necessarily be interdisciplinary. Some systems designers like to call themselves generalists in contrast to the specialist of single field. A fourth characteristic is that he is trying to optimize, i.e. to incorporate all relevant and important aspects of the planning problem at hand into one measure of effectiveness which he tries to maximize. The systems analyst deals with economics in the broad sense, not in the narrow monetary or budgetary sense: he is trying to maximize productivity in the sense of optimizing resource allocation. Of course, the systems researcher is supposed to be innovative, i.e. to develop novel solutions from the formulation of the problem, or, as it is called, from the mission of the project.

Achievements of the Systems Approach to Date

Much hope has been placed in this approach and there are spectacular examples of the application of this systems approach. For example the NASA missions would not have taken place had it not been for the systems approach, nor would the big defense systems have existed. Further applications range from scheduling of toll bridges to the layout of a production-mix for a company. More recently, proposals have been made to use this approach in other fields, for example in urban renewal, improving the environment, in tackling the nutrition problem of mankind, the health systems and even the penal and law enforcement systems. Of great importance in this connection has been the computer, which is supposed to make possible what could not be treated by the unarmed natural human brain.

Let us step back a little and look at this development in a retrospective approach. In general it can be said that the era of hope and expectation set into this systems approach has been followed by an era of disappointment. There is, particularly in the United States, a severe hangover about the possibilities and usefulness of this type of systems approach if applied to problems of the latter kind. In general it can be said without exaggeration that the classical systems approach has not yielded what was expected of it and in a number of large projects can only be considered as a failure. Furthermore, there are indications that confidence that this approach will be useful on a large scale and on many occasions is diminishing; for example, in the United States there have been cutbacks and even cancellations in the budgets of many of the large projects for applications of the systems approach. Many of the think-tanks and bodies that have been selling this approach to various governmental and industrial agencies are in very bad shape and are reducing their size. There is, additionally, considerable unemployment among those people who call themselves "systems researchers." Those who have done this kind of work in the aero-space industry have lost their jobs by the thousands. After all, it becomes evident that they are not at all the generalists who can attack any problems because of their approach but rather that they have become very narrow specialists in, for instance, missile guidance systems or in certain systems of spacemanship.

Before looking at the consequences of this development. I would like to analyze the characteristics of the traditional systems approach and why this approach has not worked as expected. For the sake of clarity I call this systems approach the systems approach of the first generation and I would like to contrast it with the systems approach of the second generation.

Steps in the First-Generation Systems Approach

The systems approach of the first generation is characterized by a certain mode of procedure, by a certain sequence of steps or phases for attacking a planning project:

1. The first step, which has been given different names by different authors, is *to understand the problem.*
2. The second step is *to gather information*, particularly to understand its context from the viewpoint of the problem. Then for some people (though others deny this) something happens called the "creative leap," the great idea.
3. The third step is to *analyze the information.*
4. The fourth step is *to generate solutions*, or at least one.
5. The fifth step is *to assess the solutions* and to decide to take that solution which comes out best.

6. The sixth step is *to implement*, then,
7. *to test*, and,
8. *to modify* the solution, if necessary, and learn for the next time.

In different textbooks different names for these steps are found, but essentially they are the same, and there is no textbook on systems methods that does not contain a first chapter describing these phases. *Operations research* (OR) is closely related with a particular type of systems approach of this first generation with the following steps:

1. *Define the "solution space,"* this being a manifold of solutions, a set of variables, a combination of which make up the set of conceived of solutions.
2. *Define the constraints*, i.e. describe which of these solutions have to be excluded because they are not feasible.
3. *Define the measure of effectiveness*.
4. *Optimize the measure of effectiveness*, i.e. identify or search for that solution in the solution space that is within the boundaries of the constraints and for which the measure of effectiveness assumes a maximum value. Usually it has to be demonstrated within the set of feasible solutions that there is no better solution than for which optimality is claimed.

These steps of OR can be applied to or substituted for the later steps of the general systems approach described above.

Shortcomings of the First-Generation Approach: The Paradoxes of Rationality

I should like now to examine why this type of systems approach does not work for planning problems that are not found, as in the military domain, in the context of a strong autocratic decision structure as is the case for most problems of corporate and community planning.

The systems approach is based on a certain naive scientific idea that the scientist has, in addition to the traditional role of gathering or producing knowledge and offering this to the world, a further role of attacking practical problems and that the ideals and principles of scientific work are carried over into the context of planning. Why is it not possible to do this successfully in the context of the practical planning problems, corporate or other?

The most important reasons are deep-lying paradoxes connected with the concept of rationality. Rationality has many definitions and I shall choose a particularly simple one: rational behavior means trying to anticipate the consequences of contemplated actions. In other words, think before you act. The systems approach of the first generation entails this obligation to be rational, which means that you try to understand the problem as a whole, and to look at the consequences. This is a rather modest definition, and there is hardly any reason to argue against it, because if a person does not try to be rational in this sense he can be considered irresponsible, not bothering about the consequences of his actions. Let us assume somebody seriously attempts to be rational in this sense. He would then try to anticipate the consequences of the alternative courses of actions: "I can do this, or that, or that, but before I make my choice I must figure out what the consequences will be." In doing this, he finds out that anticipating the consequences is consequential by itself because it takes time, labor, and money to trace consequences because it is work.

Therefore, before I can start to trace the consequences of my actions, I should trace the consequences of tracing consequences of my actions. This is, of course, in turn consequential, because I invest time and money in tracing the consequences of tracing the consequences; therefore, before tracing the consequences of tracing the consequences, I should trace the consequences of tracing the consequences of tracing the consequences. And each next step is not necessarily easier or simpler than the previous one, because the questions to answer become more and more fundamental. *Therefore there is no way to start to be rational*: one should always start a step earlier.

The *second paradox of rationality* can be demonstrated as follows: let us assume that somebody manages in some way to be rational. He is then in the middle of tracing consequences, which means that he comes to the insight that every consequence has consequences, which in turn means that there is no reason for him to stop at any point in time tracing the consequences, because every consequence can be expected to have further ones. Therefore, once he has managed to start being rational, he cannot stop it anymore, because he stops it only for extra-logical or extra-rational reasons, e.g. he has run out of time, money, or patience. Yet from within the nature of the logic of the problem, there is no reason to stop the tracing of consequences. Therefore once it has been started it can no longer be stopped.

The *third paradox of rationality* is that the more one succeeds in being rational (and I assume that this is possible), the more it incapacitates one. This is so because the further one develops causal chains of consequences into the future, the more the effects of uncertainty will come into effect and the further into the future a chain of causal effects is developed, the less one can say which of these terminals will eventually become the case as a consequence of a particular course of action. This means that the better one succeeds in being rational, the less one can derive from that what one should do now. In the long run, we are all dead; it does not matter what we do now. Therefore, if we succeed in being rational it does not help us.

A *fourth paradox of rationality* is that of self-containment. In order to study the consequences of contemplated actions, a model (a causal description of the phenomena which are affected by the contemplated actions or affect the actions) is needed. Now this model should, because one is worrying about all consequences, contain and describe all those factors or phenomena that are important. But what is more important than the causal model itself which determines what can be traced as a consequence? Therefore the model should be part of the model, because it influences what can be figured out as a consequence. In other words, a model should contain itself, and that is impossible.

Wicked Problems and Tame Problems

These are the most serious objections to the systems approach of the first generation. Speculating about paradoxes is not a philosophical game but a matter of extreme practical importance. Let us look at it from another viewpoint by studying the *nature of planning problems* and contrasting them with the problems of the scientist, the engineer or the chess player. I should like to describe and contrast two kinds of problems: the one is called "*tame*" *problems* (TPs) and the other the "*wicked*" *problems* (WPs).

Most research about creativity and problem-solving behavior is about "tame" problems, because they are so easy to be manipulated and controlled. Unfortunately, little is known about the treatment of "wicked" problems or of people actually dealing with them, because "wicked" problems cannot be simulated in a laboratory setting. Yet all essential planning problems are wicked, whereas the systems approach of the first generation is good only for more or less tame problems (for instance a quadratic equation or a chess problem, or a problem of chemical analysis, or a problem of optimization of OR).

Properties of "wicked" problems and "tame" problems contrasted

1. The first property is that a tame problem can be exhaustively formulated so that it can be written down on a piece of paper which can be handed to a knowledgeable man who will eventually solve the problem without needing any additional information. This is not so with wicked problems. When I tell somebody the problem is that we need a management information system in our company or whether to introduce a new product into our production line, I can write it down on a piece of paper, give it to him, and lock him up. But it will not be long before this person will come out again and ask for more information: What kind of a new product are you talking about? How will it affect the other production lines already in operation? What markets do you expect for your product? etc. You could say that I could have listed this information ahead of time, anticipating that the man might need it. But the irritating thing is that, depending on the state of solution, the next question for additional information is unique and dependent on the state of solution you have already reached. For example, now you have developed your solution of introducing a new product to the point that you say, "Alright, I want five machines of type 'A' which must be bought." Then the next question depends on this decision, because it has, for example, to be determined whether the ceilings in the third floor can carry these machines. This is a question that you would not have asked if you had not decided to have these machines and to have them there. This question depends on your state of solution at that point in time and the next question could not be anticipated at the beginning by the formulator of the problem. In order to give exhaustive information ahead of time for a wicked problem you have to anticipate all potential solutions first in order to think up all questions, which means that you do not have to delegate the problem anymore, because you can solve it yourself.

The first property is that *WPs have no definitive formulation*. This is a serious objection to the systems approach of the first generation, which has as a first step of the box-car train of phases "understand the problem" before you go on and solve it. This consideration shows that you cannot understand the problem without solving it, and solving the problem is the same as understanding it. But how can you understand the problem if you cannot have sufficient information without solving the problem?

2. The second property in contrast to tame problems is that *every formulation of the WP corresponds to a statement of the solution* and vice versa. When I say the problem is to get a machine carrying out a million operations, then this machine is a solution; if I say this machine should not be heavier than 500 kg, then this is exactly the solution. This means that understanding the problem is identical with solving it. Whichever statement is made about the problem is a statement of solution. That is very different from tame problems, where one thing is the problem and another the solution, and very different from the notion of a problem as the proponents of the first-generation approach had in mind.

3. The third property is that *there is no stopping rule for wicked problems*. If you have a chess problem made in three moves, then you know once you have found the combination of moves you are through with it and you have solved your problem; if you have an equation, and you have something like x = y, then you know that you are through. But this is not so with a wicked problem: you can always try to do better and there is nothing in the nature of the problem that could stop you. You stop for any planning problem, because you have run out of time, money, or patience; but that has nothing to do with the logic of the problem, and you can always try to do better.

4. The fourth property: given the solution to a tame problem you can test it, assign to it either of the two attributes "correct" or "false" and pinpoint mistakes and errors. This is not so with wicked problems. The categories of true or false do not apply: we cannot say that this plant layout or a plan for a city is correct or false. We can only say that it is good or bad and this to varying degrees and maybe in different ways for different people; for normally, what is good for A is not at all good for B. This is the fate of all solutions to wicked problems: there is no criterion system nor rule which would tell you what is correct or false. I can only say, "I think it is pretty good even if you say it is not so." So: to *WPs correct/false is not applicable.*

5. For tame problems, there is an exhaustive list of permissible operations. To take the chess problem as an example: at the beginning of a chess game you have a choice of twenty moves, and in chess it makes no sense to invent new moves during the game; or in a chemical analysis there is the choice of several hundred things you are allowed to do, though you are not allowed to tamper with the instruments or to alter the setting of a meter. But it is different again with wicked problems. *There is no exhaustive, enumerable list of permissible operations*; everything goes as a matter of principle and fantasy.

6. A problem can be stated as a discrepancy, as something as it is compared with something as it ought to be. The next consideration in problem solving of this kind is to ask "why is it not as it ought to be?" and you look for reasons for the existence of this discrepancy, the cause, and the explanation. And the trouble is that *in wicked problems there are many explanations for the same discrepancy* and there is no test which of these explanations is the best one. For example, if you say that our production is not efficient enough, you might decide that it is because our machines are too old, or because our scheduling system is not adequate, and you can try to find evidence for this; but you can also say that it is because the director of manufacturing is not the right person. Depending on which explanation you choose for the discrepancy, the solution will be led into different directions. If you think that it is the director's personality, then he will be fired; but if you think that the equipment is not adequate you will buy new equipment or look for possibilities for substituting for that equipment. The direction in which the solution goes depends on the very first step of explanation ("why is there a problem?"), which is the most decisive step in dealing with a wicked problem.

7. Every tame problem has a certain natural form and there is no reason to argue about, for example, the level of the problem. But *every wicked problem can be considered a symptom of another problem* and, of course, since nobody should try to cure symptoms you are never sure that you are attacking the problem on the right level, for curing symptoms can make the real disease worse. Therefore, never be too sure that you should tackle the problem as stated. If somebody says "we have trouble in our inventory and we have delays due to inventory," we can always understand this as a symptom of, for instance, the general personnel policy or of the organization of the purchasing department. We should not conclude too early that we need to reorganize our inventory, for maybe we should rather tackle the more comprehensive system. Every problem can be considered a symptom of another.

8. As I said before, the solution to a chess problem can be tested. For a wicked problem *there is neither an immediate nor an ultimate test to the problem*, because each action which was carried out in response to the problem can have consequences over time—next year there may be another consequence that contributes greatly to how you assess your plan. There is no time limit for the potential consequences of a problem and therefore there is no ultimate test, because there can always be additional consequences which might be disastrous and which result from what turns out to be a very bad plan.

9. A chess problem can be played over and over again; if an equation is not solved at the first attempt, try again; it only takes a bit of paper, a pencil and time. If you have solved one quadratic equation, you have solved them all because the trick of solving one is the trick of solving the whole class of equations of the second degree. There are prototypical solutions for all classes of tame problems. However, one can only anticipate or simulate potential consequences to a certain extent in order to get an idea whether something is or is not a good

response to a wicked problem, for a wicked problem cannot be repeated. *Each wicked problem is a one-shot operation.* You cannot undo what you have done in the first trial; each trial matters and is very consequential: you cannot set up a factory, see how it works, demolish it and rebuild it over again until it works. There is no trial and error. There is no experimentation in dealing with wicked problems.

10. *Every wicked problem is essentially unique.* This is very irritating because you cannot learn for the next time; you cannot easily carry over successful strategies from the past into the future since you never know whether the next problem does not have a characteristic, a property which is sufficiently different from the previous problems to make the old solution no longer work. Seemingly similar problems ask for transfer of a solution from one context to another and only a closer analysis shows that there are other factors which are so important, distinct in both these situations, that such a transfer is unadvisable. In the treatment of wicked problems you should never decide too early what the nature of the solution should be, and whether an old solution can be used again in a new context.

11. In contrast to the tame problem solver who may lose or win a chess game without being blamed for it or may state a wrong hypothesis which will be refuted by someone else, *the wicked problem solver has no right to be wrong.* He is responsible for what he is doing.

The Consequences of these Properties of Wicked Problems for the Systems Approach

If you remember the box-car train of steps or phases given earlier and compare it with the eleven properties of wicked problems, then you will see that there are various contradictions that are responsible for the uselessness of the first generation method approaches to wicked problems—*and all our problems are wicked*.

The first step was "understand the problem." But according to properties 1 and 2 of our list you cannot understand and formulate the problem without having solved it. If we cannot understand a problem, step 1 cannot be carried out without having gone through step 6 in the old list. So you cannot get information without having an idea of the solution, because the question you ask depends on the nature of solution you have in mind.

Then the generation of a solution manifold is not a separable step: it goes on all the time. With the first step of explaining the problem you already determine the nature of the solution. The first statement of problem is already a statement of solution. You cannot separate the generation of solutions from understanding the problem, etc. You can play this with all these eight steps of the first-generation approach and I claim that there is sufficient evidence to reject the first-generation systems approach for the treatment of wicked problems.

Let us now look at operations research, which is connected with this approach and in which there are also various steps: determine the solution space, determine the measure of effectiveness, determine the system of constraints, etc. Once all this is done, OR starts: you start to optimize, using linear programming, etc. This means that information gathering has to be carried out before OR can start. But is not the generation of this information (which solution shall I consider as alternative, what shall be considered good or best, and what are the constraints of my problem?) the difficult question? Once you have answered this question most of the problems have been solved, and what is left over is a search process for a well-defined optimum. But OR starts once the wickedness is out of the problem, once you have said what a good admissible, feasible solution is. You can say, "Constraints are naturally given." But that is not so. Every constraint represents a decision, mainly a decision of resignation. To give an example: a company producing pre-fabricated parts for building wants to transport these on trucks. The trucks have to cover a certain area. The lowest underpass in that area determines the maximum height of truck plus component. That is a constraint: truck, loading surface, plus height of the component should not exceed the height of the underpass. But you have implicitly decided not to remove the critical underpass: you could raise it somewhat if it is important enough to make the component a little bit taller or higher. It may pay off to carry the component over the underpass with a helicopter or to lift the underpass somewhat. It is by no means a natural constraint; it is only that you resign yourself to the irremovable existence of a critical circumstance. The constraint is not at all a technical and objectively given logical entity; *every constraint or limitation I pose on my action space is a decision, or at least an implicit indication of resignation.*

Some Principles of the Systems Approach of the Second Generation

1. The knowledge needed in a planning problem, a wicked problem, is not concentrated in any single head; for wicked problems there are no specialists. The expertise that you need in dealing with a wicked problem is usually distributed over many people. Those people who are the best experts with the best knowledge, are usually those who are likely to be affected by your solution. Hence, ask those who become affected but not the experts. You do not learn in school how to deal with wicked problems; you learn something about inventory systems, about OR, or about manufacturing technology, but not the appropriate thing to do in a particular setting of an organization. (I exaggerate deliberately.) The expertise and ignorance is distributed over all participants in a wicked problem. There is a symmetry of ignorance among those who participate because nobody knows better by virtue of his degrees or his status. There are no experts (which is irritating for experts), and if experts there are, they are only experts in guiding the process of dealing with a wicked problem, but not for the subject matter of the problem.

2. The second principle of the second generation rests on the insight that *nobody wants to be "planned at."* The most dramatic examples for this are the American urban renewal projects where people revolt against being planned at. The buildings that are constructed can be as nice and inhabitable as you want, but the fact that they have been imposed from top makes them obsolete. The consequence of this is that planning methods of the second generation try to make

those people who are being affected into participants of the planning process. They are not merely asked but actively involved in the planning process. That means a kind of *maximized involvement*. And this seems to be the case even of corporations that the planning from top (imposed planning) becomes less and less popular.

3. The next principle is that when you develop a solution to a wicked problem, at every single step a judgment is made that is not based on scientific expertise. There is always an "ought-to-be" statement involved. For each step there is a conclusion that ends with "do this and that." This is a so-called "deontic premise," i.e. a personal premise of the "ought-to-be" nature that is not justified by professional expertise but is only an indication of political and general moral and ethical attitudes. Therefore, if you look only at the outcome of the planning process, you cannot reconstruct which deontic statements have entered into the argument leading to the solution. Therefore you can no longer control the wicked problem solver because of all these more or less implicit deontic assumptions he has made on the process he was going through. If this is so, then on the one hand there is one more reason to have others participate in order to bring out these premises and, on the other, there is the need to look for methods which show some *transparency of the planning process*. These methods should lead to a situation where every step of the planning process is understandable and communicable or "transparent."

4. As has already been said, an essential characteristic of wicked problems is that they cannot be correct or false, but only good or bad. But who says whether a plan and the solution to a problem is good or bad? In fact everybody has the authority to say if he is being affected positively or negatively by the plan and there is no way of saying that A's judgment about this plan is superior to B's judgment. There is no authority to say that, because there are no experts anymore. (This is different from the doctor's situation, for he is an expert.) If A says it is a grand plan and B says it is lousy, who is right? Therefore we should draw the conclusion and say, "everybody is entitled to exert his judgment about the plan. We need procedures that enable us to explain to each other why I think that it is great and you think it is lousy.

Many methods deal with the problem of helping the process of making the basis of one's judgment explicit and communicating it to others. We call this process "objectification." This differs from making something objective, because making something objective in the scientific sense means that you invent a procedure, the outcome of which becomes independent of the person who carries it out. For example, you say in measuring technology you have succeeded in making a thing objective if it does not matter who carries out the measurement. We talk about an objective situation or an operation leading to objective statements: the less it matters who carries it out the more objective the outcome would be. But as we have seen, here it matters who judges, or who makes the statement, or who goes through the planning process. We can never be objective in planning in the scientific sense and therefore there is nothing resembling scientific planning. This is very different from carrying out science, because it matters who carries out the process and who is involved; by "objectification" we mean that we must successfully exchange information about the foundations of our judgment. If you can tell me why you say that plan A is great, and I understand your judgment, you have succeeded in objectifying your space of judgment to me. And although I might not share your judgment and might not be convinced, I understand you now. The systems researcher of the second generation hopes that better mutual understanding of the bases of judgment of others at least does not make it less likely that people come to an agreement. More deliberation does not lead to agreement, though it may lead to understanding; one cannot enforce agreement, but the likelihood of agreement and the effect of learning from each other is greater.

The hope in this process of objectification is:

- To forget less: if you tell me your version or story, maybe I forget less than I would otherwise.
- To stimulate doubt: if you have to tell your story it is likely to stimulate doubt, and this is good because only doubt is a test of plans.
- To raise the right issues: objectification will help you identify those questions which are worthwhile, which have the greatest weight and where there is the greatest disagreement. If we agree, we do not have to discuss or analyze something. If we disagree considerably and it is important we have to discuss and analyze it.
- To control the delegation of judgment: if I let you plan for me, then you had better objectify to me how you proceed, because I want to have some control about the delegation of judgment.
- The belief that explicitness is helpful which is not so in all matters of life. There are some situations where we had better not be explicit.

5. Another principle of the systems approach of the second generation is that *there is no scientific planning*. After these considerations it is pretty self-evident, but people often talk about "scientification" of planning (dealing with practical problems in a scientific fashion). Dealing with wicked problems is always political. There is not that detached, scientific, objective attitude in planning; it is always political because of these deontic premises.
6. This planner is not an expert and he sees his role as somebody who helps to bring about problems rather than as one who offers solutions to problems. He is a midwife of problems rather than an offerer of therapies. He is a teacher more than a doctor. Of course, it is a modest and not a very heroic role that such a planner can play.
7. Another characteristic of this man is that he makes careful, seasoned respectlessness, i.e. casting doubt on something, a virtue. Although he knows his dilemma of rationality and the nature of wicked problems, he must be at least moderately optimistic. Moderate activism and optimism is part of his attitude. He knows that responsible planning is important, because one cannot be

rational; on the other hand one is obliged to be rational, although it is impossible, which is a difficult situation. Either one must give up the treatment of wicked problems and of planning altogether or one must come to the conclusion to try something in any case.

8. *Moderate optimism*, a further characteristic, has been mentioned above.

9. The model you might use instead of the expert model of the first generation can be called a *conspiracy model of planning*. This means that, because we cannot anticipate all the consequences of our plans, every plan, every treatment of a wicked problem is a venture, if not an adventure. Therefore, let us share the risk, let us try to find accomplices who are willing to embark on the problem with us. For one person it is too risky, but maybe if we join our forces we may take the risk and live with the uncertainty and embark upon the venture. This seems to be a somewhat tenable position to justify the courage in planning at all.

10. Whereas the planning process of the first generation can be carried out in solitary confinement with long sequences of steps where you can proceed according to the rules of the art, the planning process of wicked problem solving must be *understood as an argumentative process*: one of raising questions and issues towards which you can assume different positions, with the evidence gathered and arguments built for and against these different positions. The various positions are discussed, and after a decision is taken one proceeds until the next question arises within the process. For instance, the issue could be the location of a plant. You can, of course, take the view that this is the wrong question, that one has to discuss first of all whether one should build a plant at all. Let us assume, however, that we say "yes, we want to build a plant." There might be three possible locations. We can then collect or set up the different positions for and against these three locations and then arrive at an argument as to which one of these might be the best. Once we have made up our mind as to which one to assume as the best, we go ahead. Shall we make it a one or a two-storey building?—so the whole thing starts all over again. Each question of decision can be combined with an argument and actually we do this all the time: we deliberate our judgment and what is deliberation other than identifying and weighing pros and cons, simulating debates and arguments in your head? Systems methods of the second generation are trying to make this deliberation explicit, to support it and to find means in order to make this process more powerful and to get it under better control. Planning is an argumentative process.

These are the main principles of the planning process of the second generation, particular versions of which are described in this report.

The Intuitive versus the Research Approach to Planning

I hope I have shown that you cannot be rational in planning: the more you try, the less it helps. On the other hand, this does not imply that you should do whatever comes into your mind, based on intuition. Certainly that is not the conclusion one should draw from this. There is actually no polarity between what you might call an intuitive approach to problem solving and on the other hand a controlled, reasonable, or rational approach. The more control you want to exert and the better founded you want your judgment to be, the more intuitive you have to be. Let me demonstrate this.

We can look at the *planning process as a sequence of events*. For example, whenever you tackle an activity for which you are very experienced, you go ahead by what you might call a routine or rote process—whenever you think that somebody has style, that means that he has well-developed routines.[1]

Now let us look at another type of problem solver. Here the man runs into a problem and he does not see any immediate way out. He then *scans his mind for a way out*, and he gets his first best idea (and usually we try the first idea assuming it is the best). Then he goes ahead and runs into the next problem. Maybe he has to scan a long time until he finds the next best idea, etc. Now, it may happen that scan as much as he might, he runs into a dead end. What does he do in such a case? Either he keeps scanning and tries to generate a potential way out or he avoids this problem and goes back to the previous problem and decides that the solution was not so good after all because it led him into a dead end. Therefore he should look for a second chance and pursue this one in order to avoid this dead end. And I would say that most of our practical problem-solving behavior is of this type.

The third approach is that the man runs into a problem and looks for a way out. But before he pursues his first idea he *develops a whole set of alternative ideas* and looks for reasons to exclude all except one. He does this by constructing filters of criteria through which he passes all these alternatives, i.e. he uses all the aspects in assessing the merits of the various alternatives with the hope that one passes. He then goes ahead until he runs into the next problem. Certainly in this case we have fewer feedback loops than in the previous case because we check more things before we go ahead. What can happen in the ideal case is that only one solution passes. At the other extreme many will pass and then you either choose at random, for instance by tossing a coin, because all the reasons you have for choosing one or the other are incorporated into these criteria, and there is therefore no good reason any more to prefer this one or that one; or you find additional criteria until only one solution is left over. The third and very frequent case is that none of the alternatives pass: the criteria are contradictory or no solution happens to be good enough. Then you either quit and say there is no solution to this problem, or you generate more solutions. You could also relax your criteria saying that you should not ask for too much.

There is a fourth possible approach: that you begin to develop alternative courses of actions, but before you move or make your choice, you see which next actions you can take, like a chess player who tries to think several moves ahead. You take a big battery of criteria, and then one hopes some alternatives, the best ones, will pass, and then you proceed with the same argument as before. If I could do this over the whole span of the problem, I would not have any loops any more. The trouble is that this process proliferates into tremendous numbers of possible courses of actions and is no longer very handy.

The "rational" man tries to develop a style more of the fourth than of the second type and you can see that this process can be regarded as consisting of two alternating basic activities. One is what you might call the *generation of variety*, i.e. having ideas to develop courses of action and ideas of solution.

The other one is a *reduction of variety,* which means constructing evaluation filters. The hypothesis of the second generation of systems analysis is: to generate variety, to have ideas, is the easiest thing in the world; even a computer may be capable of helping there. However, it can do nothing in the second part, that is in the reduction of variety, which is essentially the same as the exertion of judgment. To show the complementarity between the intuitive and the systematic, a short look is needed at the *structure of judgment*.

There are various kinds of judgments. If somebody asks you how you like the soup, it does not take you a moment to say whether it is good or bad. These are what we might call "*off-hand*" or "*intuitive*" judgments. On the other hand you might say, "Wait a minute, I must first think about it," and look for the pros and cons before you make up your mind and say whether A is good or bad or whether A is better than B. These are *deliberated judgments*. The deliberated judgments are substitutes for the offhand judgments. You make a deliberated judgment because you do not trust your off-hand judgment. You would say off-hand, "I think it is okay but should like to check it." Another and also very important opportunity for deliberation is that you have to explain your judgment to somebody else. You say, "I think it is great"; the other person asks "why?" and you have to deliberate your judgment in order to explain to somebody else why you arrived at this judgment.

Another distinction is between *overall* (final) *judgments* and *partial judgments*. Each solution has certain virtues and certain disadvantages compared with the other solutions. But you have to come up in the end with an *overall* judgment. You have to make a decision: X and Y is good or plan A is the best or is sufficient. If you cannot make an off-hand judgment, you must deliberate before you say whether for instance plan A is good enough, i.e. you must look for the reasons contributing to the quality of the performance of A, and these reasons are X1 (capital costs), X2 (maintenance costs), X3 (safety), etc. You must judge the object under all of these aspects independently and you must in some way integrate all these partial judgments into one judgment, the overall judgment. But you may want to deliberate even further. For instance, you may be unwilling to make spontaneous judgment on capital costs and distinguish instead between construction costs X11, site costs X12, roofing costs X13, etc. and make partial judgments on these. And then you must bring these second-order partial judgments together again into a partial deliberated judgment on capital costs which in turn contributes to the overall deliberated judgment whether plan A is good enough or not.

The point I want to make here is only that the more you try to deliberate, the less you trust your off-hand judgment. If you want to base your judgment on looking at all the pros and cons very carefully, the more you do it the more of a tree you get. The more systematic you want to be the less intuitive or off-hand you want to proceed. But the terminals are always off-hand judgments. This means that the more systematic you want to be and the less you trust your off-hand judgment, the more off-hand judgments you have to make. This is the point I wanted to make with regard to the correspondence between these two styles of judgments.

Let me summarize. What I wanted to do first was to demonstrate that the systems approach of the first generation, which all of you know, is not suitable for attacking planning problems of your kind. The second point was to show that there are reasons for the failure of these procedures: on the one side the dilemmas of rationality, and on the other, the wicked nature of problems. The final part demonstrated the characteristics of approaches of the second generation, the assumptions made and the foundations of the systems approach of the second generation.

Note

1 Style and routine are the same. Style is no longer necessary to solve problems: it is usually an indication of age. [Rittel's note]

Part Three

Design Reasoning

As we have seen in the Science and Design seminars, especially Seminar 1, Rittel wanted to create an overall system for innovation—not just a complete system for design, but one that would incorporate a system for design (see our discussion of optimism in Seminar 10). Rittel made extensive notes on this innovation system. But, even within the Science and Design seminars, even the closing seminar, Seminar 10, as he called for the overarching innovation system, he realized that such a system was impossible.

The problems with such systems were eloquently stated in his work on wicked problems. But there was another aspect to his recognition of the difficulties in creating a system for design: in looking for a system, he came to understand the structure of the reasoning involved in design. This work was derived from his studies of knowledge systems and his attempts to help develop systems to capture the complexity of group design activities.

The work on wicked problems, as we have seen, focuses on conditions of the problem (e.g. the project is a one-shot operation and the designer has no right to be wrong) and matters of logic and logical process (there is no definitive formulation; there is no stopping rule). Rittel's focus is on the activity and on the conditions of the problem.

"On the Planning Crisis," in addition to describing types of problems, is also, itself, motivated by a perceived problem. This is apparent in the title of the article and in the title of the more famous "Dilemmas in a General Theory of Planning," the article most widely known as the source of the idea of wicked problems. The problem was that the methods being applied—those of the "first generation"—were not suited to the type of problem they attempted to resolve.

To Rittel, the first generation applied methods that presumed tame problems while trying to resolve wicked ones. Such were the root causes of the failures of the great planning projects of the latter half of the twentieth century.

But Rittel was not merely working destructively. His intention was, as previously noted, to develop systems to help design. Rittel's second generation was not merely supposed to plunge into the fray carrying the banner of wickedness— which might be construed as suggesting that methods are not applicable (which indeed was the position of some—witness Feyerabend's *Against Method*—though this somewhat misconstrues Feyerabend's project)—Rittel was searching for tools that could actively support designers.

He based the search for tools on understanding the nature of problems, and by understanding the nature of the intellectual issues that researchers and designers faced (as can be seen in his work studying knowledge management in chemistry research and in American research institutions). It is difficult to know how much the practical aims formed the theoretical statement, and vice versa. But the theory was structured like the tool, the IBIS.

The basic theory is described in "Structure and Usefulness of Planning Information Systems," the first paper included in this section. This piece, published in the same Norwegian journal as "On the Planning Crisis," presents the main concerns that Rittel applied to the relevance of information systems. It is a development of the idea of argumentation described in the last few paragraphs of "On the Planning Crisis." This article, the first of three included in this book that cover similar material, looks at the subject from a general aspect. The second looks at the subject from the perspective of trying to implement the theory in a workable system. The third looks at the theory from the perspective of the individual.

Having discovered wicked problems, having discovered that there is no one correct answer, and that part of the problem is the number of different ways of looking at it, Rittel begins to see that we cannot pursue the artificial intelligence agenda of Herbert Simon: machines cannot make the decision, because the decision is inherently both personal and political. "Structure and Usefulness of Planning Information Systems" examines the general theoretical issues that surround the use of such systems and presents the basic theoretical backbone of design as a process of argumentation.

This process is described as having three basic elements: issues, positions, and arguments. The issues are the questions of concern; the positions, the varied responses to the question; and the arguments, the reasons offered for the positions. Any of the elements can lead to a new issue. This creates the openness suggested in wicked problems, the unlimited possibility that a new perspective will be adopted. He would come to call this the "epistemic freedom" of the designer: the designer is ultimately choosing the problem to be solved. Because of this freedom, Rittel sees a role for information systems as aiding the management of the argumentative structures of design. This led to the creation of his tool, the IBIS.

The IBIS, or Issue-Based Information System, first described in the 1970 working paper "Issues As Elements Of Information Systems," was a system for handling design knowledge. It was a system for capturing and recording the deliberations of design (or research) groups or institutions, a system for recognizing and laying out all the questions that were raised in the design process. These questions were the fundamental "issues" that gave the IBIS its name. IBIS records the issues, positions, and arguments of the design. In the process of recording this design knowledge and representing it, the different issues are brought together so they can be seen all together rather than as a series of separate questions and so that they will be heard and not forgotten, and thus it is hoped that the design decisions will be more successful.

IBIS is essentially a mnemonic aid. It is not an attempt to provide a full representation of knowledge, like semantic networks (e.g. Minsky), nor a foundation for computerized intelligence. IBIS does not claim to provide a semantic foundation—human intelligence is needed to make sense of the issues in an IBIS. Nor is it akin to expert systems—IBIS does not attempt to make suggestions to the user; it does not say what the right thing to do is, it simply attempts to present all the issues, positions and arguments that the designers can think of, all the arguments and positions that look at the different sides of a given issue. IBIS is a tool for the "objectification" that Rittel described at the end of "On the Planning Crisis."

IBIS would serve as the foundation for a number of related information systems that Rittel worked on. For example, APIS (Argumentative Planning Information System) was developed within the framework of the project "Scientific and Technological Information in the European Community" of the Directorate General of the Commission of European Communities.[1] Another example, UMPLIS (Umweltplanungs-infromationssystem) was designed to coordinate the environmental activities and policies of various government agencies, the executive and the legislature of the German government (Rittel and Kunz 1973).

These systems were practical in intention, and aimed at large groups of designers and institutional design settings. But the work also led Rittel inwards: the argumentative structure of design—which is discussed briefly in "On the Planning Crisis"—can be seen as applying, not only to the design reasoning of a large group, but to the reasoning of an individual designer.

"The Reasoning of Designers" was originally published as a working paper late in Rittel's career—it is the latest of the works we present. The paper we have is from 1988—one of his last papers before his death in 1990.

Rittel's examination of the reasoning of designers is limited—it does not attempt to examine or explain psychology or philosophy of mind. It is a schematic description of the related ideas, premises, and logical elements that make up the decision-making process. It is descriptive of reasoning processes without trying to explain them. Psychological issues, such as a designer's potential unconscious motivations or such can be left out of the discussion of reasoning—they may, in fact, be thought to be something other than reasoning—emotion, reaction, habit—and the thought process becomes reasoning at the point the designer takes a definite position regardless of whether that designer has any conscious or logically cogent supporting argument.

The argumentative structure that Rittel attributes to the reasoning of the individual is essentially parallel to that of the IBIS.

Rittel's interest in the designer as a person was not limited to this one article—he also shows this focus when he writes, "Principles for the Design of an Educational System for Design." It was, however, on the larger group design processes that he focused most of his attention.

The argumentative structure—in contrast to systems based on first-generation thinking—is able to handle and incorporate incommensurable ideas: they are simply different positions on an issue. The argumentative structure does nothing to eliminate logical contradiction or any of the logical failures that cause problems for logic-based systems.

But these logical failures did not worry Rittel: he presumed their existence. In all three of these articles, Rittel's aim is not to eliminate logical error, but rather to reveal the reasoning that has been used and to make transparent the different arguments that are considered.

Note

1 Unpublished.

Structure and Usefulness of Planning Information Systems

Horst W. J. Rittel

In my introductory lecture I tried to demonstrate that planning can be understood as a process in which problem-relevant information can be produced and processed. One of the points was that problem formulation is identical with problem resolution. It follows that, from the viewpoint of the "second-generation" systems researcher, the design of a planning system is the same as the design of the planning information system. We can thus limit ourselves to considering the characteristics of planning information systems whenever we want to talk about the possibilities of improving planning. Hence it can be said that the search for better planning systems is identical to the construction of better planning information systems. Let me go over the grounds for this.

Planning System = Planning Information System

First, given the characteristics of "wicked" problems, the planner must remain continuously in touch with the surroundings of the problem being considered. Secondly, objectification in planning means exchanges of information among those concerned in order to reach mutual understanding. Learning from one another is based upon information. Thirdly, the subject of planning is only partially known and hence during the planning process there are changes in the criteria for considering the subject and in the knowledge of the subject of planning through information. From this we concluded that planning can be understood as the generation of ideas and of an understanding of what is instead of that which ought to be and how to bring about what ought to be the case. This process of generating ideas is obviously an information process. In the best cases this information process takes place through comprehension, unlike the other possibilities of learning.

There are various types of learning. The first type is learning through conditioning: someone is shown something until he can do it. Then there is conditional conditioning: during this process of conditioning, reward or punishment is given as it was to Pavlov's dog. Something related, which in general is only expected of human beings, is persuasion: someone is told about something until he believes it. This is the normal advertising approach. All these steps are characterized by the learning process taking place gradually, with responses that are increasingly in accordance with those expected by the teacher.

Finally we reach planned conviction. This means that, on the basis of an argument, there is suddenly an "aha" effect when something is seen to be like this and not like that; systematic planning is based upon the fact that this is possible.

The difference between the first groups and planned conviction consists thus in the fact that in the first knowledge is gradually produced, a sort of stimulus-response relationship is created, whereas in the second case there is something such as an "aha" effect.

It is on the conviction rather than the persuasion processes that planning methods can and should be based. The reason is that the desired form of planning should try as little as possible to persuade and condition those involved but to have as many comprehension processes as possible to reach a state of knowledge through an "aha" effect.

When we speak of a planning system we appear to contradict the already stated fact that all planning tasks are unique; for a system is an institution that remains in general terms. Whether or not a planning system can be created to deal with one class of problems or remain valid over a specific time period is a serious problem. The consequence is nevertheless that whenever we speak about planning systems we should not be talking about the content of planning (for instance about planning a specific institution, town or factory) but rather everything said in this connection about planning should be seen from the viewpoint of the subject as normative and factually independent. Furthermore, whatever is said should be true for all planning and not for planning of a specific task. In this meaning planning can be considered in general and the considerations concerning the methods of planning can be universalized.

I have attempted to show that the planning system is the same as the planning information system when we look at it from the viewpoint of the second-generation systems analysis. This is not so in the first generation for there the planning system is the manipulation of given or specifically processed information, as is the case, for instance, in operations research. The main concern there is to process the information and to draw conclusions from it. But since it has been shown that in the second-generation systems research the planning approach is more or less the same as the information process, things cannot be tackled in the same way here.

What is Information?

There is an information theory that defines information. But this description of information is not suitable for our purposes for it is concerned exclusively with measuring the choice which someone involved in the communications process has when he enters into communication. With every word I speak or sound I emit I have to make a choice among the mass of words or noises at my command and the measure of information is concerned only with this procedure of choosing. Shannon and Weaver's classic measure of information is a measurement for the decision range that I must take with every news item that I send over a specific channel. This theory allows for only more or less choice in informing and communicating. When one uses this fine word "information" in another less narrow and specialized way, it must be redefined.

For us, information is a process that leads to changing somebody's knowledge, not a sub-stratum, nor some sort of material that can be shoveled round. We say that an information process has taken place when for instance an individual who knows something at a specific point in time "t"—that all bodies are heavy and fall to the center of the earth—at the time "t" + "t" no longer knows this or knows something more. This definition has many consequences. When I tell somebody what he already knows, then I have not informed him. Or when I tell somebody something so that he no longer knows what he knew previously, I have informed him, although I have in fact taken knowledge away from him; this is called disinformation.

There are, furthermore, elements of knowledge: sentences, statements, which someone agrees to subscribe to. Let us take the sentence: the earth is round. We can be sure that people who have subscribed to this sentence by signing in general know that the earth is round (although this is a superstition). One can also prove the reliability of knowledge, the existence of elements of knowledge, in that people are willing to bet on them. The higher the bet is (that somebody is willing to subscribe to a sentence that represents an element of knowledge) the more certain he is of this element of knowledge. Thus one can introduce a degree of certainty "c" from an element of knowledge "K_1"; for some things we know more certainly than others and one can imagine that this can be made measurable in some way or other, for instance through betting experience or a collection of signatures. The planning process can be understood as the production of such elements of knowledge which are specific for a given planning problem or for the context of a given planning problem.

Now there are various sorts of information processes. The first consists in the degree of certainty over an element of knowledge "K_1" becoming greater than it was previously. We already knew that the earth is round, but this has been reconfirmed.

The second case is just the opposite: the degree of certainty about something previously known diminishes. This case of becoming doubtful is obviously also a case of information.

The third case consists in something which was already known, changing radically into its opposite. An example of this is the following: in every textbook of chemistry it is stated that noble gases combine with nothing and are hence noble. There are good reasons for this: the outer ring of electrons is saturated and therefore there is no reason for electrons to be exchanged with other atoms. This can be found in all the text books so that in fact there is no reason to test whether this is really the case . . . at least until a disrespectful young American researcher got the idea of testing this and came to the conclusion that noble gases in fact combine.

The next case is clearly the scrapping of a whole knowledge edifice (K). This fourth case, the so-called "paradigmatic revolution," means that information can lead to a whole complex of learning (for instance that the world is in order and that all is working properly) falling apart without a substitute. Clearly, resistance to this is still greater than resistance to the previous sorts of information.

And the least likely case of all is when a new complex of information springs up from nothing that one synthesizes completely anew the conception of a whole part of the world.

Learning becomes increasingly difficult and information increasingly resisted the farther up the scale one goes: we prefer to absorb information that confirms what we already know. To unlearn something is much more difficult.

Now there is *internal and external information*. One can change one's information in that one cuts oneself off from outside communication and comes to conclusions simply through reflection and reorganizing one's knowledge and inspiration. These are processes of internal information. What is of interest to us and can be organized and manipulated when we want to plan better are processes of external information, i.e. changes in information that are introduced through external causes; this does not mean that these external causes cannot also have internal information as a consequence.

What is an information system? An information system is an institution that is intended to serve the improvement and the support of outside information. If what has been said above is correct, a planning system is a system that should contribute to the better external information of a planner, i.e. to a planning information system.

Types of Knowledge

The knowledge needed by the planner can be separated into the following five types. Planning consists in creating and developing all these types of knowledge during a project.

The first type of knowledge is what is known as factual knowledge (F-knowledge), recognized by sentences with the following form: x is, was or will be the case. Whether in a concrete case this is really so or not is another question. We have said that we do not have a monopoly in claim to determine what really is the case or should be the case, but rather that the expertise about this is evenly spread among those involved in planning.

The second type of knowledge is called "deontic knowledge." Deontic knowledge reflects our convictions over what should be, or should become the case. The standard form is: x should be, or should become the case.

As we have already seen, a necessary condition for the existence of a problem is that there is a discrepancy between factual knowledge ("that which is") and deontic knowledge ("that which should be") concerning a given subject. Without such a discrepancy there can be no problem at all, and hence we cannot plan at all.

The third category can be called explanatory knowledge. This type of knowledge informs us why what is there, or should be there, is as it is or as it should be. It has the general form of: x is the case because y . . . We have already seen that we always use this type of knowledge to find a solution to our problem. In the very instant we explain why it is not as it should be, we have laid down the direction in which to look for the solution.

Now this third type of knowledge is obviously not enough. We certainly know that everyone dies because we cannot live forever, but that does not help us very much to do something really instrumental to combat this. A specific amount of knowledge is characterized by providing us with the ways in which we can change something: instrumental knowledge. It has the form: when x is done, y is the consequence. Given Z—Z is the condition under which this instrumental knowledge can be used. When coffee powder and water are put together and are heated, we have coffee, provided that the heating is enough, that it takes place under normal atmosphere, that we have a saucepan available, etc . . . A planning task has been resolved when a series of sentences of this sort have been put together in such a way that one can expect to do away with the discrepancy between the "is" and the "should be" situations. A plan is a semi-ordered amount of instrumental knowledge that is brought up to date to resolve a problem. By implementing all these instructions it is expected that the original discrepancy between a piece of factual and a piece of deontic knowledge about a situation can be overcome.

The fifth and last category is "*conceptual* knowledge," knowledge on the meaning of words and other vehicles of communication that we have to use to make ourselves understood. When we speak about "productivity" the conceptual knowledge is that that is understood by the concept "productivity." As you know very well, there are many concepts of productivity, and whenever we talk about productivity we have to think about which concept of productivity is being used. We are talking here about a specific sort of knowledge that provides the string of signs of verbal communication which is devoid of content with meaning so that specific combinations of noises are not only words but that these words have also meaning. As everyone knows from experience, most discussions arise from the question "what do you really mean by it?" the outcome of which is an attempt to provide "conceptual knowledge."

Should it be so desired, further sorts of knowledge could be differentiated. One could for instance say: there is also "knowledge about the future." But this could be countered since expectations about the future can be considered as not very strongly assured elements of factual knowledge: for instance, that in 1985 every family in Central Europe will on average have 1.9 cars. The less substantiated an expression about the future appears, the more limited is the level of certainty over factual knowledge that deals with the future. We could differentiate between factual knowledge about the past, the present and the future (as we have done above). And this knowledge must be well differentiated from "should be" knowledge about what has happened, is happening and will happen. The main critique that we have recently raised against the Delphi method is precisely that it makes no distinction between "should be" knowledge about the future and factual knowledge about the future. However, for our purposes this fivefold classification of knowledge is sufficient.

Characteristics of Planning Information Systems

Our hypothesis is that the planner has, during this process, to do no more than to produce and to manipulate these five sorts of knowledge. He starts with a discrepancy between factual and deontic knowledge, seeks out explanations why things are so and how they should be, and these explanations give him hints about the instrumental knowledge he needs to overcome this discrepancy. And now and again or constantly he must ask himself what he is in fact doing, what he in fact means by productivity, or neighborhood, or an operating town? He then produces conceptual knowledge that he exchanges with others.

A planning information system (PLIS for short) can be differentiated from other types of information systems. For instance, there is something called a "scientifico-technical information system," where one gets a book out and, usually, finds factual or explanatory knowledge. Deontic knowledge, such as how the world should be, cannot be found nor learnt from a scientifico-technical information system. In general it is assumed that the reader himself can derive the instrumental knowledge from the explanatory knowledge. Now one must obviously see that not all explanations, i.e. explanatory information, are already instrumental. We know why people die, but that in no way tells us what we have to do to combat this. On the other hand, we know how to use a lot of things, i.e. we have a lot of instrumental information, without knowing why these things function, i.e. without having the relevant explanatory information; for instance, we know that when we cross our fingers it helps in carrying out specific activities, but no one knows why this is so.

A PLIS must provide not only factual information on the subject but also data on its "should be" situation. The main criticism of planning information systems to date, for instance urban information systems, is that they limit themselves to the collection of factual information, statistics, etc., whereas planning obviously needs all sorts of information.

The first component required for such an information system is certainly the ability to help in the production of factual knowledge about the future, a sort of forecasting sub-system. Perhaps this can even be arranged "conditionally" so that it can be said: if I use this or that element of instrumental knowledge and if this or that is really the case, then the following will certainly (or with a higher degree of probability) happen. This sub-system should preferably be dependent on the possibility of up-dating all instrumental knowledge used for a given operation.

But what is needed above all, and is postulated by the systems approach of the second generation, is that deontic knowledge should be much more explicit and externalized in the planning system than was the case until now. In the period of belief in the compulsory character and objectivity of planning, it was quite obvious what the case should be. But this is no longer so now, and the less this is the case, the more the preconditions of the systems approach of the second generation come into play, the more important it becomes to externalize the deontic knowledge about the subject and to make it a part of the information system. What should be the case becomes less and less clear and hence what the case should be must be stated, written down, and discussed.

In contrast to systems research of the first generation where one says: collect your information and then plan, our starting hypothesis is that planning consists of *producing* knowledge and not just storing and handling it, thereby enabling planning to take place. Hence a useful planning system must guarantee the feedback between those who plan and those for whom the planning takes place. All possible measuring places and communication points are thus parts of this planning information system. Hence, a survey sub-system is needed in a planning system that is concerned with the production of data. For instance, measurement is made of the weather or what people think about a specific question or how many children there are per capita. A common error of those who believe in the first generation of systems analysis is that it is, for instance, possible to collect and make available (on online computer) all information needed for planning, i.e. information on the population, the economic situation, the working situation, social habits, etc. In general, these very costly attempts to make available planning data banks, which are supposed to be useful for whole classes of planning tasks, can be considered to have failed. The source of information that is required in special situations cannot usually be provided through this data bank system. In town planning for instance, just about everything has been counted: you can find statistics about cholera cases since 1880, and although there has been no case of cholera in Central Europe for 30 years, the counting still goes on. On the other hand, it might very well be useful to know in connection with a concrete question, for example, how many stray female dogs there are in a town, and such information is often not to be found. Hence a planning information system should not only embrace a constantly accumulating data collection system that collects the same data on given categories for tens or hundreds of years, but also a data production system that works according to categories depending on the given situation. It is precisely here that there is an obvious bottleneck in statistics and in statistical methods: we need, but have not yet got, more sampling methods by which we can cheaply and quickly obtain a rough order of magnitude of a given phenomenon in the context of a specific subject. This is the data production system which should belong to a planning information system.

Contrary to a handbook or to a scientifico-technical system, a planning information system is always *full of contradictions*. One person says a town is overpopulated whereas another says it is underpopulated. Since we have said that we accept the "symmetry of ignorance," we leave both opinions in our information system. Hence it is of considerable importance to know who has introduced an item of information into the system.

An additional very difficult problem of planning information systems, especially when many people are participating, is how to keep the planning process moving and to ensure that the process does not fall apart. Hence it is important for a planning information system to have something like a *monitoring system* by means of which one can organize what should happen within the planning process. In a scientific information system, for instance, that is not necessary. But it is necessary in a PLIS which sets down instrumental specifications for the future and then helps to check whether these happenings have in fact taken place and whether they have led to the desired results.

Issue-Based Information Systems (IBIS)

There are many other characteristics of planning information systems, but these can be skipped here so as to make the following considerations. In my introductory lecture, specific methods of systems research of the second generation were examined and a group of these were called an IBIS, an issue-based information system. I should like to examine a little the theory of this system.

The ways and means for building up an IBIS are based on the fact that there are the five sorts of knowledge mentioned above and as a consequence five sorts of questions that can arise in a planning process. These questions cannot be answered by the available information. As has already been seen, the answers to these questions are or can be controversial. Whenever the answer to a question can be considered as controversial, we can speak of an issue, and whenever the answer to a question is not controversial we are faced merely with a question. There are at least two answers to an issue, and for these at least two different parties must be represented. If I ask someone what the time is and he answers without being contradicted 10.18 a.m. then there is no issue, merely a factual matter. But when someone says it is 10.18 a.m. and another 10.19 a.m. and the difference is important for one reason or another (perhaps because you want to launch a rocket), then this question about the exact time becomes an issue. The answer to *any* question can be contested; consequently every question can become an issue.

Now to the *mechanics of such a system*. On every issue there are *positions*, which represent the various points of view taken towards this issue. And for every issue there are *arguments*, i.e. the foundations of this position. Planning is a sequential process: on every issue raised there are positions, which are argued (arguments for and against the positions are collected), and, in one way or another—formally through voting or through conviction—a decision is reached and so on until a new problem arises where there is a further discrepancy between the "is" and the "should be," which leads to a further issue enabling various positions to be brought forward again, which can be argued about until the next decision is reached, etc. This is the picture of the planning process of the second generation, which we have made into a method, the IBIS approach.

On deontic issues (should, for instance, private cars be done away with in Karlsruhe?) there are at least two possible positions: a "yes" and a "no" position. But there is a third possible position, namely, to reject an issue as being unimportant, irrelevant or false. This is a perfectly legitimate position. It leads from the issue to a further question which is considered to be more important. For each one of these positions there are lists of arguments and these arguments can be continued until nothing new comes up or until time has run out and when there has been sufficient discussion, in the case of discord, a vote will have to be taken.

According to the type of the knowledge that is contested, there are various types of issues. There are *factual issues* where there are arguments for and against: Is the number of cars in the inner town of Karlsruhe too high? Then there are *deontic issues*: Should the inner town of Karlsruhe be cleared of vehicles?

Then there are *explanatory issues*: Why is the inner town of Karlsruhe overpopulated twice daily? There is a whole variety of possible answers: because of too-high trading tax in the outskirts, because cars are too slow, because the streets are too narrow, because all the shops open and close at the same time, etc. Explanatory issues do not have just two positions but a whole list of them. One can have many reasons for explaining a given situation.

Then there are *instrumental issues* concerning what one should do to get rid of a discrepancy. Here there are generally whole lists of possibilities that can be used.

The same is more or less true for *conceptual issues*, those which are concerned with what is in fact meant. Before you can, for instance, discuss whether productivity should be increased or not, you should first of all agree what the concept in fact means.

The object of the methods training is to demonstrate a system that uses these five types of issues and their interrelationships, which gets all those involved in the planning to contribute issues and to express themselves in the form of arguments on the issues in the right place. There is a to-and-fro process between question and answer that is characteristic for this type of planning process.

One example of the ways in which an IBIS can be used is at present being worked out: an environmental planning information system for the Federal Government of Germany. The Ministry of the Interior is the overall sponsor for the establishment of this system and we are suggesting how it can be established. We are presenting the IBIS as a central tool for such a system. Positions on environmental questions are never scientific or technical. They are purposeless in as far as the deontic questions are not made a part of the planning system. Environmental questions are political questions and political questions are deontic questions. Therefore we are suggesting such an IBIS system firstly to be used to bring up environmental questions. The production of problems is also a problem. For who says that mercury in salmon is a problem? Who has the right to bring up such problems? Some sort of sub-system is hence needed in the environmental planning information system which supports the production of problems. Further sub-systems must, for instance, decide upon the priorities of issues, document the resources that exist to overcome environmental problems (this of course being with all the pros and contras) and produce factual data about the success of measures for which deontic data is needed in order to be able to define "success."

Chapter 3.2

Issues as Elements of Information Systems[1]

Werner Kunz and Horst W. J. Rittel

Abstract

Issue-based information systems (IBIS) are meant to support coordination and planning of political decision processes. IBIS guides the identification, structuring, and settling of issues raised by problem-solving groups, and provides information pertinent to the discourse.

It is linked to conventional documentation systems but also activates other sources. Elements of the system are topics, issues, questions of fact, positions, arguments, and model problems. The logic of issues, the sub-systems of IBIS, and their rules of operation are outlined.

Three manually operated versions of IBIS are in experimental operation by governmental agencies; computerization of system operations is in preparation.

Argumentative Processes

1.

This paper introduces a type of information system meant to support the work of cooperatives like governmental or administrative agencies or committees, planning groups, etc., that are confronted with a problem complex in order to arrive at a plan for decision. The concept of these issue-based information systems (IBIS) rests on a model of problem-solving by cooperatives as an argumentative process.

2.

An initially unstructured problem area or *topic* denotes the task named by a "trigger phrase" ("Urban Renewal in Baltimore," "The War," "Tax Reform").

About this topic and its subtopics a *discourse* develops. *Issues* are brought up and disputed because different positions are assumed. *Arguments* are constructed in defense of or against the different positions until the issue is settled by convincing the opponents or decided by a formal decision procedure. Frequently *questions of fact* are directed to experts or fed into a documentation system. Answers obtained can be questioned and turned into issues. Through this counterplay of questioning and arguing, the participants form and exert their judgments incessantly, developing more structured pictures of the problem and its solutions. It is not possible to separate "understanding the problem" as a phase from "information" or "solution" since every formulation of the problem is also a statement about a potential solution.

3.

Four categories of information exchange occur during this process:

- between the participants (opinions, expertise, reference to previous questions and decisions, similar questions, etc.);
- with the experts about specific questions;
- information from documentation systems (for literature support of a position, for factual reference, etc.);
- in the case of dependent cooperatives: with the client or decision maker (directives, quest for decisions, reports, etc.).

IBIS is designed to support, to document, and to coordinate these information processes.

4.

There are various reasons for the design and implementation of IBIS-type systems. First, there is a "missing link" between the organization of conventional documentation systems and the structure of the discourse in such cooperatives. To many questions arising descriptor strings selected from a thesaurus cannot be adequately designed.

Thus, the issue "Shall we legalize private manpower banks?" is not sufficiently represented by the descriptors "Legalization," "Manpower Banks," "Private." Depending on the participants' image of the problem, the relevant context may become the associative neighborhood of "Equal opportunity," "Private Eyes," "Exploitation of the Needy," "Systematic Unemployment," etc. A very precise picture of the state of discourse must be conveyed to the documentation system incessantly. Second, the description of the subject matter in terms of librarians or documentalists may be less significant than the similarity of an issue with issues dealt with previously and the information used in their treatment. Third, the discourse developing is notoriously centering around concepts expressed by ad hoc vocabulary which is rapidly changing, defying thesaurization. Many central terms used are proper names for long stories specific of the particular situation, with their meaning depending very sensitively on the context in which they are used.

Another reason is the desire for a more transparent working procedure for such cooperatives. IBIS ought to stimulate a more scrutinized style of reasoning that more explicitly reveals the arguments. It should help to identify the proper questions, to develop the scope of positions in response to them, and assist in generating dispute. The role of external experts also deserves clarification. Precise questions should be directed to them that have their well-defined place within the problem-solving process. IBIS is also a documentation and reporting system that permits fast and reliable information on the state of discourse at any time.

The Logic of Issues

5.

Issues are the organizational "atoms" of IBIS-type systems. Among their properties are these:

- Issues have the form of questions.
- The origins of issues are controversial statements.
- Issues are specific to particular situations; positions are developed by utilizing particular information from the problem environment and from other cases claimed to be similar.
- Issues are raised, argued, settled, "dodged," or substituted.

6.

There are several kinds of relationships between issues, forming networks between the items of the "issue bank" which can be used to aid the search for similar issues, the history of an issue, the consequences of previous decisions, etc.:

- Issue I_2 is a *direct successor* of issue I_1: I_2 challenges a statement made in support of one of the positions maintained in view of I_1.
- Issue I_2 is a generalization of I_1.
- I_2 is a *relevant analogy* to I_1: the arguments used in I_2 are transferred into arguments regarding I_1, *mutatis mutandis*.
- Positions taken in response to I_1 can be *compatible*, *consistent*, or *incompatible* with a position assumed in response to I_2 (by the same or another proponent).

7.

With regard to content, the following types of issues can be distinguished:

- *factual issues*: "Is X the case?"
- *deontic issues*: "Shall X become the case?"
- *explanatory issues*: "Is X the reason for Y?"
- *instrumental issues*: "Is X the appropriate means to accomplish Y in this situation?"

To each issue a logically closed set of possible positions or an open list of possible positions may be assigned.

8.

Other elements of the system are these:

- *Topics* as introduced above serve as a crude organization principle for denoting the foci of concern.

- *Questions of fact* (F-questions) request information that is not assumed to be controversial. Doubting the credibility of an answer leads to an issue.
- *Model problems* are not specific to a particular situation. They correspond to scientific or managerial models meant to deal with whole classes of problems (location models, cost-benefit models, etc.). Much literature is dealing with model problems. Since they are always defined over a closed set of descriptors (variables), their usefulness for structuring a particular problem depends on the importance of those factors that have not been included.

The Structure of IBIS-Type Systems
9.
IBIS-type systems contain several sub-systems:

S-1: Issue bank: file of living (S-11), settled or abandoned (S-12), and latent (S-13) issues.

S-2: Evidence bank: file of F-questions and their answers (S-21, answered; S-22, open).

S-3: "Handbook": collection of model problems.

S-4: Topic list.

S-5: Issue map: representation of the various relations between issues, F-questions, etc., by graphic display of the state of argument.

S-6: Documentation system: search and analysis in view of living or latent issues and positions (S-61), descriptor index and thesaurus construction (S-62), regular scanning in view of the topic list (S-63).

10.
All the items are numbered consecutively to ease reference. The formats for describing issues, F-questions, model problems also indicate the various relationships between them, defining an "IxI-Matrix" for each of the types of relationships between issues and "IxT-Matrix" (assignment of issues to topics), etc. These matrices are used for tracing connections between items and for constructing issue maps (S-5). In addition, literature sources are assigned (by accession number) to the various items and vice versa. In this way, several layers of search networks are established.

Operation of the System
11.
To describe only the main operations, "treatment of issues":

0–1: Participant M_k raises the rth issue I_r in the context of topic T_J. An "issue form" is filled in, identifying the preliminary issue, the list of alternative positions, administrative indicators.

0–2: I_r is edited (in contact with M_k), relationships to other issues are established (aided by S-1, S-4, S-5, S-62).

0–3: For each position P_{rs} an "argument sheet" is prepared. Sources are mainly the deliberations between M_k and his opponents.

0–4: File I_r is processed by S-61, where supporting evidence and opinion is retrieved from the literature (the argument sheets are amended and literature evaluation sheets are added to the file).

0–5: The issue map S-5 is updated.

0–6: File I_r becomes the basis for discussion. I_r is either settled by accepting one of the positions or further evidence is requested from an "expert" (through F-questions which are treated similar to the processing of issues), or a supporting statement for a defended position is challenged, thus leading to another issue (GOTO S-1). Finally, the significance of I_r can be denied and substitute issues may be introduced (GOTO S-1).

Further Developments
12.

Currently three IBIS-type systems are operated experimentally. IBIS-1 serves a supranational agency in order to support the development of recommendations for information policy. IBIS-2 is used by an interdepartmental government committee dealing with a national plan for information networks. IBIS-3 is applied in a project of university planning. These systems follow the principles outlined, but each of them had to be tailored to the specific conditions of application. The most astonishing result is the eager acceptance by the users, although the implementation induced major changes in organization and working styles. Still being operated manually, computerization of several operations is being programmed. Publication of the theory of IBIS and the systems manuals is in preparation.

Note

1 This paper was originally published as Working Paper No. 131, Berkeley: Institute of Urban and Regional Development, July 1970; reprinted May 1979. We wish to thank Messrs. H. Dehlinger, T. Mann, J. P. Protzen, and Miss G. Mattei, whose exploratory work has contributed significantly to the results outlined here.

References

Kunz, W. and Rittel, H. (1968) "Zur Logik von Forschung und Dokumentation." *Die Naturwissenschaften*, 55(8): 358–361.

Kunz, W. and Rittel, H. (1969) "Die Informationswissenschaften." Report, Heidelberg and Berkeley.

Kunz, W. and Rittel, H. (1970) "The Changing Information Environment." Report, Heidelberg and Berkeley.

Rittel, H. (1966) "Instrumentelles Wissen in der Politik," in H. Krauch (ed.), *Wissenschaften und Politik*. Heidelberg: Studiengruppe für Systemforschung, pp. 183–209.

The Reasoning of Designers

Horst W. J. Rittel

1. The Universe of Design

It is one of the mysteries of our civilization that the noble and prominent activity of design has found little scholarly attention until recently. During the last decades this has begun to change (1962 was the first conference on design methods in London).[1] The present conference here in Boston is an indication of a sudden burst of interest across numerous disciplines. Perhaps, the reason is not just intellectual curiosity, but also widespread dissatisfaction with our ability to design the worlds we live in.

Everybody designs sometimes; nobody designs always. Design is not the monopoly of those who call themselves "designers." From a downtown development scheme to an electronic circuit, from a tax law to a marketing strategy, from a plan for one's career to a shopping list for next Sunday's dinner—all of these are products of the activity called design.

The scope of entities designed is vast and the knowledge employed in design is very diverse, ranging through all aspects of human experience. Only if there is some specific commonality between these activities in spite of the great diversity of the objects they deal with, it is justifiable to talk about design in general terms. I contend that there are such characteristic commonalities which demarcate design from other forms of coping with difficulties.

What are these commonalities? All designers intend to intervene into the expected course of events by premeditated action. All of them want to avoid mistakes through ignorance and spontaneity. *They want to think before they act.* Instead of immediately and directly manipulating their surroundings by trial and error until these assume the desired shape, designers want to think up a course of action thoroughly before they commit themselves to its execution. Designing is plan-making. Planners, engineers, architects, corporate managers, legislators, educators are (sometimes) designers. They are guided by the ambition to imagine a desirable state of the world, playing through alternative ways in which it might be accomplished, carefully tracing the consequences of contemplated actions. Design takes place in the world of imagination, where one invents and manipulates ideas and concepts instead of the real thing—in order to prepare the real intervention. They work with *models* as means of vicarious perception and manipulation. Sketches, cardboard models, diagrams and mathematical models, and the most flexible of them all, speech, serve as media to support the imagination.

Design terminates with a commitment to a plan that is meant to be carried out.

The act of designing can be fun: what would be a more rewarding pastime than to think up some future and to speculate how to bring it about? However, what is troublesome is the recognition that the plan may actually be carried out. If so, the designer faces two possible kinds of failure. A type-1 failure has occurred if the plan does not accomplish what was intended. A type-2 failure has occurred when the execution of the plan causes side and aftereffects that were unforeseen and unintended, and prove to be undesirable. Normally, mainly the fear of the latter type of failure spoils the fun of design: have I forgotten something essential? Designers worry.

Many forms of mental activity take place in the course of design. Designers think more or less coherently; they figure, they guess, they have sudden ideas "out of the blue," they imagine, speculate, dream, let their fantasy wheel freely, scrutinize, reckon, they "syllogize." Much of the mental activity (some would say most) resides and occurs in the subconscious. We certainly do not understand, and we may never know, everything about all the intricate workings of our mind. But a very significant part of design happens under conscious intellectual control. Since design is intentional, purposive, goal-seeking, it decisively relies on reasoning.

Studying the reasoning of designers becomes a way of attempting to understand how design happens—possibly the only way. We may not know much about reasoning either, but at least it is not nothing.

2. Design as Argumentation

Are there any discernable recurring patterns in the reasoning of designers? Is there a logic of design? Here, "logic" is not meant in the sense of a formal logic, but as a certain way of reasoning, a philosophy guiding a mode of conduct (as in "the logic of driving a car," or "The logic of your argument is odd").

"Reasoning' pertains to all those mental operations we are aware of, can even communicate to others. It consists of more or less orderly trains of thought, which include deliberating, pondering, arguing, occasional logical inferences. Imagine a designer thinking aloud, arguing and negotiating with himself (or with others), trying to explain or justify what he is proposing, speculating about future consequences of his plan, deciding the appropriate course of action.[2]

The picture obtained by analyzing this mental activity is not that of the "classic" problem solver, who first defines his problem in clear terms, obtains the information deemed necessary, and subsequently searches for a solution in the then well-defined "solution space."

The designer's reasoning is much more disorderly, disorderly not due to intellectual sloppiness, but rather to the nature of design problems.[3] There is no clear separation of the activities of problem definition, synthesis, and evaluation. All of these occur all the time. A design problem keeps changing while it is treated, because the understanding of what ought to be accomplished, and how it might be accomplished is continually shifting. Learning what is the problem IS the problem. Whatever he learns about the problem becomes a feature of its resolution. From the beginning, the designer has an idea of the "whole" resolution of his problem which changes with increasing understanding of the problem, and the image of its resolution develops from blurry to sharp and back again, frequently being revised, altered, detailed and modified. His focus alternates continually from small component parts, back to the whole problem, and back to other details.

This picture defies description in terms of discernable grand phases of task organization. Only at the micro level can we identify patterns of reasoning corresponding to recurring difficulties of the process. Over the course of the project, the scope of the difficulties may change, but their nature remains the same throughout.

The designer's reasoning appears as a process of argumentation. He debates with himself or with others; issues come up, competing positions are developed in response to them, and a search is made for their respective pros and cons; ultimately he makes up his mind in favor of some position, frequently after thorough modification of the positions. In this model of design as argumentation, the various issues are interconnected in intricate ways; usually several of them are "open" simultaneously, others are postponed or reopened.[4] He finds himself in a field of positions with competing arguments which he must assess in order to assume his own position.

The most frequent typical issues are:

- What is or will become the case?
- What is the reason that something is the case?
- What should be accomplished?
- Which ways are there to accomplish what ought to be accomplished?

At the same time, a whole family of "meta-issues" lurks in the background, such as:

- Am I dealing with the appropriate problem, or is this problem only a symptom of some other, higher-level problem which I should attack instead?
- Is this problem too comprehensive to cope with? Should I reduce its scope?
- This leads nowhere. Should I start all over again?
- Is it advisable to cut off deliberation now, or should the search and analysis for more solutions be continued?

3. Figures of Reasoning in Design

The fine structure of reasoning is best demonstrated in terms of a typical recurrent issue. Consider a designer who is contemplating whether a certain measure A (a component, a procedure, a trait) should become part of the plan. He faces the issue "Should I incorporate A into my plan?" Figure 3.3.1 shows the (somewhat simplified[5]) web of alternative courses of reasoning in this situation.

His response to this issue (*) may be clearly and spontaneously affirmative and he goes ahead with A. If his judgment is negative, there are three options to proceed (x):

- to abandon A and seek alternative means A to the same end (which leads to another issue of similar structure);
- to trace back the reasoning that led to the present issue and take another path which bypasses the present issue;
- to conclude—due to frustration—that if there is no resolution to present issue then the whole project should be given up.

Frequently, however, he will be unsure of the appropriateness of A. Then he can ask himself any one of five subsequent questions:

1. "Are you confident that A will work?," i.e. will A actually accomplish what it is intended to accomplish?
2. "Will the prerequisites (ingredients, conditions, input states) for A be available?," i.e. whether A will be actually executable in the context of the present project.
3. "Will there be undesirable side and aftereffects of A?"
4. "Do you expect the advantages of A to outweigh its disadvantages?"
5. "Is there some better way, A, to accomplish what is to be accomplished by A?"

The deliberation of any of these will lead either to abandonment (x) of A or back to (*). If still undecided the same or another one of the questions is to be dealt with. This process proceeds until the designer has made up his mind about the original issue (*).

A little journey through this web may help to clarify its significance. Assume our undecided designer asks himself whether the prerequisites for employing A will be available (2). If he detects that it is not so, he may either give up the pursuit of A, or he might raise a new issue "Is there an acceptable way, B, to provide the missing prerequisite?" This issue is treated in a similar way while (*) is dormant. Let us assume that perhaps after extended deliberation (possibly diverting through several other subordinate issues) he has found an acceptable measure B. He returns to (*) and might find himself still uncertain about the appropriateness of A.

This time his uncertainty might pertain to A's side and aftereffects (3). Assume that he detects some consequence of A which he judges very undesirable. His pondering of pros and cons will lead him to make up his mind whether:

- to "live with this consequence," perhaps unhappily (back to (*));
- to search for some measure C which alleviates the ill effect (thus raising the side issue of finding such a remedy);
- to reject A because of this effect (go to (x)).

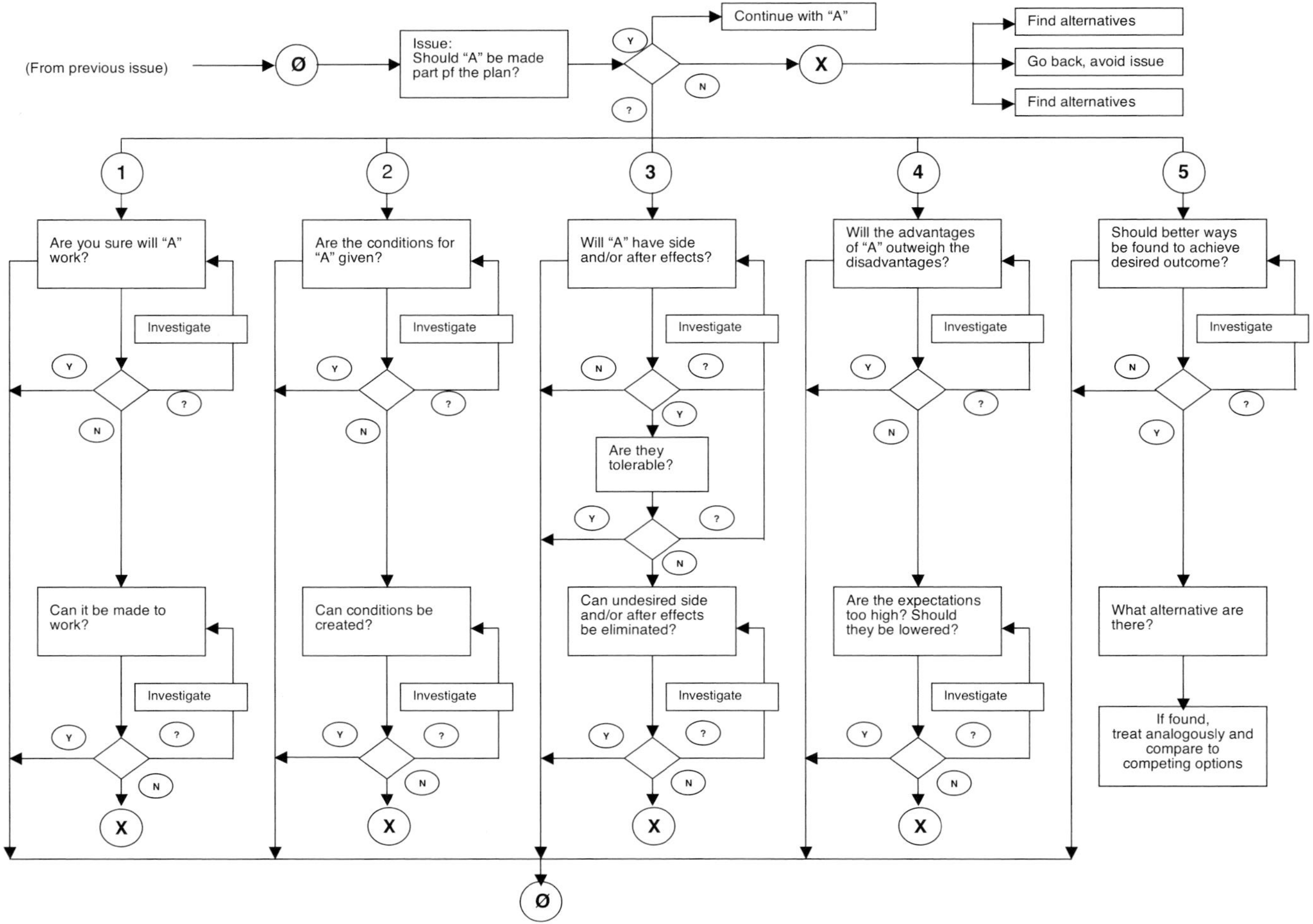

FIGURES OF REASONING

Figure 3.3.1

And so on and so forth. In any round of deliberation, he may ask himself whether there is not a better way than A to accomplish the same ends (5) and proceed accordingly.

This description has been deliberately abstract in order to underscore the claim that there are universally recurring difficulties and ways to cope with them. Any number of examples can be easily found in any realm of design.

4. Epistemic Freedom

This exemplary analysis shows the argumentative nature of the designer's reasoning. The process appears as one of formation of judgment, alternating with the search for ideas. The understanding of the situation changes with the alternatives seen in pursuit of the plan. Different facts and different ought-to-be questions come up depending on the means to accomplish these ends.

It also shows that all deliberations terminate with judgments (e.g. "Good enough!") which may be "based" on the deliberations, but are not derived from them. Looking at the various pros and cons, the designer has "made up his mind." How this happens is beyond reasoning.

The analysis reveals the awesome *epistemic freedom* in designing: there are no logical or epistemological constraints or rules that would prescribe which of the various meaningful steps to take next. There are no "algorithms" to guide the process. It is left up to the designer's judgment how to proceed. There is no—logical or other—necessity to want or to do something particular in response to an issue. *Nothing has to be or to remain as it is or as it appears to be*; there are no limits to the conceivable. There is a lack of "sufficient reason" which would dictate to take a particular course of action and no other.

It is not easy to live with epistemic freedom, therefore many designers are grateful for what the Germans call *Sachzwang*. It is a device to "derive ought from fact" (Rittel 1976). For example "Because 58 percent of the population say they want a freeway, I shall seek to provide it." Or "Since the demand for electricity is increasing by 7 percent per year, by 1995 we must build new 8 nuclear power plants." Obviously, these are fallacies. If demand threatens to exceed supply, you might also try to reduce the demand. The hidden deontic premise in the first example is "Thou shalt give all the people what the majority say they want"—a debatable principle which certainly does not follow from the facts. Nevertheless, *Sachzwang* is very popular among politicians and planners, because it reduces the epistemic freedom and releases the designer from responsibility. He has no choice.

5. The Varieties of Reasoning in Design

How does one explain the huge variety of styles of designing? Why are design products for seemingly very similar situations so vastly different?

The preceding considerations should have demonstrated that the course of designing depends decisively and at every step of reasoning on the *world view* of the designer. There is no neutral, objective design. *Design is subjective*. Of course. Why shouldn't it be?

What the designer knows, believes, fears, desires enters his reasoning at every step of the process, affects his use of epistemic freedom. He will—of course—commit himself to those positions that match his beliefs, convictions, preferences, and values, unless he is persuaded or convinced by someone else or his own insight. Design is associated with power. Designers plan to commit resources and thereby affect the lives of many. Designers are actors in the application of power.

Take a few examples. An important aspect is the division of phenomena into *changeables* and *invariants*. Whether somebody regards the Building Code as an immutable given, as a source of rigid constraints to abide by, or whether he considers its regulations as negotiable claims (you can always seek an exception) makes a great difference for the range of resolutions that might be considered. Some people see gravity as an inescapable fate, while others try to invent anti-gravity devices or put their production lines into outer space.

Constraints are decided, selected, and self-imposed, and not implied, derived or logical necessities. Every constraint is something the designer does not want to change.

Another source of variety in design are the guarantors used by designers as unquestioned sources of reliable knowledge. It can be tradition ("We have always done it this way"), the state of the art ("Nowadays, we do it this way"). It can be science, common sense, or the spirit of progress. Sometimes it is conscience, gut feelings, or revelation.

Obviously the designer's outlook on life, and his personality traits play a significant role. Thus the optimist will often assume the "It will work!," and proceed accordingly, while the pessimist is constantly nagged by the suspicion that "Nothing works as intended." The role of hope, self-confidence, and courage on the designer's reasoning is apparent.

It is no wonder that every designer wants to sell what he knows best. Thus an architect will hardly ever discourage a client from new construction, and a real estate agent would suggest looking at the buildings already on the market. This is a problem of the predominant aspects. An economist sees only economic problems, an engineer sees only engineering problems, and a manager only managerial problems, while all the other aspects remain in the background to be dealt with later (if at all; Darke 1979). But design problems are usually all-encompassing and don't fit neatly into pigeon-holes of the professions.

The question "What ought to be accomplished?" is easy for some. They know what is good for mankind, and for you and me specifically, while for others this is a most tortuous question. Some see their peers as their predominant audience, others put themselves before the judgment of history, others are satisfied with pleasing their client, and still others want to be loved by everybody.

What has been called "cognitive style" (Cross 1983) in design can be analyzed in similar ways. Some start with the issue "What shall the whole thing be like?," while others work from the bottom up, starting with "What shall the parts and components of the thing be like?" Some like to dash into depth pursuing a particular aspect, while others work "breadth first" (McCall 1978).

It is easy to compose the world views that guide the common caricatures of designer types, such as the "*Masterminder*," the "*Technocrat*," the "*Bureaucrat*," the "*Visionary*," and so on.

Fortunately for all of us, most designers don't succeed in shaping the world their way. Design takes place in a *social context*. Virtually all plans affect many people in different ways. Plan-making aims at the distribution of advantages and disadvantages.

No plan has ever been beneficial to everybody. Therefore, many persons with varying, often contradictory interests and ideas are or want to be involved in plan-making. The resulting plans are usually compromises resulting from negotiation and the application of power. The designer is party in these processes; he takes sides. Designing entails political commitment—although many designers would rather see themselves as neutral, impartial, benevolent experts who serve the abstraction of the common good.

6. Science of Design?

Do these considerations about the nature of reasoning in design render the attempts to develop a science of design futile? Not at all. On the contrary, our abilities to design or to shape the human condition are not so perfected that we can live comfortably with the usual ways of muddling through, and ignore the difficulties of the activity of design. The economy, environment, international affairs, our institutions, and the world of artifacts surrounding us all suggest that the art of design leaves much to be desired. Besides its intellectual appeal (what could be more fascinating than studying peoples' ways of shaping their futures?), the science of design might even prove to be useful. Even if it helps us to find out only how *not* to design.

The science of design has three tasks. First, to further develop the theories of design, to learn more about the reasoning of designers. Secondly it should pursue empirical inquiries into how plans come about, and what the effects of plans are in comparison with what they intended. Finally, on this basis, it should look for tools to support designers in their work. The human mind is fallible. Methods ought to be sought to amplify its abilities, even if it's only to keep us from falling prone to our idiosyncrasies.

Even if such remedies cannot be found easily, can we afford not to keep searching?

Notes

1 The proceedings of this conference are documented in Jones and Thornley (1962). It is interesting to compare the issues of that conference with those at the present conference. [Rittel's note]

2 This is only a thought experiment, assuming that the designer is telling the truth, and does not attempt to construct "post facto rationalizations" for his decisions, etc. If used as a practical research method, many obstacles have to be taken into account: "mental reservations" of the talking subject, the effects of "talking about what you think making you think about what you talk," etc. [Rittel's note]

3 Design problems (which can be called "wicked problems") have specific difficulties that make them different from "tame problems." For a discussion of wicked problems and their characteristics, see Rittel and Webber (1973), or Rittel (1972). ["On the Planning Crisis" (in this volume, pp. 151–65); Rittel's note]

4   An information system to guide and to monitor the process of argumentation and to administer the evolving network of issues has been developed called IBIS, for issue-based information system. Computer-controlled versions of this system have also been realized. Further readings about the structures and uses of IBIS can be found in Dehlinger and Protzen (1972); Kunz and Rittel (1970); Kunz and Rittel (1973); McCall (1978); and Reuter and Werner (1983). [Rittel's note]

5   For the sake of legibility some less frequent though realistic options have been omitted, such as "Giving up 'A' because one cannot sufficiently remove the uncertainties associated with it," "Accepting 'A' in spite of doubts in its workability (Let us hope that it works!)," etc. [Rittel's note]

References

Cross, N. (1983) "The Relevance of Cognitive Styles in Design Education." *DMG Journal*, 17: 37–49.

Darke, J. (1979) "The Primary Generator and The Design Process." *Design Studies*, 1: 36–44.

Dehlinger, H. and Protzen, J.-P. (1972) "Debate and Argumentation in Planning: An Inquiry into Appropriate Rules and Procedures." Institute of Urban and Regional Development, University of California, Berkeley, 1972, IURD Working Paper 178. (Also: IGP S-78–3.)

Jones, J. C. and Thornley, D. G. (eds) (1962) *Conference on Design Methods*. Oxford: Pergamon Press.

Kunz, W. and Rittel, H. W. J. (1970) "Issues as Elements of Information Systems." Institute for Urban & Regional Development, University of California, Berkeley, Working Paper No. 131.

Kunz, W. and Rittel, H. W. J. (1973) "Information Science: On the Structure of its Problems." *Information Storage and Retrieval*, 8: 95–98, 155–169.

McCall, R. J. (1978) "On the Structure and Use of Issue Systems in Design." Ph.D. Dissertation, University of California, Berkeley.

Reuter, W. D. and Werner, H. (1983) *Thesen und Empfehlungen zur Anwendung von Argumentativen Informationssystemen*. Institut für Grundlagen der Planung, Universität Stuttgart.

Rittel, H. W. J., (1972) On the Planning Crisis: Systems Analysis of the First and Second Generations. *Bedriftsoekonomen*, 8: pp. 390–396.

Rittel, H. W. J. (1976) *Sachzwaenge—Ausreden für Entscheidungsmuede*. Institut für Grundlagen der Planung, Universität Stuttgart.

Rittel, H. W. J. and Webber, M. M. (1973) "Dilemmas in a General Theory of Planning." *Policy Sciences*, 4: 155–169. (Modification of a paper presented to the Panel on Policy Sciences, A.A for the Advancement of Science, Boston, December 1969, Institute of Urban and Regional Development, University of California, Berkeley, Reprint # 86, 1972.)

Part Four

Consequences of Design

In this final interlude, we turn from the reasoning of designers to outcomes of design. The two articles in this section look at the wide-ranging ramifications of design, and especially the unanticipated outcomes. The first article looks at how new technologies create change, prompting the reader to look beyond whether new technologies simply accomplish what they have been designed for, to see what their wider consequences are. The second, written by J. P. Protzen from Rittel's notes, examines how plans go awry and the attitudes of designers that contribute to unforeseen, undesired consequences, if not calamities. Rittel called these attitudes pathologies of design.

"Technological Change and Urban Structure" ("Technischer Wandel und Stadtstruktur") was Rittel's last published article in German. Its concern is not directly with pathologies, but with unforeseen outcomes more generally. He examines the reciprocal interactions between new technologies with the social and physical fabrics of the urban areas.

Starting in the early 1980s, Horst Rittel, in his seminars on the "Logics of Planning" in the Departments of Architecture and City and Regional Planning, introduced a chapter on the failures of planning. He found many reasons for why plans go awry; prominent among them were the many human frailties, which led him to investigate the "Pathologies of Planning."

To some extent, Rittel's interest in the pathologies was linked to his involvement with the energy politics of Germany. He was concerned by the unquestioned acceptance of socio-economic trends as if they were inescapable constraints (*Sachzwänge*), like natural forces such as gravity: for example, it might be argued that between then and now energy consumption has increased by X kw/capita, therefore to satisfy demand so many years hence we will need to provide Y kw/capita, that is, we must build Z more power plants. Rittel gave expression to his concerns in 1986 at a congress,[1] under the title "Design der Zukunft—wie stellt es sich in unseren Köpfen dar?" ("Design for the Future—how is it represented in our minds?"). A revised version of Rittel's paper was subsequently published as "Energie wird rar? Sachzwänge oder der Krieg um die Köpfe" ("Energy becomes scarce? Inescapable trends or the battle for the minds," 1987), in which he publicly outlined some elements of the pathologies of planning, but he never had the chance of writing up a more extensive treatment of the subject matter in either German or English.

The article on pathologies included here is not a translation of the above-mentioned papers, but rather represents the recollections, reflections, and interpretations of the author (Protzen), who had participated in the early seminars and discussions on the pathologies. In addition, in writing the article, Protzen had the benefit of some of Rittel's unpublished notes and manuscripts.

Shortly before Rittel passed away he introduced the author to the book *Das Menschenrecht auf Irrtum* by Bernd Guggenberger (1987), which is concerned with the questions of how to avoid major planning disasters. This text matched Rittel's preoccupation with the pathologies of planning and seemed to provide further insights into his thinking about the subject.

An early version of the present article was read by Protzen at the 36th Annual Conference of the Association of Collegiate Schools of Planning in 1994 and later published as a joint paper with Niraj Verma in *Planning Theory* (Protzen and Verma 1997). The current version is a revision of these earlier papers.

Taken by themselves, the pathologies paint a rather grim picture—they show what goes wrong—but they also are the stuff of daily newscasts. Together with the properties of wicked problems, they may lead some planners to resignation and inaction. Others may simply dismiss the notions as mere philosophy, irrelevant to practice, and ignore them. Rittel intended neither of these attitudes and he certainly did not embrace either. He was an engaged person, always involved in public affairs, from the design of information systems for the Organization for Economic Co-operation and Development (OECD) and the German government, to the development of blueprints for the teaching of information sciences at German universities and the implementation of new curricula for the education of designers. Rittel took his insights into the nature of design problems and his experience with the pathologies of design as a starting point to formulate and develop strategies and methods to cope with wicked problems and to avoid or counteract the pathologies.

As a planner Rittel shunned neither decisions nor risk; his entire work was directed at minimizing the chance of forgetting relevant factors, encouraging the search for the idoneous purposes,[2] and facilitating the search for possible consequences, good and bad—in short, to combat the pathologies of planning.

Our look at the pathologies brings again to the fore the seeming contradiction in tone and spirit, especially of Rittel's later work. The importance of the pathologies is negative, but they are examined out of a spirit of optimism: by understanding them better, we are to be better able to move forward with the hope of avoiding such failures. To use a motto often attributed to Antonio Gramsci, Rittel allied the "pessimism of intelligence with the optimism of the will."[3]

Notes

1   Forumkongress des Internationalen Design Zentrum Berlin e.V. in Berlin in December of 1986.

2   For an explication of "idoneous purposes" see Protzen (1981).

3   Gramsci himself attributed the motto to Romain Rolland, but "it is not known exactly where Romain Rolland used this maxim or from what source Gramsci learned about it" (see Gramsci 1992: 475).

Chapter 4.1

Technological Change and Urban Structure[1]

Horst W. J. Rittel

1. Techniques and Technology[2]

1.1 Instrumental knowledge

It is obvious that technological change goes hand in hand with urban changes. Currently, technological change is particularly rapid. What kind of urban change can be observed or are to be expected as a consequence?

In preparation for the discussion, some preliminary remarks—possibly trivial, perhaps heretical—are in order.

Technology (*die Technik*) is the arsenal of techniques at the disposal of a culture at a given time, the aggregate of instrumental knowledge, the collection of its recipes for the manipulation of the living conditions. In this sense, the technology of the Etruscans includes, among other things, the practice of "reading" the liver of a sacrificial animal to predict the future.

Techniques can be exported from one culture to another. Did Marco Polo export ravioli to China, or did he import the wonton to Europe? Today, the consolidated technology (*die Technik*) of the industrial countries is being exported to third world countries and is assimilated with their technology.

A technique is a piece of know-how, a prescription whose application is meant to bring about an intended goal. The application of a technique requires the investment of resources (installations and machines, materials, skills). If these are not available, one might look for other techniques to procure those resources or to substitute them.

There are hard and soft techniques, the boundaries of which are not always sharp: a stone hammer, a diesel engine, and a microchip are hard; shamanic practices, value-added taxes and FORTRAN are soft; techniques such as parking meters, artificial fertilization, and organic farming comprise both aspects.

A technique produces nothing. It is meant to make possible or facilitate something. Only its application has effects. Therefore, instead of talking about the consequences of a technique it would be more tedious but more accurate to talk about the consequences of the application of a technique. Someone—an actor—who has the requisite knowledge, skills and resources for a given technique (its "ingredients" so to speak), will apply it with the hope of achieving the desired effect. When trying to determine the consequences of the application of a technique one, therefore, should look out for the one who applies it and not its inventor. *Cherchez l'homme!* It is not the invention of the gaslight that brought general street illumination to the city, it is the effort of the city's citizens and its administration, as well as the willingness of the industry to adopt and market this technique.[3]

Admittedly, the mere existence of a technique may lead to its application. Curiosity, play instinct, and the lust for adventure have forever been strong motives for explorative actions. Every toxic mushroom has been eaten at least once, and every admiral would like (at least in secret) to sink a ship with the newest rocket.

As a matter of fact: there are no technological compulsions, no iron-clad necessities, *Sachzwänge*, for the application of a technique; it is always people who want to apply a technique.

1.2 Mechanics of technological change

In every culture techniques get invented, accidentally discovered, developed, imported from other cultures, and occasionally forgotten.

Technological change is not an autonomous, predestined process. Technology in the industrialized nations is characterized by the fact that its change is purposefully and systematically pursued. In this, the odd inventor and the casual discovery play hardly any role. Rather, Research and Development (R&D) are determinedly, systematically pursued and at great cost. This is made possible by a new kind of technique, techniques of a second order, so to speak.

There exist techniques for the development of new techniques. These R&D techniques facilitate custom-made discoveries, inventions and developments on demand: techniques (apparatuses, methods) for the discovery of new elementary particles, the development of new materials, or electronic switches with pre-established properties. Equally, and foremost, "soft techniques" need to be mentioned: methods, organization, coordination, and management of R&D, as well as *social technologies* of the *think-tanks*, large research institutions and technology centers. The massive application of techniques of the second order made possible the "exponential" acceleration of technological change.

What was postulated above applies also to these techniques: Their impact depends on who applies them for what purpose. Because they require enormous resources as "inputs," almost only governments and large firms can afford to apply them. Only occasionally, a David succeeds in bypassing these Goliaths and achieves a technological breakthrough. The technique of micro-computers is such an example.

The most important impact of the application of these techniques is that the intensity and the direction of technological change—also called technological progress—has become a problem of politics and of planning: "which techniques are in fact desirable?" The democratic control of technological change has become as important as its application.

The significance of this can be appreciated if one contrasts it with an understanding of technological change as it appeared in the Enlightenment, and which in its variation is still popular today. Let us call it the "trickle-down" model of progress.

This vision postulates a *techno-scientific era*, in which technology and its change, in conjunction with the natural sciences, assume the role of the autonomous primary cause of social development. Following its own logic, science determines what the next question is. The "answers" then trickle down through the applied sciences into the technological development where they then find their implementation. The technological change so engendered is seen as an autonomous (self-regulating) event that guarantees progress. Technology evolves according to a Darwinian process. The best ideas impose themselves in the competition with others (or otherwise they would not be the best). And where does this progress lead? Forward, of course. One only needs to stick one's finger into the wind of change and the direction of progress reveals itself.

Admittedly, this process has its victims, but, it is argued, the bottom line of the last two centuries is a spectacular improvement in living conditions. In this view, it is not without reason that this technology, a child of Europe, has found global acceptance as *the* technology per se. Technophobia, therefore, is not only stupid but immoral.

This doctrine today has little plausibility. It is obvious that the application of R&D technology in nuclear techniques produces a different technological progress than an investment into marine biology, hydrogen techniques, or cosmetics. R&D technology is the basis of a growth industry, which lives off its orders.

1.3 The consequences are diverse

The primary effects of the application of a technique are its raison d'être. They are not always achieved. A technique has failed—be it because it has not been properly applied (human failure),[4] or because it does not always work, i.e. it does not reliably produce what it promises.

Secondary effects accompany the application of any technique. They are of different kinds.

Side effects are concomitant with its application. Where one is planing, there are shavings. Resources are used up; side products arise. *After- or late effects* are the consequence of the primary or side effects of the application: e.g. the technique of raising taxes at source impedes tax evasion of dividends, yet it stimulates the flight of capital to foreign countries. Cumulative effects arise from the application of a technique on a large scale: a single car does not produce traffic congestion, a can of hairspray an ozone hole.

Secondary effects may have been anticipated or they may appear unexpectedly in the aftermath. They may be desirable, tolerable, or undesirable. The latter can be accepted, or one can hope that it will not be too bad, or one can search for techniques that will mitigate or eliminate them. The *technique-consequence-repair-technique* has become a growth industry: drinking-water purification, three-way catalysts, and underground garages are examples. The applications of such techniques naturally bring about their own secondary effects. Sometimes the secondary effects cancel out the primary effects: the addition of lanes to a freeway for the purpose of easing the traffic flow encourages commuting from even farther away, thus creating additional traffic to the point of creating traffic congestion as bad as or worse than before—an improvement for the worse (*eine Verschlimmbesserung*).

Undesirable, unanticipated secondary effects (which, perhaps were at first considered acceptable) are what constitute the environmental crisis.

Sometimes one hopes that certain cumulative secondary effects actually arise. The lowering of the prime lending rate (a soft technique) is meant to stimulate investment, which in turn will stimulate the economy.

Different people are differently affected by the consequences of the application of a technique. It is empirically well documented that hardly any technique that is beneficial for some, or even large numbers of people, is without detrimental consequences for others—especially if the technique is applied on a large scale. Not all techniques find application ("acceptance") immediately and everywhere, and their application can have very different consequences in different locations.

To sum up: it makes no sense talking about *the* consequences of the application of a technique. The consequences are diverse, ramified, and disputed.

1.4 Cause or effect?

What presents itself as an overall development (say of a city) is the result of innumerable efforts to intervene in the course of things to change it in view of someone's interests. Clear cause-and-effect relationships are thoroughly confused because there are too many reciprocal relationships and amplifying effects. The chicken-and-egg (better yet the hen-rooster-egg) problem thwarts the search for causal one-way streets. What we observe, all in all, are only episodes, statistical indicators, and snapshots in an incalculable manifold of social processes.

Did motorization enable suburbanization, or did suburbanization demand a more comfortable means of transportation? Or was the state sponsorship of the bourgeois ideal of home ownership with one's own yard, the "rooster" that engendered it?

This is a bitter lesson for planners. They want to solve a problem by attacking its cause, but for this they depend on a plausible causal model. For example, liabilities imposed on perpetrators of environmental damage, as posited by the principle of responsibility (*Verursacherprinzip*), are meant to discourage such actions. But who is the responsible party in the case of the cumulative effects of air pollution? Is it the driver of a car, the manufacturer of the car, or of the fuel? Or is it the planner who, through his support of urban sprawl, has brought about the traffic problem? In practice every party has its own model into which it can mold the data. Which model is ultimately adopted for planning purposes is subject to arduous political confrontations. Think of the energy planning of the last decades, in which a causal coupling between the primary energy consumption and the GDP was postulated to have global validity. An understanding or model such as "a lavish lifestyle stimulates energy consumption" would certainly have led to a different energy policy.

2. Technology and Changes in Urban Structure

2.1 Urban technology

All the techniques used by a city government in planning, management, and administration can be subsumed under the notion of urban technology. Examples for hard techniques are garbage collection, traffic controls, street illumination, urban freeways, fire fighting; examples of soft technologies are bridge tolls, building permits, zoning ordinances, property taxes, truancy laws, etc.

Urban technology—as these examples show—has changed dramatically over the last decades, and this not only in the industrial nations. As a consequence, cities have undergone multiple structural changes.

A change is a *structural* change if the values of essential variables, say of the economic or social structure or of the lifestyle, show shifts of some order of magnitude or when longstanding trends show a reversal. New phenomena that suddenly appear on the agenda, too, can be understood as structural changes: drug scenes, second or third family cars, condominiums, and homelessness clearly are such structure-changing phenomena.

Looking out the window, the city "in principle" looks exactly as it did 50 years ago. "Technically absolutely feasible" visions for the layout and "hardware" of the city as promised by e.g. Soleri or Archigram in the 1950s have nowhere materialized. Pneumatic people movers, helicopters in the backpack as a popular transport system with landing pads on the roofs, megastructures into which individual dwellings could be hung on demand, gigantic domes under which cities create their own climate, are techniques that have little chance of implementation in the immediate future.

The to-be-observed changes in the structure of cities are in the main not the consequences of the primary effects of the technological change. There is good evidence to argue that the structural change of our cities is predominantly the consequence of secondary effects of applied techniques that were chiefly not urban techniques. The structural effects are primarily shifts in demography, changes in the economic structure, changes in living patterns with their manifold effects on city budgets, infrastructure (provision and disposal, schools, traffic, etc.), as well as the "character" of a city.

2.2 Effects of some techniques on urban structures

Let us take a look at some "key techniques," the application of which over the last 200 years explain many drastic structural changes in many cities. The significance, the disparities of who gets affected, and the ambivalence of causal interpretation will become evident.

The perfection of artillery made ramparts obsolete and thereby made the territorial expansion of cities possible. Until then the expansion of cities was tied to very costly extensions of the ramparts. Now the uninhibited, amoeba-like expansion at low cost is feasible. Yet, not all cities made use of this possibility. Avignon is an example thereof.

The steam engine liberated industrial cities from their dependence on water-driven mills and thus opened up locations independent of a water course. This did not mean that cities already built on the shores of rivers were abandoned.

Gaslights enabled the cheap illumination of the streets but also of large inside spaces. It also enabled (around 1810 in England) the 12-hour factory workday, in two shifts. In addition, it stimulated child labor: it was shown that children did not—as until then assumed—only grow in sunlight; 12 hours of work under gaslight remained without impact on their growth (Singer *et al.* 1958: 442). Also, evening schools soon became popular in "worker formation clubs" (*Arbeiterbildungsvereine*) (the consequences of which are well known). Since there were now evening reunions, family life "after work" underwent fundamental changes.

Central drinking water supply and sewer techniques brought about a drastic reduction in the threats of epidemics and thus facilitated the formation of cities with millions of inhabitants.

Or is it perhaps the awareness of the importance of hygiene that fostered these techniques? At any rate, city administrators and legislators in many cities made substantial resources available for the implementation of these techniques. The chance of a cholera epidemic in, for example, Hamburg today, is negligible. On the contrary, in the third world there are continuously growing cities without such supply and disposal systems that have extensive coverage: they lack the resources and one hopes to counter epidemics in an emergency case with some health technology—which often does not work.

Reliable central electricity supply systems offered ubiquitous availability of energy without the transport of bulk goods (say coal). The choice of industrial location become even more "arbitrary"—i.e. more independent of transportation costs.

Rapid and cheap public transport systems—primarily made possible by the electricity supply—facilitated the separation of home and workplace. This urban technique enabled the realization of the dream of the separation of urban functions. Commuting becomes part of the workday. Nothing now prevents the formation of purely residential districts and suburban settlements. Yet, in the Ruhr cities, for example, the worker districts remain in the shadow of the mills and the mines.

The safe elevator enabled rapid and comfortable vertical transport and opened up the third dimension to construction, which, in turn, brought about the densification of the central city under the pressure of rising land prices.

Even this technique was not applied immediately and everywhere. It took 20 years before it was seriously applied and it is not until the middle of the twentieth century that high-rise buildings were built in numbers in Europe. On the other hand, since the time of Babylon, there existed numerous settlements with high-rise buildings without elevators. The residential towers built for the nobles of Tuscany often reached heights above 50 meters; a residential house in Siena typically had eight floors. People who like tall houses are not afraid of climbing stairs.

Another example of the hen-rooster-egg problem: was the elevator invented because of rising land prices, which made it advisable to intensify land use? Or is it the wide use of elevators that raised land prices in the inner cities, because land became more valuable due to this technique? Or was it the Babylonian urge [to reach for the sky] that animated the inventors?

The mechanization of agriculture released a labor force, which enabled the rural exodus, and thus facilitated industrialization and urbanization. Or was it the more attractive living conditions in the cities and the better salaries in industry that triggered the rural exodus and thus motivated the search for less labor-intensive agricultural techniques?

The automobile was a technique, which by its nature (its primary effects) was unsuitable for movement in the cities. Because the automobile—as a symbol of unlimited self-determination through rapid access to destination choices—gained wide popularity, it was determined in many places that the urban structure needed to be changed to accommodate the universal application of this technique.

In many places this credo was elevated to a rigorous program: Los Angeles of the 1930s and Stuttgart of the 1950s were rendered automobile-friendly. Not every one followed this logic: Zermatt long ago settled on [public sector] electro-mobiles only; Munich refused to improve or extend its street network; and in increasing numbers of cities one notes a renunciation: in view of unbearable environmental stress, damage to buildings and traffic congestion, the automobile—after 30 years of euphoria—is repentantly banned from the inner cities.

Two "bio-techniques" were particularly significant.

The universal application of antibiotics has considerably raised life expectancy. The successful combat against infectious diseases—together with improved nutrition and hygiene—caused considerable "demographic unrest," which brought about clear shifts in housing demand and also the pension problem.

The distribution of estrogen as a contraceptive delivered [sexual activity] from its fatefulness and allowed "efficient" family planning. The birthrate in the industrial nations is falling dramatically. At the same time there is an emancipation push: innumerable women of childbearing age now have the opportunity to enter the labor force. A strong rise in GDP was to be observed in the aftermath of the acceptance of this technique (as is well known, housewives don't contribute to this glorified planning goal), but also a "school drought," a widely experienced lack of daycare centers, and an increase in car ownership (the second car is a complement to the "working wife"). This delighted the car dealer; but school and kindergarten teachers lost out. In the long run the "pill boom," in conjunction with rising life expectancy, will threaten social security systems.

In the industrial nations the application of the estrogen contraception technique is no longer as popular as in the sixties because of its side and after-effects. Yet the idea of family planning and the "naturalization" of the idea that women—even young mothers—can and should have their own careers, has taken hold in many countries.

The argument can be turned around even in this case: the push for emancipation was long overdue and unstoppable. Estrogen as a means to this goal came just at the right time.

In many developing countries this technique did not find widespread distribution. Reinforced by better medical care (antibiotics), population growth remains unfettered.

These retrospective examples show the continued tendency for many new techniques to bring about greater freedom of movement and availability, but also the impact of manifold and far-reaching secondary effects on the urban structure, as well as the ambiguity of these consequences for the diversity of affected people.

2.3 What High Tech could accomplish

Currently we are experiencing the rapid development of a whole range of techniques called "state-of-the-art technologies," "high technology," "technologies of the future" or, using an Anglicism, simply "High Tech." Included are microelectronics, telecommunications, and other computer, material, energy, and biological technologies. Because of many overlaps and their application in many "classical" techniques (mechanical engineering, optics, medicine) they are difficult to define and classify. A common trait of these technologies is the intensive application of the before-mentioned R&D techniques in their development, their close connection with "hot"—primarily physical—basic sciences, as well as the central role of electronic techniques.

The spectrum of new possibilities that these techniques will open up for all kinds of domains is incalculable. Let us consider some whose application could be especially relevant for the structure of human settlements.

Automation of industrial production and of office work can free people from repetitive work. At the same time this leads to a higher demand for highly qualified, well-paid professions. Industrial production plays an ever-diminishing role in the post-industrial economy, while the service sector is expanding. The liberation from work permits more leisure time and the opportunity for self-determination. The new media open up an inestimable manifold of possibilities for information and entertainment, as well as the possibility of instantaneous worldwide communication for the leisured society. The citizen of the information society has the chance (and the time) to participate efficiently and knowledgeably in the affairs of the polis. "Community without propinquity": a world in which spatial distance is irrelevant for the exchange of ideas; long-distance transmission of knowledge and collaboration becomes "technically possible."

In particular, the possibilities of *substituting transportation with communication* could have an impact on the city: homogenizing, reducing, or even eliminating commuter and freight traffic. *Teleconferencing* renders business trips obsolete; *telefax*, the letter carrier; *teleshopping*, the trip to the store; *telebanking*, the bank. More significant yet is the possibility of collaboration without spatial proximity. A lot of "paper work" (accounting, financial transactions, correspondence, computer programming, administration, design and planning) does not require physical proximity with a collaborator. An individual *workstation* connected to a network allows work to be performed anywhere—at home or in "work-houses" rented by the firm in the residential areas of its collaborators. Eliminating the reasons for trips, the great number of such workplaces could drastically reduce workday traffic. The same holds true for communication among business entities: there is no need for a headquarters under one roof; subsidiaries can be located anywhere—especially if communication with the clients is carried out electronically. The reasons for the centralization of business life in the city would disappear. The distribution of many centers over the region could homogenize traffic, reduce the concentrated traffic loads, leading, perhaps to the end of the rush hour?

The miniaturization of many products may make possible the decentralization of "hard techniques" and their location almost anywhere. Hardly any voluminous mass products need to be moved. Cheaper and faster transportation— e.g. by airplane in conjunction with motor vehicles—enables the division of labor among spatially widely distributed production units. Surprisingly, automation does not imply a monotonous stereotyping of products: each piece could be unique. The variation of products is facilitated by the possibility of rapidly reprogramming production lines. Besides rapid redisposition of production lines, smaller production lots become economically viable, which in turn entails smaller stocks. And so on and so forth.

All this and much more could be enabled and facilitated by the application of High Tech.

The rapidity and the large scale with which these techniques are implemented everywhere is astounding. Many effects become the stuff of headlines and are reflected in statistics. What are the consequences for the cities—primarily of the secondary effects? I recommend a look at the USA, the country of origin of High Tech. There one can observe clear changes in the social and economic structure—and therefore of the cities—due primarily to technological change. As has been the case often before (think of environmental problems and the energy crisis), America has a lead of several years on the problems—which does not imply that solution proposals developed there can simply be imported elsewhere. The developments in California offer a particularly constructive example. The resulting picture is extremely complicated and differentiated. It is resistant to an overall description with a few tendencies and clear lines of developments. I will therefore sketch out a few "clusters" of phenomena, episodes that illustrate the kaleidoscope of possibilities. Several of these occurrences are emerging in Europe in similar ways.

3. Spotlight: USA

3.1 Consequences of the techniques of technique development: California

In the 1950s California became a favorite location not only for modern industries (airplane construction, electronics, nuclear and rocket techniques), but also for innumerable R&D outfits of government and industry. "Think-tanks," such as the RAND Corporation and the Systems Development Corporation, were supposed to think about the next possible wars even in peace time; other research institutes developed the NASA programs; large firms established their research centers there (IBM, GE); others, such as the Stanford Research Institute, carried out contract research for the government and industry at the forefront of scientific-technological development.

The motivations for this concentration were, on the one hand, to provide a pleasant ambience for the "high carat" and scarce experts to work in, and, on the other hand, the desire for proximity to the renowned and productive universities (Stanford, University of California in Berkeley and Los Angeles, University of Southern California, etc.). This R&D industry—in its absolute magnitude—does not

207

play a big role, but it acts as a catalyst for a new style of economy, which elevates permanent technical innovation to a principle. A new "knowledge-intensive and service-based" industry is developing around the development of new techniques.

California became the symbol of a new industrial society and of an optimistic lifestyle, the promised land of a new American way of life. Immigration and a baby-boom brought about a strong population growth; an unprecedented wave of suburbanization led to an enormous increase of the settled land surface and numerous new cities as a consequence. Large, continuous agglomerations grow around the core cities (especially Los Angeles, San Francisco, San Diego).

The middle class departed the old cities for the suburbs, leaving the old cities impoverished and bleak. In 1950, San Francisco had 775,000 inhabitants; in 1980 there were only 679,000—in spite of the baby-boom. At the same time, the population of the San Francisco–Oakland–San Jose agglomeration increased from 3.2 million (1940) to 5.8 million (1986). Affluence establishes itself at the gates of the city.

The automobile makes it possible. An excellent system of freeways permits any choice of workplace and dwelling. Public transport is almost dead. *Industrial parks* sprout between the suburbs, where numerous, diverse and "clean" trades and service outfits settle. A glance further back into history may illustrate the strange ways in which such urban structures developed.

3.2 The key technique: the streetcar in Los Angeles

The megalopolis Los Angeles is known worldwide as a gigantic horizontally expanded city, the functioning of which is (supposedly) guaranteed by the automobile. Less known is the fact that this city owes its current layout and structure not to the car but first to the railroad and then primarily to the electric streetcar.

By 1870 some entrepreneurial capitalists—soon in fierce competition with each other—had built a few railroads that connected first the Pueblo de Nuestra Señora Reina de Los Angeles with the port of San Pedro, and then with some equally insignificant surrounding settlements—with many stops in the (not so) "green field" in between. Around 1885, a "spider" with five legs defined, in essence, the axes and centers of today's agglomeration. Soon thereafter this system was connected (also in fierce competition) to a supra-regional system. This competition at times resulted in extremely low fares ($1 for a Kansas City–Los Angeles ticket), which in turn strongly stimulated the mass migration mostly out of the Midwest.

The operators of the railroads were often also real estate or development companies, or else worked closely with such. The consequences? A dense development around the stations in the areas thus opened. Since about 1875 an ever more ramified network of streetcars, first horse-drawn and then electrified, come into being. The service was cheap, on time, frequent, fast, and comfortable. It did not matter whether one lived on the edges of the agglomeration or in its "nucleus" (to come from "outside" was even more comfortable than from the edge of the center).[5] By the turn of the twentieth century the system was consolidated (bought up and expanded) into Pacific Electric (PE), whose Big Red Cars served the whole territory on standard gauge track. The profitable system was most efficient and popular. Many lines had their own tracks besides the roads. In 1923 the total length of the system measured about 1,850 km.

Around 1915 the automobile appears. Conflicts (delays, accidents) develop at the crossing of the two modes. The Automobile Club of Southern California demands clear roads (*Freie Fahrt*). *Jitneys*—taxi-like limousines—run alongside the tracks of the streetcars and pick up passengers waiting at the stations at a cheaper price—this, of course, only along profitable routes. The recession and an understandable, but shortsighted, business strategy ruined the financial situation of PE.

In 1919, the government realized that public transportation had become a public task; public commissions then regulate the operation and the fares, and, in following years, direct and indirect subsidies became the norm.

In 1936, the bus manufacturer General Motors, the tire manufacturer Firestone, and a few other firms, bought PE, with the intention to replace it with a bus system. Their expectation resides less in the hopes for profits from the operation as from the sales of busses, tires, gas, etc. The busses replace the streetcars; the streetcars get scrapped. Anti-Trust trials ensue. The last streetcar run is in 1961.

The first automobile-appropriate road (*miracle mile*) was built in 1928: the Wilshire Boulevard. The adjoining businesses are obliged to provide parking for their customers. The "Linear Downtown" becomes possible and usual. A massive freeway construction program follows in the 1950s and 1960s—approximately along the former Big Red Cars' lines and beyond, into the desert: "on reserve" so to speak, presuming that some day someone will live out there. This hope was not disappointed.

However, with the Red Cars one got from Pomona to Santa Monica in 45 minutes; today on the freeway with normal traffic it takes 90 minutes (if all goes well). The irony: since the early 1960s planning efforts have been underway for a fast, railroad track bound public transportation system, which thus far has led to nothing: LA belongs to the automobile. The public transport system (the busses) withers away.

Today one speaks of a "Rail Renaissance" for Los Angeles. Currently, a 1.25-billon-dollar fast train and electro bus system, Metrorail, is under construction, which more or less also follows the Red Car system, but which is much less extensive. The rail cars are built in Japan. The construction noise is considerable. Lesson: sometimes the new is the enemy of the good. Occasionally, belated regrets appear.

3.3 High Tech and downtown: San Francisco

Since the beginning of the decade [1980s] San Francisco has been on the rise again—at least according to the usual indicators. Prosperity is conspicuous. Is this the effect of technological change and its consequences, or merely the expression of the economic climate under Reaganomics? Analogous changes can be observed in Boston, Houston, Los Angeles—yet other cities, like Detroit, are hardly showcases.

The appearance of the city has changed markedly. The massive skyline of downtown, when coming from the East Bay over the bridge, obstructs the famous view of the city's hills. A dense wall of skyscrapers offers a collection of the architectural styles of the twentieth century. Next to the witnesses to sober internationalism one finds ever more diversified exemplars of postmodernism: the window matrices have a pasted-on feeling; majestic porticos adorn the entrances; on dizzy heights "rooflets" appear; semi-cylindrical green houses or cupolas are crowing decor. The many antennas and satellite dishes—reminders of High Tech—connect the resurrected financial center to the rest of the world. In most offices there are computers and terminals.

How to explain this massive concentration, when—as discussed above— the new techniques enable an advantageous decentralization? High taxes, a stifling lack of parking, and a growing resistance of the citizens are weighty arguments against a continued *Manhattanization*. It is astonishing to find such a dramatic concentration in the wake of computerization in a branch of the economy that makes such an intensive use of computers.

This phenomenon is yet another example of the fact that not all the possibilities offered by a new technique will always and everywhere be fully exploited and that other, thus long-secondary, considerations top the "classical" notions of choices of locations.

First, it must be noted that many new centers have been built on "green pastures" in the environment surrounding the city (e.g. in San Leandro, with 40,000 jobs). Many old and established—also big—firms, such as the regional telephone company, have, for reasons mentioned before, moved their centers to suburbia. Although many, like the telephone company, kept their headquarters in San Francisco, many others have left the city. The economic expansion is much stronger in the surroundings than in the city.

As it is, businesses sort themselves out: those with intense client contacts keep or establish their downtown presence, whereas activities such as telephone information and exchanges, accounting, and catalog mailings are transferred to suburbia.

The immeasurable value, yet high desirability of many of the city's amenities of a downtown location become apparent. It is only there that one can meet unplanned, *over lunch*, one's attorney, get a tip on the stock market, receive insider information, and hear the latest gossip. The probability of a fruitful chance encounter, the chance for informal and undocumented contacts, and unplanned communication due to the high density, cannot be replaced by telecommunication. Important information, anyway, is not transmitted over official and formal channels. It is remarkable that the stock market in spite of all the electronic possibilities still requires the simultaneous physical presence of its actors.

Also, the large numbers of specialized services offered by a "naturally" grown city provide an invaluable locational advantage: shopping options, restaurants and bars, as well as photocopiers and blueprint businesses, notaries and money changers, cleaners and translators, debt collectors and priests are to be found within 100 meters of vertical or horizontal distance. The classic skyscraper harbors not only its "main tenant" but also hundreds of mostly small enterprises. In the suburb all this needs first to be planned and then implemented.

Last but not least: the prestige value of a downtown address is not

to be underestimated. "200 Montgomery Street, San Francisco" is more attractive than "15390 Main Street, Jonesville." One is ready to pay for this prestige
advantage. Downtown prestige is so valuable that cities that for a long time have
been "downtown free" have—on the instigation of their chambers of commerce—
built brand new skylines to improve their image; Los Angeles and Phoenix are
examples.

Office space in San Francisco has grown by more than one-quarter since
the late 1970s. Because this space has been built "in reserve" and because the
demand has not kept pace with expectations, 20 percent of this space is vacant.
Nevertheless rents remain high ($20/m^2 per month or more).

The massive commercial construction boom irritated the citizens.
Because of an overburdened infrastructure (traffic, supply, and disposal) and its
costly consequences, doubts arose whether the additional business taxes will ever
compensate these costs. The fact that the "downtown friendly" mayoress reduced
the yearly quota of new business space to 250,000 m^2 and reduced this by half
again did not appease the citizenship. In a referendum, this quota was reduced by
yet another half with the additional requirement that new buildings could not cast
shadows on public spaces.

3.4 De-industrialization?

In San Francisco there are about 600,000 workplaces, almost as many as there
are citizens. 100,000 of these, primarily in the service sector, have been newly
created since 1979. At the same time, 84,000 jobs were lost to rationalization
(*Gesundschrumpfung*), and to the moving out or closing of firms, for a net growth
of only 24,000 jobs. Surprisingly, two-thirds of the new jobs were created by small
or medium-sized firms—a fact denied by the chamber of commerce and industry,
because the development efforts primarily benefited the big firms.

San Francisco has changed from a "blue collar" economy to a financial,
service and commercial center, with an increasing portion of well-paid "professionals." Here, as in the rest of the country, the production plants are disappearing—a
symptom of de-industrialization.

3.5 Traffic

Public transportation in San Francisco has recovered. The modernized MUNI is
covering the city with a dense net that is connected with several systems to the
surrounding area. The service is frequent and fairly punctual; several lines operate
24 hours a day; a single fare of $0.75 allows any number of trips within the center
of the city during a two-hour window; a monthly pass costs $25. The number of pas-
sengers has grown by about 30 percent to 800,000 since 1978. A capable manager
completely revamped this system, which some years ago was decrepit. The adjacent
system, AC Transit, which serves neighboring Oakland and its surroundings was long
seen as a model. In recent times, however, this has been run down by scandalously
incompetent management.

The regional rapid transit system BART is a High Tech product of the
1960s, admired worldwide and considered a model, has been in operation—als

Torso—since 1972. In spite of continued difficulties—the consequences of overdeveloped High Tech in a rough environment—the system has gained acceptance by the commuters. On workdays 210,000 used the system in 1985. A 30 percent fare increase, however, reduced this number to 195,000. Some anticipated secondary effects have materialized. The routes have become development axes—but also generators of an unexpected increase in road traffic. The catchment area for commuters has considerably increased. The system is subsidized by several sources, among them portions of the bridge tolls and of the sales taxes. Scurrility: a homeless person in Oakland, who has no reason to use BART, is subsidizing the banker who commutes from far-away Orinda to his office in San Francisco with his food purchases.

In spite of the high user rate of public transportation, private transportation has grown considerably. Rush hour is always a nightmare. Mile-long traffic jams for crossing the bridges and on urban freeways are the rule. There are commuters who get on the road at 5 a.m. to be in their office on time at 8 a.m. (which they then reach at 6.30). If they started later they would be late for work.

Without public transportation, traffic would collapse completely. Some "soft" urban techniques were invented to ease that traffic problem: computer-supported car sharing programs, the privileged use of bus lanes on the bridges for cars with three or more passengers, etc.

The formation of business and industrial centers in the surrounding areas has indeed brought about certain homogenization of commuter traffic—however, without reduction of the traffic to the main centers. Today, the number of out-commuters from San Francisco amounts to about a third of in-commuters. Traffic jams in both directions are a daily experience.

4. Life with Confusion (*Unübersichtlichkeit*)

Considering the last hundred years, what has changed in the structure of technological change and its effects? Could not structural changes similar to those discussed here be observed all along, i.e. during industrialization? I don't think so, and here are some theses.

The rate of structural change has accelerated as a consequence of spontaneous and global communication and its accompanying "epidemic" spread of news and ideas, followed by abrupt changes of behavior. If in earlier times demographic indicators, such as birth rates, varied by only fractions of percentages per year, today these change considerably within a few years both in direction and intensity. The courses of economic barometers and of stock market values resemble infarct cardiograms. The "micro-computer revolution" established itself in less than ten years. If formerly, long-lasting trends facilitated the life of planners, today the beneficial inertia of social processes is entirely lost. The variety of lifestyles and norms of behavior continues to multiply. Social events can no longer be brought to fit simple classification schemes; belonging to different and varied "sub-cultures" has become the norm. Simultaneously, the incidences in which very many people want to do the same thing at the same time (and often in the same place) are increasing—take a vacation, go to the bathroom at halftime in a football game, withdraw money from their bank accounts.

The readiness to confidently accept the plans of a presumably well-meaning and knowledgeable authority is waning. Cautioned by gigantic planning failures and the obvious incapacities of those responsible, the alert, well-informed and enlightened citizen becomes distrustful. Planning measures, which are proclaimed in the name of an overarching "common" interest, are thwarted ever more often by initiatives, appeals, and a general rebelliousness, the ruthless exploitation of legal procedures, the public media, and even the practices of civil disobedience. The critical citizen suspects specific group interests behind such measures.

Many politicians and planners bemoan this "new confusion," because, they say, it complicates planning and governing in our community, even calls into question the notion of government.

Not only the citizens have changed. The application of technology has itself contributed significantly to the new confusion. Some examples:

Our century [the twentieth] was the century of urban technological patent recipes for restructuring cities. Universal solutions for a manifold array of urban problems have been proclaimed in a plethora of manifestos: the garden city, separation of functions, development axes, satellite towns, the automobile-correct city, urban renewal, pedestrian zones, etc. It is remarkable and irritating that all these "fads," proclaimed with such admirable self-confidence, were immediately implemented on large scales and the world over. Their average life expectancy was a few years before they were replaced by the next patent solution. Many cities suffer considerably from the consequences of these urban technological concepts.

Karl Popper called this planning style "utopian engineering" and has shown why such "masterminded" schemas are condemned to failure, even if for epistemological reasons alone.

Many techniques are hastily implemented without a careful exploration of their secondary effects—only to bring about catastrophic consequences. Examples: asbestos, fluoridal carbohydrates, PCB.

Megalomania ("big is beautiful; bigger is better") as a strategy for the implementation of infrastructure projects (energy supply) has not only brought about a sensitive susceptibility to breakdowns (blackouts) and the danger of catastrophes of continental dimensions (Chernobyl, CIBA-Geigy), but also reduced to notion of the "human right to err" as a consequence of the intimate and non-transparent connections of technological installations. An action that is harmless per se, a small, generally pardonable inattention, can have catastrophic consequences.

The hypertrophy of the techniques to eliminate the consequences of the application of techniques/technologies has led to absurdly complicated "systems." The processing of drinking water, garbage disposal, and the reprocessing of nuclear waste, are grotesquely complicated processes, which in turn require other control and elimination techniques—with a positive effect on the Gross National Product.

The new confusion is presumably the (unintended) most consequential effect of the technological and social change on the structure of our polities. It demonstrates that the conventional ways of planning and governing are no longer workable. In matters of the *polis*, the *symmetry of ignorance* reigns: I don't know what is best for you or for all of us, but you do not know either. Only a permanent argumentation over what we ought to want can diminish the probability that we engage in something that, *post factum*, none of us did want. Presumably nobody can conclusively estimate the secondary effects of the application of any technique. The implementation of any new technique is an adventure—and (ad-)venture—with uncertain outcomes. Therefore, everyone has the right to intervene in such planning and bring to bear his/her point of view as loud as he/she can, and this in the interest of everybody, for the dissident could well contribute an aspect which otherwise may be overlooked or swept under the carpet. Technocratic calculi cannot overcome the fact that the introduction of any new technique will have its beneficiaries and its victims. Accordingly, there is no objective calculus for the determination of the "objectively" best location for a toxic waste disposal site. Even a majority decision does not deserve the aura of higher wisdom. It does not matter what people say or mean; it is the convincing power of what they communicate that matters.

The assumption of the "old clarity" was that social conditions, however complicated, were understandable, configurations that could be governed by simple concepts. This assumption is less justified than ever. Let us hope that the old clarity and orderliness have been overcome. The new confusion may be a nuisance and on occasion destructive, but let's learn to live with it.

"History teaches us that it is not the rebels and the dissidents that threaten society; it is the non-thinking, the non-questioning, the obedient, the silent and the indifferent."

Notes

1 Originally published as "Technischer Wandel und Stadtstruktur," in R. Wildenmann (ed.), *Stadt, Kultur, Natur. Chancen zukünftiger Lebensgestaltung* (Baden-Baden: 1989). Translated by Jean-Pierre Protzen.

2 The German subtitle is "Techniken und die Technik". In its strict sense, "die Technik" designates the whole of technological knowledge, capacities and possibilities and is to be distinguished from "Technologie," which designates the science of "die Technik," i.e. the study of the conditions, application, and possibility of "Technik." In English, this distinction cannot be made. Interestingly, this distinction is starting to disappear also in German, where now often the term "Technologie" is substituted for "Technik." In its broad sense "Technik" designates a particular procedure, or what in English is a technique. [Translator's note/JPP]

3 It is to be admitted that the threat of applying a technology or the fear of its consequences have their effects. An example of this is the Cold War, where the threat of a nuclear attack kept the superpowers at bay. [Rittel's note]

4 The argument of human (as opposed to technical) failure stands on shaky ground. After all, a technique is the work of a human being. Would its inventor, developer or operator not have had to anticipate its fallibility? Technical failures are equally human failures. [Rittel's note]

5 For a good description of this development see Banham (1973). [Rittel's note]

References

Banham, R. (1973) *Los Angeles: The Architecture of Four Ecologies*, Harmondsworth, UK: Penguin Books.

Singer, Charles *et al.* (eds) (1958) *A History of Technology*, vol. 4. New York and London: Oxford University Press.

On Rittel's Pathologies of Planning[1]

Jean-Pierre Protzen

Introduction

If design is the attempt to shape the human condition to suit our intentions and desires then, Rittel argued, we have failed miserably. The evidence he found in what he called the "scandals of well-to-do societies": homelessness, extreme poverty amidst plenty, rape of world resources, massive pollution of air, water, and land, and so on and so forth. Furthermore, with our advanced science and technology, we have—within the last 80 to 100 years—brought about a historically new situation, one without precedent and beyond comparison with any earlier period: we have acquired the ability to destroy the world and ourselves through our own actions or inactions. Planning failures today have the very real potential of having catastrophic consequences.

Rittel recognized planning failures of two types: first, a plan, when implemented, yields the desired situation, but is accompanied by undesirable side and aftereffects, and second, a plan, when implemented fails to bring about the desired situation. An example of the former is the use of DDT (Dichloro-Diphenyl-Trichloroethane), which (nearly) wiped out malaria (the desired outcome), while causing considerable environmental damage; an example of the latter is the "war on drugs" which, thus far, has failed to reduce drug traffic and use.[2]

There are several ways to explain planning failures. There are epistemic failures: failures to recognize the limits of our models, such as limits imposed by the paradoxes of rationality,[3] which show that our models cannot be complete. In the case of DDT, an epistemic failure would have been to use DDT under the belief that all significant consequences of its application had been predicted. There are empiric failures: inadequate or insufficient knowledge of the facts, especially of cause and effect relationships. In the case of DDT, empiric failure would have been caused by failure to trace the effects of DDT through biological and ecological chains: it was not known that massive application of the chemical hindered formation of calcium in living organisms and that it accumulated through the food chain. Finally, there are *human weakness* failures: failure to sufficiently protect against problems because of the lure of personal gain. In the case of DDT, any number of short-term goals might have caused such a failure, from the noble aim of wiping out malaria, to the baser motive of corporate profit.

Pathologies

Although Rittel proposed that the whole gamut of human fallibilities was available to explain planning breakdowns and strange forms of institutional behavior, he isolated and discussed some salient planning pathologies. One need only read the daily press to find illustrations of these pathologies. Listed below are the pathologies identified by Rittel, using the names he gave them.

1. Patent medicine: what is good for one is good for all

What is good for the developed countries, the US in particular, is good for the developing countries. The World Bank and the International Monetary Fund have been operating under this belief. In exchange for approving loans, they request that the recipient country privatize its state-owned industries, devaluate its currency, curb government spending, and encourage exports. Measured by some indicators, this neoliberal program seems to have been a roaring success. In the developing countries I know best, Bolivia and Peru, hyperinflation was curbed, currencies have stabilized and foreign investments soared, new jobs were created, and GDP grew by 3 to 4 percent yearly in the last few years. But as a *New York Times* headline noted, this "Latin Economic Speedup Leaves Poor in the Dust." In the drive for austerity, more jobs are lost than gained and many already precarious social services further reduced, wages are falling, and the price of basic commodities is rising. The economic growth is lopsided, the rich get richer and the poor get poorer. The treatment of the small farmer in remote areas goes from benign neglect to total abandonment. The quickening pace of industrialization is accompanied by rapid and severe environmental degradation, etc. That the neoliberal patent medicines of the World Bank and the International Monetary Fund are working to the detriment of the developing countries and to the advantage of Wall Street has been well documented by the Nobel Prize-winning economist and one-time member of the World Bank, Joseph E. Stiglitz (2003).

2. Inability to stop the implementation of a plan although it is obviously failing

"All the sacrifices could not, and cannot have been for naught." War memorials are tragic examples of this mentality, particularly if the war was lost. This attitude is often reinforced by "the want to 'save face', the notion that admitting to a mistake is to give leverage to the opponent."

2a. Throwing good money after bad

Everybody is familiar with this pathology. I will mention only a company that insists on continuing the development of its own software for handling its inventory, when there are now readily installed, easily adaptable, cheap and superior products available on the market.

2b. Heroic foolishness

In 1994, Gustavo de Greiff, then Colombia's prosecutor general, saw that the war on drugs had brought no victories, only defeats. No matter what had been done— eradication programs, seizures of shipments, prosecution or killing of drug lords—the prices of drugs seemed unaffected. The illicit trade reaps immense profits for the traffickers with which they corrupt the police, custom agents, airport authorities, etc.[4] De Greiff's arguments for legalization seem to have found a sympathetic response from mayors and police chiefs in the US, but legislatures are not about to follow suit. The same morality that brought about prohibition is still deeply ingrained. In spite of the failure, and its associated social and economic cost, the same principles are righteously adhered to.

It is one of the ironies of the "war on drugs" that the new "war on terrorism" in Afghanistan, according to the United Nations Office on Drugs and Crime (UNODC), has led to opium production in Afghanistan, which equals nearly double the estimated annual global consumption.[5] Economic wisdom would have it that such an oversupply should send the price of the drug plummeting. But apparently that is not so. Antonio María Costa, the UNODC executive director, suspects "that the big traffickers are hoarding surplus opium as a hedge against future price shocks and as a source of funding for future terrorist attacks, in Afghanistan or elsewhere."[6]

3. Failure to plan, to take action

3a. Ostrich policy, or burying one's head in the sand

In the debate over US national healthcare reform, the "'no crisis' minimalists won" the battle. They argued that the country was "by and large, happily ensconced in a fee-for-service system with full freedom of choice over which doctors people see, and full access to the wonders of technology."[7] But, as Drew Altman, head of Kaiser Family Foundation, remarked, "when it comes to health care reform, you can run but you can't hide. The problems that put this on the agenda are going to get worse."[8] He was referring to the rising costs and diminishing services even to the currently insured. These problems, indeed, have not gone away; they are still with us today, almost 15 years later. How to control the costs of healthcare and how to provide coverage for all emerges again as a major issue in the US presidential elections of 2008.

3b. Allergy against bad news, or the palace guard is blocking your view

"The allergy against bad news already existed in classical Antiquity and in the ancient Orient. The messenger who transmitted the bad news used to be beheaded." Today, the whistle-blowers get fired and disgraced, and the critics are dismissed as irrelevant or their loyalty, sincerity, or patriotism is called into question. Under these circumstances, it is not surprising that more often than not, the heads of firms, organizations, agencies, or governments remain unaware of the catastrophes towards which they are drifting or which have already hit them.

3c. Good old habits, or staying the course in a changing sea

Continued success makes complacent, cripples the ability for critical self-evaluation, and dulls the awareness of the surroundings. One happily pursues the course that has proven itself and misses the changing currents. IBM's decline as the dominant computer firm can be traced to its stubborn reliance and insistence on mainframe computers, while the world was increasingly working with mini and micro computers.

3d. Running with the pack

Analogous to the good old habits but leading in the opposite direction is the practice of joining in with every latest development, of following whatever is "in"; after all, one cannot fall behind the times or lose out on potential profits. The current financial upheavals due to major financial institutions the world over jumping onto the band-wagon of sub-prime mortgages are an example of this pathology.

3e. Après moi le déluge

When the People's Republic of China decided to make its auto industry into a "pillar industry" to help sustain economic growth into the next millennium, many saw this development to be a big mistake, for China is "already suffering from traffic con-gestion, choking pollution and dwindling supplies of oil." In spite of this and other serious arguments against the plan, a Chinese automaker is quoted as having said "the Chinese auto industry is just at the beginning stage of development and there is no necessity to worry about some problems that will crop up in the future"![9] The very same attitude today pervades the US Government when it comes to global cli-mate change, only here it may mean après *nous* le déluge—in an all too real sense.

4. *Obsession with order and simplicity*

The workings of modern social entities often appear too complex for our compre-hension. When the impenetrable diversity, heterogeneity, and disorder become unbearable, we succumb to simplifying the world. The quest for moral clarity and expressions such as "you are either with us, or you are against us" are current exam-ples of the reduction of complicated situations to simple notions and dichotomies.

4a. Reduction to indicators

A favorite method of simplifying the world is the attempt to describe complicated phenomena with indicators: GDP, literacy rates, productivity indices, unemployment figures, etc. It is easier to deal with indicators than with the underlying phenomena. However, these simplifications raise the temptation "to cure the indicators rather than that which they indicate . . . One can also change the definition of the indica-tors to produce a prettier world. If there are too many unemployed, one can reduce their number by eliminating from the statistic those who have given up the search for employment." (Rittel 1992a: 386).

4b. Inability, fear, or unwillingness to recognize complexity

The US military engagements in Iraq and Afghanistan speak to this pathology. To bring the expressed goal of liberty and self-determination to an oppressed people may be noble and straightforward, but to achieve this goal with military might alone clearly shows an inability and an unwillingness to understand the complexities of the larger context of cultural, ethnic, religious, political, and historical factors in which these conflicts take place.

4c. *Sachzwänge*

There is no proper translation for the German word *Sachzwang* (plural *Sachzwänge*), which is of rather recent coinage since it is found in only a few of the more recent dictionaries, where it is generally translated as "practical constraint." This translation, however, does not even come close to the power of its German meaning. Rittel tried to translate it as "coercive fact," but suggested that the word be adopted into the English language without translation, just as zeitgeist, angst, and other such words have. Here I follow his advice.

We frequently hear arguments like "Because of rising healthcare costs, we *have* to raise our insurance premiums." Such sayings betray how policymakers, planners, politicians, etc., construe an observable fact into an inevitable and inescapable *Sachzwang* akin to a law of nature such as the law of gravity. It is obvious to any one that, in the above example, reining in the healthcare costs would be another option for action. By declaring the rising costs a *Sachzwang* the policymakers clearly simplify the world and their task: they avoid the careful analysis of healthcare costs and the confrontations with the pharmaceutical industry, the manufacturers of medical equipment, particular medical practices, etc. *Sachzwänge* have become a favorite "instrument for the justification of political strategies, planning measures, and pressing actions" (Rittel 1992b: 271). But *Sachzwänge* are often nothing more than either excuses for laziness or cowardice, or fabricated justifications for special interests (Beck 1996: 280–282).

4d. Obsession with overriding aspects

Globalization and the new economy are spawning uncertainties and insecurities: Will I still have a job tomorrow? Will I find one after I graduate? Will the banks foreclose on my mortgage? Will I be safe in my home, on the street? Will my pension plan be taken from me? Who will care for me when I am sick, getting old? Too often, to assuage their anxieties people turn to immigrants, legal or illegal, as the perceived overriding cause for all their fears and troubles. This obsession, which can be observed throughout the United States and Europe, found one of its uglier illustrations in a campaign poster used during the 2007 parliamentary elections in Switzerland which depicted a bunch of white sheep kicking a black sheep off of a Swiss flag.

5. *Megalomania*

The "ever bigger and better" syndrome leads us into designing systems whose complexity we no longer grasp, and whose behavior is beyond our predictive powers. Salient examples can easily be found in the field of biotechnology where grand plans abound. From plans to eliminate world hunger to attempts to create synthetic life itself,[10] the aspirations of biotechnology are often grand, and all depend on manipulating genetic material in ways in which the outcome is uncertain.

The various pathologies presented above are not exclusive of each other. In fact, several of the examples may fit more than one pathology and may be interpreted as resulting from a combination of pathologies. Rittel's pathologies resonate ominously with Jared Diamond's analysis of why societies make disastrous decisions, decisions that lead to their collapse (Diamond 2006). Some of Diamond's findings expand on Rittel's pathology of "Failure to Plan, to Take Action." We may fail "to perceive a problem that has actually arrived" because the problem may be "literally imperceptible" or because of "creeping normalcy." An example of the former is the mercury content of seafood that only chemical analysis can reveal; an example of the latter is gradual suburbanization. Most people will not remember, "how different the landscape looked 50 years ago" (Diamond 2005: 424–425). Another of Diamond's reasons for our failure to take action is what I would call "resignation" (or perceived impotence), that is "the problem may be beyond our present capacity to solve, a solution may exist but is prohibitively expensive, or our efforts may be too little and too late" (436). Another of Diamond's important reasons for planning failures is "reasoning by false analogy" (423). False analogies may not be so much pathologies as they are examples of epistemic failures. Yet, many of the pathologies are the result of using false analogies, for example, patent medicine, which assumes that a single instance provides an appropriate model for all other cases.

Corrective Strategies

"All these forms of behavior are, of course, common occurrences in daily life. They are considered to be neither particularly wise nor morally commendable, but they also are not seen to be particularly abhorrent or even criminal." They represent nothing more than ordinary human weaknesses. Why then should we worry?

In daily life, the damage and injury caused by such behavior is kept within bounds, and are limited to the few. However, if large political institutions, nations, or corporate entities are managed in this way, considerable damage is not unlikely (Rittel 1992a: 388).

Human weakness may be a fact of life, but planning failures need not happen. To mitigate human fallibilities and to make it more difficult for planning failures to occur, Rittel developed an arsenal of attitudes, actions, and strategies ranging from questioning authority, unveiling ulterior motives, systematic doubting, to producing counter-expertise. Furthermore, his entire second-generation approach to planning must be interpreted as an effort to reduce the risk of planning failures.

1. Cherchez l'homme (ou la femme)

Rittel taught his students that systems, i.e. organizations, governments, corporations etc., do not make decisions, people do. His advice was often cast in the form of one-liners, such as: "Who has a motive?", "Always ask who is promoting a course of action and how it matches the promoter's interest. Are these interests compatible with the public interest?", "Whoever demands sacrifices in the public interest, is not usually one to sacrifice!"

2. Keep the questions alive, or "spit into their soups"

"There is a flaw in every plan. Find it!"

"Watch for attempts of deriving 'ought' from 'is'!"

"Be skeptical of and unimpressed by hypertrophic scientific or techno-logical vocabulary: it usually hides ignorance, or possibly sinister schemes!"

"Know your Machiavelli. Be familiar with the arsenals of power, and the techniques to generate or deflate power!"

3. Doomsaying

Are the growing ozone holes, global warming, and changing weather patterns indica-tors that our atmosphere is undergoing drastic, maybe incorrigible, changes at our hands, or are they just the effects of random fluctuations? Should we just sit back, wait and see, or should we act now?

Considering what is at stake, namely life on earth, it would behoove us to adopt the worst-case scenario and act now, even if it should turn out that no action was required. This strategy is similar to one proposed by Kenneth Boulding to defuse social conflicts before they degenerate into violence (Boulding 1962). He advocated the installation of an early warning system. Such a system may produce two types of errors: first, it may sound a false alarm, prompting us into action, although none was needed. Second, it may fail to warn us, in which case we take no action, although action would have been needed. The two types of error are not independ-ent; diminishing the number of false alarms may result in higher failed alarms, and vice versa. Boulding argued in favor of false alarms, as in the long run they might be cheaper.[11]

Questions arise to the reliability of large-scale software systems that comprise hundreds of thousands of lines of code and that run on several hundreds of microprocessor. Such systems are in charge of the safety of nuclear reactors and their security systems. How reliable are they? Bev Littlewood and Lorenzo Strigini, in their article "The Risks of Software" (1992), reported several breakdowns of large-scale software systems that disrupted telephone systems and delayed shuttle launches. The fact is that "it is not feasible to assess the number and kinds of soft-ware errors, that remain, if any, after the completion of system design, development and test." In other words, we cannot know whether a system will break down until it does, and then the results maybe catastrophic. Therefore Littlewood and Strigini recommend "[c]onsidering the levels of complexity that software has made possible, we believe being skeptical is the safest course of action."

Typically, the promotors of genetically modified crops argue that they are the answer to, and salvation of, a starving world population. Their critics argue that these crops will continue to evolve and that we have no way of knowing where this evolution will take them nor how these crops will interact with natural species once they are released into the wild. They could bring about disruptions of the ecosystem of unknown proportions.

In view of impending disasters, Bernd Guggenberger, invoking Hans Jonas's "Imperative of Responsibility" (Jonas 1979), admonishes us that:

> Wenn bei grosstechnischen Entwicklungen nicht weniger als Alles, das Ganze auf dem Spiel stehen kann, dann gebührt . . . der 'Unheilsprognose' prinzipiell mehr Gehör als der Heilsprophezeihung.
>
> (Guggenberger 1987: 125)

> [When large-scale technological developments have the potential of threatening everything, to put at stake the whole, then . . . on principle, the doom prognosis warrants more attention than the salvation prophesy.]

Second-generation Systems Approach as an Attempt to Overcome Pathologies

The express purpose of planning approaches of the second generation is to assist planners, through participation, argumentation, and objectification[12], in:

- forgetting less: by comparing notes, swapping ideas, and comparing interpretations of a problem with others, planners may learn about the problem's scope and be less likely to forget, overlook, or ignore, important aspects;
- identifying the right issues: argumentation is likely to bring out a wide variety of issues and to highlight the "questions which are worthwhile, which have the greatest weight, and where there is the greatest disagreement."
- stimulating doubt: the more diverse understandings and interpretations of a problem are obtained, the more doubt will arise about any specific course of action, making the planners more cautious;
- explicating judgments: through objectification, the participants are likely to learn more about each others' bases of judgments. This in turn may lead to an understanding, if not appreciation, of different value systems.

Thus, second-generation planning methods, if applied, are likely to bring about the questioning of "patent medicines," the shaking up of "good old habits," the breaking of the "obsession with order and simplicity," the unmasking of "*Sachzwänge*," or the deflating of "megalomania."

"I can, therefore I ought"?

Reflecting on the pathologies of planning and their prevention, Rittel observed that the scope and scale, intensity and frequency, of planning endeavors have increased drastically during the last century. Ever more phenomena, which used to be considered fate or destiny, have become planning problems, problems for deliberate and purposeful intervention:

- genetic traits of one's offspring;
- procreation beyond one's own death;
- distribution and allocation of deadly risks (toxic dumps, nuclear plants, etc.);
- the "natural" balance of ecosystems;
- the size of the world's population;
- the survival of species, including our own.

To date, most theoretical and methodological investigations on planning have concentrated on the question of "how to plan," regardless of what is planned. But "the curse of feasibility"[13] as Rittel called the loss of destiny, raises the question of "what to plan, and what not to plan." Should every domain enter the realm of planning, just because we think we know how to manipulate it? Should we follow Edward Teller's advice that "technical man ought to apply what he has come to understand" and this "without setting himself any limits" (1975: 116)?

What to plan and not to plan

Rittel was not given the time to design his proposed "system to determine what to design," but hints of what some of its elements might have been may be gleaned from similarities between Rittel's work and the writings of Bernd Guggenberger.[14]

Rittel was deeply involved in the debate over the German energy policy, in particular its nuclear component. In this context he wrote: "nuclear power plants were designed with the certainty that the problems of the intermediate and final storage of spent fuel, as well as its enrichment, would be solved in due time." This expectation, of course, never materialized, and indeed, the "self-assurance of those planners, who implemented energy policies based primarily on an untested, and surely immature technology, is remarkable" (Rittel 1992a: 375).

We live in an era of mediated reality. We are instantly informed of events around the globe; we know about famine here, civil strife there, a volcano eruption yonder, genocide somewhere else, but very few of us have first-hand knowledge of these events. This loss of reality, Rittel cautioned, may become an impediment to our ability to judge the appropriateness and impact of our actions, for we have lost the "feel" for it. The hesitations, stumblings, and fumblings of many European governments and the bewilderment of their people in the aftermath of Chernobyl are an example of this. How is one to deal with a reality that manifests itself only as numbers on dials of sophisticated scientific instruments?

Likewise, Guggenberger is concerned with the widespread application of knowledge that has not undergone experiential validation, and the fact that more and more of our large-scale interventions are beyond preliminary testing. Fast breeders cannot be experimentally tested in laboratories as a complete installation, nor can World Bank fiscal policies be tested on a small-scale local economy; their first test runs are in real time and real life. In such situations one cannot afford to make mistakes; one is no longer at liberty to experiment and learn from experience.

Because to "err is human," and because learning by trial and error is a fundamental epistemological principle, Guggenberger pleaded for the restoration of the human right to err and the creation of a planning environment in which failures do not, and cannot, have catastrophic consequences, one in which we can still learn from experience, and correct our mistakes, one in which we do not have to pay the ultimate price for being mistaken.

There is a striking similarity between Guggenberger's position and Popper's arguments against large-scale planning efforts, or "utopian engineering." Popper insisted that trial and error is essential not only for the acquisition of scientific knowledge, but also to solve practical problems. But if the practical problems we try to solve are radical in the sense that they aim at remodeling "the whole society," there is not much room for trial and error, for "it is very hard to learn from very big mistakes" (Popper 1961: 88).

From his position, Guggenberger derived some practical advice regarding the question of "what to plan and what not to plan," which may be summarized as follows:

- No measure shall be implemented which has not been submitted to an appropriate period of "trial and error," or which, for technical, or any other reasons, cannot be submitted to such.
- No measure shall be implemented in which there is not, at least in principle, the possibility of acquiring first-hand experience with the knowledge or technology applied.
- Spatially dispersed, temporally staggered, and locally diversified measures are, in general, to be preferred over ubiquitously and simultaneously applied, centrally administered, uniform solutions.
- No plan shall be implemented whose consequences cannot be reversed[15] or corrected within an adequate time frame.

Guggenberger further suggested an ethical principle that should guide what planning efforts should be undertaken, and which should not:

> No generation shall pass on to the next generation more difficult to reverse conditions than it had inherited itself.
>
> (Guggenberger 1987: 111)

Rittel often enough argued that our actions today may limit the options of future generations, and that, therefore, planners were accountable not only to their contemporaries, but had an obligation to the yet unborn. But Guggenberger's other propositions seem antithetical to Rittel's understanding of planning problems as "wicked problems."

"There is no immediate nor an ultimate test for a solution to a Wicked Problem" (Rittel and Webber 1973: 163): the waves of consequences of solutions to wicked problems keep on crashing onto the shores of the far future. An implemented plan may be successful in the beginning only to show undesired consequences much later, as in the above-mentioned example of the application of DDT. What then constitutes an "appropriate period of 'trial and error'"? When the undesired consequences start to show, it may be already too late for any remediation; the damage has already occurred.

"Every wicked problem is a 'one-shot operation' . . . there is no opportunity to learn by trial and error, every attempt counts significantly . . . It leaves 'traces' that cannot be undone" (Rittel and Webber 1973: 163). No planning action, however benign, is ever without consequences and these consequences are irreversible. Rittel interpreted "reversible" in a stricter sense than Guggenberger (1987: n. 23). All mechanical, electrical, or magnetic phenomena are reversible, as long as no temperature differences are involved. Thus, a tensioned spring will return to its original, relaxed state without the expenditure of additional energy and without permanent state change in the spring. In planning there are no analogues to these reversible phenomena. An architect who does not like the wall that was just erected can sign a change order and, thus, restore the "original" state (reversibility in Guggenberger's sense). But he cannot do so without the expenditure of additional energy and other resources, and without leaving traces, for example, demolition debris. In this sense all (planning) actions are essentially irreversible, which led Rittel to argue that irreversibility of action ought to be an axiom of any theory of planning.

Because "every wicked problem is essentially unique" (Rittel and Webber 1973: 164), meaning that there "are no classes of wicked problems in the sense that principles of solution can be developed to fit all members of a class," Rittel challenged the opportunity, and usefulness, of learning from experience with regard to planning problems.

And finally, Rittel was emphatic about designers having no right to be wrong: "Planners are liable for the consequences of the actions they generate; the effects can matter a great deal to those people that are touched by those actions" (Rittel and Webber 1973: 167).

Are Guggenberger and Rittel's positions as irreconcilable as they appear?

Rittel did not rule out the possibility of learning from experience, he only cautioned against a premature transfer of experience gained in one planning situation to another, no matter how similar the two situations may appear. "Despite seeming similarities . . . one can never be certain that the particulars of a problem do not override its commonalties with other problems already dealt with." To emphasize the similarities over the difference is what may lead to drawing false analogies.

Rittel further noted that planners have very little opportunity to learn from past projects because of the long half-lives of consequences, especially of large-scale projects. A project may have beneficial effects at the outset, only to have catastrophic consequences many years, even decades later. The lag between planning and implementation, which also may range from many years to decades, further adds to the difficulties of learning from practice.

Underlying Guggenberger's insistence on the right to err is the assumption that people will actually learn from their mistakes. But, as we know and Dietrich Dörner has convincingly shown in his *Logik des Misslingens* ("Logic of Failures," 1992), this is not necessarily true. Unanticipated and undesired consequences can easily be ignored, displaced, marginalized, or even embellished. The same pathologies that have brought about planning failures can be applied to the unanticipated and undesired consequences. As Friedrich Hegel noted, what "we learn from history is that we do not learn from history."

"The effects of an experimental curriculum will follow the pupils into their adult lives." Indeed, the consequences of planning actions cannot be undone. Yet, if it is true that no action can be undone, it is also true that it is sometimes possible to mitigate, or even correct undesired consequences. Again, Rittel did not deny this possibility; he only cautioned that every attempt at mitigating or correcting old mistakes was a new planning project, one that was as likely to engender undesired consequences as the one that brought about the first mistakes. More recently, Ulrich Beck argued that our contemporary society is caught up in a vicious cycle of problem solving–problem generation—that is, every problem we solve creates new problems. Instead of attacking problems at their root we only cure symptoms. Instead of abandoning our habit of polluting, we focus on how to clean up the mess we leave behind with new techno-scientific means. The new means benefit the industries involved, but also may have undesired and unforeseen consequences of their own, which will need to be fixed in turn, and so the cycle goes on (Beck 1996: 295).

Rittel himself struggled with the notion of "less planning." Recognizing that our ability to plan is limited (i.e. subject to failure), he argued that perhaps we ought to reconsider the scope of what we try to plan. Is there some middle ground between seeking the impossible "maximal intervention," that is perfection and completion of the whole, or Popper's "utopian engineering," and the shortcomings of no intervention, leaving everything to market forces? Not unlike Guggenberger, Rittel was searching for planning strategies that would reduce the incorrigibility of undesired consequences, strategies that would make it possible to interrupt the implementation of any plan, at any time without leaving irreparable damages, that is, damages that could not be repaired within a reasonable time frame and at acceptable costs.

To this point, it is possible to construe Rittel's arguments not as a refutation of Guggenberger's proposal, but rather as a positive critique that uncovers the theoretical and methodological difficulties underlying any "system to determine what to design." There remains, however, the question of the planner's responsibility.

If the empirical evidence that people err is elevated to a human right to err, as proposed by Guggenberger, then nobody can do wrong, and nobody can be held responsible for making mistakes. Rittel did not see it that way. Planners cannot shed the responsibility for their actions. This, however, does not prevent the search for a planning environment in which failures do not, and cannot, have catastrophic consequences, one in which we can still learn from experience, and correct our mistakes. Recognizing that "trial and error" is fundamental to learning does not imply that a child who does wrong should not be reprimanded. In other words, the human right to err is not a prerequisite to a planning environment in which we can still learn from experience.

Conclusions

His analysis of "minimal intervention," or "less planning," led Rittel to the conclusion that no matter how the idea is interpreted, the search for a planning environment in which failures do not, and cannot, have catastrophic consequences, one in which we can still learn from experience, and correct our mistakes, is not only a difficult, but perhaps an impossible task. Such an environment would, like Boulding's alarm system, require great sensitivity to the possibility of something going wrong. There is no calculus to answer the question "how much planning is appropriate?" It is a question of world view, manner of thinking, and attitude.[16]

For example, if "less planning" is interpreted as "given a budget B, then it is better to pursue many projects, each using a fraction of B, than spending all of

B on one project." "Instead of attempting to pool the resources for comprehensive planning, many local and incremental projects should be pursued. [Compare Guggenberger's proposal above.] . . . According to this view, the 'amount of planning' is measured by the volume of resources involved . . .." This view assumes that the consequences of a project remain commensurate with the magnitude of resources that are invested in it. However, there is no correlation that would support this assumption. "Interventions which are 'small' according to this understanding can have unforeseen, immense and expensive, even disastrous consequences."

The attempt to answer the question "what to plan and what not to plan" by considering the consequences of action plans, and then weeding out those action plans whose consequences appear undesirable, incorrigible, or even catastrophic, presupposes our ability to correctly predict the consequences of our actions. Yet it is our very inability to do so that produces planning failures in the first place and leads to the search for mitigating or corrective interventions. Thus, the hope of determining "what to plan and what not to plan" by considering the consequences is gravely compromised.

To meet this dilemma, Rittel proposed an approach to planning which he called "unheroic." "The unheroic planner is not sure what the 'actual' problem is. He is not the expert for the welfare of other people. He accepts the 'symmetry of ignorance': he does not know whether he knows better what ought to be planned, than those 'for whom' he plans (who probably don't know either). He has doubts and sleepless nights, for he knows very well, that he does not control the consequences of his actions, that the 'rationally correct', or even the 'optimal' plans do not exist. He behaves modestly rather than decisive and sure. He believes that he must always learn something new, and knows that even then he does not know enough."

In this, Rittel echoes Popper. Faced with "the assumption that there can be no political move which has no drawbacks, no undesirable consequences," Popper's piecemeal engineer differs from the utopian engineer in that the former has to replace "the great art of convincing ourselves that we have not made any mistakes, of ignoring them, of hiding them, and blaming others for them . . . by the greater art of accepting the responsibility for them, in trying to learn from them, and of applying this knowledge so that we may avoid them in the future" (Popper 1961: 88).

Furthermore, "when trying to assess the likely consequences of some proposed reform, the piecemeal technologist must do his best to estimate the effects of any measure upon the 'whole' of society" (Popper 1961: 68).

This attitude towards planning may have salutary benefits, for the planners who follow it may abandon action plans for which it is too difficult "to estimate the effects . . . upon the 'whole' of society." An unheroic planner may never have engaged in implementing nuclear power plants, or may not be willing to take the responsibility for the consequences of genetic engineering. But "doing the best one can," answers the question of "what to plan and what not to plan" no more than the "consequentialist" approach.

How, then, are we expected to decide?

C. West Churchman observed that "[p]robably the most startling feature of the twentieth-century culture is the fact that we have developed such elaborate ways of doing things and at the same time have developed no ways of justifying any of the things we do" (Churchman 1964: 1). And thirty years later, in a different, yet related context, Marvin Minsky noted, that the question "bears on our right to have children, to change our genes, to die if we so wish." Minsky continues by pointing out that the challenge we face in our attempt at answering the question is that:

> No popular ethical system yet, be it humanist or religion-based, has shown itself able to face the challenges that already confront us. How many people should occupy the earth? What sorts of people should they be? How should we share the available space [and resources]?
>
> (Minsky 1994: 113)

What ethical systems or moral principles to cope with the "curse of feasibility" Rittel would have invoked in his proposed "system to determine what to design," we can only speculate. In his view, ethics were an indispensable part of any theory of planning. Inevitably, to plan is to make decisions about purposes and ends, that is, to make value judgments; there is no such thing as "objective" planning. Rittel's concern with value systems and how they mold design can be traced back to his early work[17] and ethics is a subject he regularly taught. In his work we find elements of various schools of thought. His unheroic planner may be seen as an example of an ethics of conviction or *Gesinnungsethik*,[18] that is an ethic which, in the Kantian tradition, sees morality as inherent not in the action and its outcomes, but in the autonomous good will. His insistence on the planners' accountability for the consequences of their actions to future generations is plainly inscribed in an ethics of responsibility as originally sketched out by Max Weber (1926) and later professed by Hans Jonas mentioned above. And finally and foremost, his model of planning as argumentation shows affinities with communicative (or discursive) ethics as proposed by Jürgen Habermas and Karl-Otto Apel.[19]

Rittel's model of argumentation was, in part, inspired by the works of Paul Lorenzen (1969, 1978) and Oswald Schwemmer (1971), who proposed norms of reasonable argumentation for the probing and justifiction (*Begründung*) of value judgments and of planning or political actions. Reasonable argumentation is seen as bringing about "better mutual understanding" of the participants' values, of what the perception of the problem is and how it may be solved, which in turn would lead to a reasoned consensus and idoneous decisions on what ought to be designed and what not.

But as seen above, Rittel also meant argumentation to raise doubts, to question assumptions, to frustrate pathologies, to uncover conflicts of interest, to challenge proposed means and ends, to contest arguments, in other words, not to reach consensus, but to activate unseen or unspoken conflicts.

How can this seeming paradox between reaching consensus and activating conflict be explained? "Conflict" has the common connotation of discord, dysfunction or even disease, but conflict can also be understood as an inevitable element of society (and possibly an element of all life) that acts as the motor of evolution and development. Comparing societies in which conflicts are absent or suppressed to societies in which conflicts are accepted and regulated, Ralf Dahrendorf noted that the former tend towards stagnation, even totalitarianism, whereas the latter keep changing and developing. He termed conflicts an "outstanding creative force of societies" (Dahrendorf 1965: 125). However, it is to be acknowledged that conflicts per se do accomplish nothing, at best they point out possibilities beyond a given situation. In Boulding's words, what makes conflicts valuable "is the process of conflict toward some kind of resolution which gives it meaning . . ." (Boulding 1962: 307). The model of planning as argumentation provides the grounds on which conflicts among the involved parties get articulated and avenues are opened that may lead to resolutions. A resolution does not mean that new conflicts will not arise, for planning or "[s]ocial problems are never solved. At best they are only re-solved—over and over again" (Rittel and Webber 1973: 160).

While Rittel believed in the convincing powers of reasoned arguments, his pathologies of planning reveal that he was all too aware of human frailties. People do not always argue in good faith and resolutions may not be reached.[20] Furthermore, he was under no illusion that, to help resolve conflicts, there is no overriding ethical system to be invoked: the "attempt to establish a normative value system valid for everyone and always . . . is futile. Two thousand years of frustration in occidental philosophy have shown this."[21] With this Rittel was alluding to the limits of ethics.

He sympathized with Hoederer, the main character in Sartre's play *Les Mains sales*, who questioned his comrade Hugo's insistence on purity of principle and asked him "do you really imagine that one can govern innocently?" (Sartre 1974: 194). Rittel often told his students that to engage in planning was an adventure and that like all adventures, planning entailed risks, even the risk of dirtying one's hands. More recent research on argumentation lends substantial support to Rittel's intuition. Tore Sager has demonstrated that, in analogy to Kenneth Arrow's "theorem on the general impossibility of consistent and fair social choice," argumentation, or deliberation, "cannot ensure consistent recommendation and simultaneously prepare for political decision making in a democratic manner" (Sager 2002).

I don't know whether Rittel had had the chance to read Isaiah Berlin's essay "The Pursuit of the Ideal," but I have little doubt that he would have agreed with Berlin:

> There is no escape: we must decide as we decide; moral risks cannot, at times, be avoided. All we can ask for is that none of the relevant factors be ignored, that the purposes we seek to realize should be seen as elements in a total form of life, which can be enhanced or damaged by decisions.
>
> (Berlin 1991: 18)

Notes

1 This paper is based, in part, on some of Rittel's unpublished notes and manuscripts, in particular for *The State of the Art in Design Theories and Methods* (August/October 1989), *Agenda for a Theory of Design* (October 1989), an unpublished paper "Planung und kleinster Eingriff," and

a published paper "Energie wird rar: Sachzwänge oder der Krieg um die Köpfe," in *Design der Zukunft, Architektur—Design—Technik—Ökologie*, ed. Lucius Burckhardt, Internationales Design Zentrum Berlin, Dumont Taschenbücher 202 (Köln: Dumont Buchverlag, 1987; reprinted in Horst W. J. Rittel, *Planen, Entwerfen, Design*, ed. Wolf D. Reuter, Facility Management 5, pp. 369–402 [Stuttgart: Verlag W. Kohlhammer, 1992], and on a paper presented by the author at the 36th Annual Conference of the Association of Collegiate Schools of Planning in 1994, which subsequently was published as an article jointly with Niraj Verma in *Planning Theory*, No. 18 (Winter 1997). The present version is a revision of both, the paper and the article. Quotes in the present article that appear without references are taken from a variety of Rittel's piecemeal notes.

2 In 1971, US President Richard M. Nixon named drugs "US public enemy number one" and initiated the war on drugs that has been supported by every US administration since (www.pbs.org/wgbh/pages/frontline/shows/drugs/cron/).

3 See Rittel, "On the Planning Crisis" (this volume, pp. 151–65).

4 Reported in *The New York Times*, 07 July 1994.

5 Afghanistan Opium Survey 2007, United Nations Office on Drugs and Crime

6 *Washington Post*, 25 April 2007.

7 Reported in *The New York Times*, 20 February 1994.

8 Ibid.

9 Reported in *The New York Times*, 22 September 1994.

10 For example, as reported in *The New York Times*, 25 January 2008 (p. A15).

11 One possible exception is in case of violent conflict in which either alarm may be equally fatal (Boulding 1962: 326 ff.).

12 For an explanation of these concepts, and an overview of the second-generation systems approach, see Rittel's "On the Planning Crisis," this volume, pp. 151–65.

13 Rittel called it "Der Fluch der Machbarkeit."

14 Shortly before his death, Horst Rittel presented me with a copy of Guggenberger's *Das Menschenrecht auf Irrtum* (1987), but we were not given time to discuss it.

15 Nowhere does Guggenberger discuss the notion of reversibility. I presume by "reversibility" he means something like "bringing back the original state," as for example in Nature Conservancy's effort to restore in several parts of the Midwest the prairie landscape and ecology that existed before the arrival of Europeans. Not all our actions are reversible in this sense: for example, we cannot bring back the species we have driven to extinction.

16 Horst W.J. Rittel, "Intervento Minimo," ms., p. 8.

17 Cf. for example, Science and Design Seminar 9 (this volume).

18 "*Gesinnung*" is also rendered as "disposition," "mental disposition," or "mental attitude." The problems in translating the term are discussed by Munzel (1999: pp. xvii–xviii).

19 For a critical discussion of these schools of thought, see, for example, Böhler (1994), or Benhabib and Dallmayr (1990).

20 Rittel did not buy into in the Habermasien "ideal speech situation."

21 Science and Design Seminar 9.

References

Beck, U. (1996) *Die Risikogesellschaft: Auf dem Weg in eine andere Moderne*. 2nd. ed. Frankfurt am Main: Germany: Suhrkamp (originally published 1986). In English: (2002) *Risk Society: Towards a New Modernity*, London: Sage Publications.

Benhabib, S. and Dallmayr, F. (eds) (1990) *The Communicative Ethics Controversy*. Cambridge, MA: MIT Press.

Berlin, I. (1991) *The Crooked Timber of Humanity: Chapters in the History of Ideas*. New York: Alfred A. Knopf.

Böhler, D. (ed.) (1994) *Ethik für die Zukunft: Im Diskurs mit Hans Jonas* [Ethics for the Future: In Dialogue with Hans Jonas]. Munich: C. H. Beck.

Boulding, K. (1962) *Conflict and Defense: A General Theory*. New York: Harper & Row.

Churchman, C. W. (1964) *Prediction and Optimal Decisions: Philosophical Issues of A Science of Values*. Englewood Cliffs, NJ: Prentice-Hall.

Dahrendorf, R. (1965) *Gesellschaft und Freiheit* [Society and Freedom]. Munich: R. Piper and Co.

Diamond, J. (2005) *Collapse: How Societies Choose to Succeed or Fail*. New York: Penguin Books.

Dörner, D. (1992) *Die Logik des Misslingens: Strategisches Denken in Komplexen Situationen*. Reinbek by Hamburg: Rowohlt Taschenbuch Verlag GmbH; trans. R. Kimber and R. Kimber (1996), *The Logic of Failure: Recognizing and Avoiding Error in Complex Situations*. New York: Basic Books.

Guggenberger, B. (1987) *Das Menschenrecht auf Irrtum: Anleitung zur Unvollkommenheit* [The Human Right to Err: Instruction for Imperfection]. Munich, Germany: Carl Hanser Verlag.

Jonas, H. (1979) *Das Prinzip Verantwortung: Versuch einer Ethik für die Technologische Zivilisation*. Frankfurt am Main: Insel Verlag; trans. H. Jonas (1984) *The Imperative of Responsibility: In Search of an Ethics for the Technological Age*. Chicago: University of Chicago Press.

Littlewood, B. and Strigini, L. (1992) "The Risks of Software." *Scientific American*, 267(5): 62–75.

Lorenzen, P. (1969) *Normative Logic and Ethics*, B.I-Hochschultaschenbücher 236, Mannheim and Zürich: Bibliographisches Institut.

Lorenzen, P. (1978) *Theorie der Technischen und Politischen Vernunft* [Theory of Technical and Political Reason]. Stuttgart: Philipp Reclam jun.

Minsky, M. (1994) "Will Robots Inherit the Earth?" *Scientific American*, 271(4): 108–113.

Munzel, G. F. (1999) *Kant's Conception of Moral Character: The "Critical" Link to Morality*. Chicago: University of Chicago Press.

Popper, K. (1961) *The Poverty of Historicism*. 3rd. ed. New York: Harper & Row.

Rittel, H. W. J. (1992a) "Energie wird rar? Sachzwänge oder der Krieg um die Köpfe" [Energy is Becoming Scarce? Coercive Facts and the Battle for Ideas]. In W. D. Reuter (ed.) *Planen, Entwerfen, Design: Ausgewählte Schriften zu Theorie und Methodik* (pp. 369–402). Stuttgart: Kohlhammer.

Rittel, H. W. J. (1992b) *Planen Entwerfen, Design: Ausgewählte Schriften zu Theorie und Methodik* [Planning, Envisioning and Designing: Selected Writings on Theory and Method]. Stuttgart: Verlag W. Kohlhammer.

Rittel, H. W. J. and Webber, M. M. (1973) "Dilemmas in a General Theory of Planning." *Policy Sciences*, 4: 155–169.

Sager, T. (2002) "Deliberative Planning and Decision Making: An Impossibility Result." *Journal of Planning Education and Research*, 21(4): 367–378.

Sartre, J.-P. (1974) *Les Mains sales* [Dirty Hands]. Paris: Gallimard.

Schwemmer, O. (1971) *Philosophie der Praxis: Versuch zur Grundlegung einer Lehre vom moralischen Argumentieren* [Philosophy of Practice: An Examination of the Foundations for Teaching Moral Argumentation]. Frankfurt am Main: Suhrkamp Verlag.

Stiglitz, J. E. (2003) *Globalization and Its Discontents*. New York: W. W. Norton.

Teller, E. (1975) Interview. *Bild der Wissenschaft* [A Picture of Science], 12(10): 94–116.

Weber, M. (1926) *Politik als Beruf* [Politics as Profession]. 2nd ed. Munich: Duncker & Humbolt.

Epilogue

Horst Rittel was a pragmatist in the sense that he was concerned with practical implications; Klaus Krippendorff echoes this thought in *The Semantic Turn* (2006). Rittel did not search for knowledge for knowledge's sake; rather, he sought knowledge for practical reasons. From the Science and Design seminars, through "On the Planning Crisis," the IBIS, the reasoning, and the pathologies, his interest was focused on the practical implications. Though he presented theories—e.g. the theory of argumentation or the paradoxes of rationality—they were always presented in a context that was concerned with practical outcomes.

The practical outcome, indeed, is one aspect of design—a crucial one—that defines it. Design is about how we hope or intend to change the world. Though there is a great tradition of knowledge for its own sake (not unrelated to the idea of art for art's sake), that was not Rittel's aim. His theories were not theories to prove ideas, but rather arguments to guide behavior—even, in a way, when it was the most abstract of research (e.g. the study of knowledge systems).

To Rittel, design involved a process of inquiry. Indeed, Rittel's view of design can be likened in many ways to the view of science espoused by Popper—whose influence on Rittel we have already noted. Rittel's vision of the process of design, like Popper's process of science, is a social project in which participants test ideas and accept as the standard not an idea that has been proven true, but rather the one that has withstood the most rigorous testing.

While Popper's view of science has been so widely accepted that many practicing scientists and statisticians can tell you what a null hypotheses is—which is the very foundation of Popper's principle of falsification providing an avenue to certain knowledge—often the fundamental role of the social process of choosing the best-tested theory is neglected or forgotten. To some extent, this may be because Popper himself tried to argue both that science depended on a social process and that the social process was due to conditions of scientific method:

> objectivity is closely bound up with the social aspect of scientific method, with the fact that science and scientific objectivity do not (and cannot) result from the attempts of an individual scientist to be 'objective', but from the friendly-hostile co-operation of many scientists. Scientific objectivity can be described as the inter-subjectivity of scientific method.
>
> (Popper 1966: 217)[1]

Though Popper hopes to argue that this particular social system is free of the sorts of prejudices that influence other social systems, work such as Bruno Latour's *Science in Action* (1987) has shown just how pervasive the social aspects of the scientific method can be.

But what gets even more lost than the basic principles and the philosopher who so influentially framed the idea, is the fact that Popper's theory is ultimately one that says that science does not prove any truth—"Our science is not knowledge (*epistēmē*): it can never claim to have attained truth, or even a substitute for it, such as probability" (Popper 1959: ch.10 §85)—but rather the truths posited by science are social artifacts. This is an idea familiar from such other philosophers of science as Kuhn, Feyerabend, or Latour.

Rittel's vision of design was parallel to Popper's vision of science. Design was supposed to be an open, transparent process where the different issues, positions and arguments would be available to all those crucially involved, and the decisions that were made were those that withstood the most rigorous testing. This is the implication of recognizing the wickedness of problems and the crisis in planning. This is the purpose of developing the IBIS, which was designed to capture all the positions and issues related to a project, and describing the reasoning of the designer. And it is with the intent of avoiding pathological design that the pathologies were a focus of his interest.

Recent work has shown how we, as humans, have historically destroyed our cultures by outstripping the resources available (Diamond 2005; Ponting 1991). Planning pathologies have led to problems of growing scope—the problems presented by some of the planning failures of the twentieth century far outweigh the problems of the previous centuries.

As humans we have long prided ourselves on our superiority over the "lower" animals. We believe ourselves to be like the gods—to have even been made in the image of God—but we face a situation in which we may turn out to be no more than another population that grows without restraint, destroys our resource base, and then is devastated. Are we no better than deer with no predator to keep our population in check? We pride ourselves on our intelligence, on our adaptability, on our ability to plan. But our ability to plan is serving us ill if it leads us to destroy natural sources of food, to pollute our water and air—the very sources of our life. And yet, what else can we presume from the great body of scientific evidence about our natural world?

The last half of the twentieth century was a time of great wealth and comfort in the Western industrialized world, but now the evidence suggests that to continue as we have been will lead to environmental disaster. The problem lies before us, and we still have a chance to design our future.

As Rittel showed, the problem facing humanity is not a technical one, and cannot be found in technical answers; technical answers are readily available if we are willing to change our lifestyle. The problem lies in the political and social realms.

Rittel taught us that the approach to problems and the approach to design must be through social interaction. And this, in itself, is a radical departure from heavily entrenched ways of thinking. Design is not about the materials manipulated and the resulting object, but rather it is about the people who are affected. Rittel's lesson of wicked problems and issue-based argumentation is that design lies in the social realm, and it is there that the best answers will be found. All knowledge, Rittel would say, is political.

When Rittel began his career, optimism in the use of scientific and systematic methods dominated the culture. Rationality ruled as king. It was very much the dominant spirit of the day, having grown in power and strength over the preceding century as the technological marvels of the Industrial Revolution had changed the world. And those technological marvels were seen largely as the product of rational thinking and the scientific model. Such scientific optimism entered society at large, permeating such fields as architecture and art. It is the thinking that Rittel called "first generation." As he noted in "On the Planning Crisis," there was great hope and were many successes for this approach.

It was the sort of thinking that engendered some of the great ideas of the age. The heroes of the age were scientists. From the real scientists, the living heroes—Einstein, Bohr, Heisenberg—to the fictional heroes and villains from the pages of science fiction, where scientists battled to save or enslave the world; to artists and architects like the Italian Futurists and the International Style modernists, scientists—those who unflinchingly followed logic and reason—were heroes and models to be emulated in their method. It was an age where figures like Ayn Rand's character Howard Roark, portrayed on the screen by Cary Grant, dominated the world with their unflinching pursuit of a truth—some ultimate truth that lay beyond human differences. This search for an ultimate truth was so common that Popper felt it important to observe "the old scientific ideal of *epistēmē*—of absolutely certain, demonstrable knowledge—has proved to be an idol" (Popper 1959: ch.10; sec. 85). It was an age where people began to believe that if everyone acted rationally and for their own self-interest, an invisible hand would lift the world to a state of maximum efficiency—a technical/rational utopia. It was an age where a political theorist could posit that an ultimate social truth could arise from the dialectic between conflicting classes. Rationality was thought to be the source of truth. Indeed, the period known as "the Enlightenment" is known so because, from the perspective of the present day, it represents the period in which our culture first accepted a set of ideas that still rule the present day. And what is the Enlightenment known for if not its use of reason? Not all of these ideas are out of currency today, but we can see, for example, that Enlightenment notions like Smith's invisible hand—in the form of theories that suggest the inevitable mechanical optimization of effort created by free market forces—dominates political practices in most of the world.

Rittel's philosophy grew in an age where these ideas predominated, but he matured when the claims of "technical rationality," as Donald Schon called it, were being called into question.

In the early half of the twentieth century, the cracks in the idol of perfect truth began to appear: Heisenberg's uncertainty principle, for example, makes the idea of objectivity quite problematic, and Gödel's proof of the incompleteness of arithmetic demonstrated problems in axiomatic systems. Popper's *Logic of Scientific*

Discovery, where he claims that the idol had been exposed—was written originally in 1934. Despite the successes of operations research in military efforts in World War II and in the years following, and despite the growing acceptance of these methods in government and business, the logical foundations of technical rationality, and the scholarly support for those foundations were beginning to crumble. Thomas Kuhn's *The Structure of Scientific Revolutions* was published in 1962, as was Rachel Carson's *Silent Spring*, a classic that challenged the wisdom of the technological foundations of the "green revolution." We have already mentioned Rittel's collegial interactions with C. W. Churchman and the others of Churchman's seminar. It was the age, also, that brought the beginnings of deconstruction and post-structuralism: in philosophy, Michel Foucault, Jacques Derrida were Rittel's contemporaries; in architecture, Venturi's *Complexity and Contradiction in Architecture* (1966), a seminal work of the postmodernist movement, was published in the mid-1960s. And it was, of course, only months after the Science and Design seminars that, on the campus where Rittel taught, the Berkeley Free Speech Movement claimed national prominence, introducing Berkeley as a hotbed of student political action and ushering in an era of student protest. Rittel's theories were anti-authority in their own way: he did not accept that there was any one "correct" formulation of a design problem.

Almost half a century has passed since Rittel gave his seminars to the faculty of Berkeley's College of Environmental Design. The academic credibility that non-rationalist ideas have gained is not matched by similar views in political and corporate realms. Mass-planning and mass deployments of technology have been made and continue to be made with no better justification than a cost benefit analysis prepared in a corporate boardroom or government office. And the impacts of these dubious projects is immense: genetically modified foods now make up a huge portion of food grown in the US, and little can be known about the long-term impacts of a technology that was developed less than two decades ago. And this is only one example of a mass deployment of brand-new technology. As long as some "scientific" reports—funded by the interested party, of course—claim safety over a short period, governments allow the product to be deployed—if, indeed there is any oversight at all.

Rittel spoke from a point of cautious optimism—from the perspective that we can make good plans, really good plans that will serve us well, that will serve people well for generations.

But perhaps Rittel was something of a revolutionary in that he believed that everyone's opinion should be included in the debate. Rittel did not aim to stop development or exploration and experimentation, but rather to create a context in which the massive design decisions that affect us all are made on the basis of good premises and not purely for the benefit of a small group. While Rittel would have surely been aware of just how elusive it is to try to define the common good, he still would have espoused striving for the common good rather than striving for selfish ends.

Rittel's work taught us to be careful, to respect and to hear the needs of all the people involved. In *The Fountainhead* (1943), Rand despised the work of committees—saying it drove one to the worst of all possible worlds. But Rittel would rather reject the grand schemes of a Howard Roark—at least insofar as those schemes ignore real concerns and important issues.

It is not that Rittel was opposed to grand schemes—he speaks of the need for utopian visions at the end of the Science and Design seminars—though his explanation there does not fully capture why trying to work on the problem of utopian visions is important.

While lacking an explicit statement of a utopian vision, Rittel's writing echoes a utopian vision of Rittel's colleague C. W. Churchman, one which gives an interesting perspective to Rittel's claim that utopian images are problems and "that is their main purpose". In 1978 Churchman wrote, "The future will see that problems should not 'go away' because problems are the means by which individuals can contribute to social planning and action," and "it is *contribution* which is the goal, because contribution is the full expression of each one's individuality. We create problems and attempt to solve them *in order to* contribute" (Churchman 1978: 189). The answer, in Churchman's utopia is not found by giving people material wealth or food or shelter or leisure—all of which have been identified as positive goals—but to give people's lives meaning. Rittel's work shows why such a utopian image is far more practical than many.

Rittel said that "defining the problem is the problem" and also that once you have defined the problem, you have also defined the solution. In light of Churchman's utopia, it seems appropriate to wonder whether, in a social sense, the attempt to solve wicked problems is the solution—that, indeed, a certain sort of process becomes the goal. Rittel prefigures this very question at the end of the Science and Design seminars:

> Should conflict between different images of the grand system be resolved once and for all? I think not . . . any resolution of this conflict means a 'freezing' of concepts, of ideas . . . conflict as a means to produce ultra-stability or dynamic equilibrium is essential and should be cultivated.

And then he carries this notion a little further in "On the Planning Crisis":

> planning methods of the second generation try to make those people who are being affected into participants of the planning process. They are not merely asked but actively involved in the planning process. That means a kind of *maximized involvement*.

And:

> because we cannot anticipate all the consequences of our plans, every plan, every treatment of a wicked problem is a venture, if not an adventure. Therefore, let us share the risk, let us try to find accomplices who are willing to embark on the problem with us. For one person it is too risky, but maybe if we join our forces we may take the risk and live with the uncertainty and embark upon the venture.

There is an obvious meeting of the minds between Rittel and Churchman, and Churchman's framing of this notion as a utopian vision reveal to us that aspect of what Rittel is describing. Beyond question, there are risks and ventures that lie before us, and we can see that many of them have arisen from first-generation attitudes and practices—the attempts to apply universal visions and massive "rational" planning schemes—but Rittel's work, and Churchman's utopia as well, shows us the importance of a diversity of ideas and of the necessity of the designer understanding and respecting the diversity of views, and working together to share the vision, to share the risk and, one hopes, to share the reward.

Note

1 Or, similarly: "what we call 'scientific objectivity' is not a product of the individual scientist's impartiality, but a product of the social or public character of scientific method; and the individual scientist's impartiality is, so far as it exists, not the source but rather the result of this socially or institutionally organized objectivity of science." (Popper 1966: 220)

References

Alexander, C. (1964) *Notes on the Synthesis of Form*. Cambridge, MA: Harvard University Press.

Alonso, W. (1964) *Location and Land Use: Toward a General Theory of Land Rent*. Cambridge, MA: Harvard University Press.

Archer, L. B. (1965) *Systematic Methods for Designers*. London: The Design Council.

Asimow, M. (1962) *Introduction to Design*. Prentice-Hall Fundamentals in Engineering Design Series, Englewood Cliffs, NJ: Prentice-Hall.

Boulding, K. (1956) *The Image: Knowledge in Life and Society*. Ann Arbor, MI: University of Michigan Press.

Bucciarelli, L. L. (1988) "An Ethnographic Perspective on Engineering Design." *Design Studies*, 9(3): 159–68.

Churchman, C. W. (1967) "Wicked Problems." (Guest editorial) *Management Science*, 14(4): B-141, B-142.

Churchman, C. W. (1968) *Challenge to Reason*. New York: McGraw-Hill.

Churchman, C. W. (1971) *The Design of Inquiring Systems: Basic Concepts of Systems and Organizations*. New York: Basic Books.

Churchman, C. W. (1978) "The Case against Planning: The Beloved Community." *DMG/DRS Journal*, 12(3/4): 170, 187–90.

Churchman, C. W., Ackoff, R. L. and Arnoff, E. L. (1957) *Introduction to Operations Research*. New York: Wiley.

Churchman, C. W., Protzen, J. P. and Webber, M. M. (1992) "Horst W. J. Rittel." *University of California: in memoriam*. Berkeley, CA: University of California, Berkeley, Academic Senate.

Conklin J. (2006) *Dialogue Mapping: Building Shared Understanding of Wicked Problems*. Hoboken, NJ: Wiley.

Cuff, D. (1991) *Architecture: the story of practice*. Cambridge, MA: MIT Press.

Davidoff, P. (1965) "Advocacy and Pluralism in Planning." *Journal of the American Institute of Planners*, 31(4): 331–38.

Diamond, J. (2005) *Collapse: How Societies Choose to Succeed or Fail*. New York: Viking.

Faludi, A. (1973) *Planning Theory*. Urban and Regional Planning Series, vol. 7. Oxford: Pergamon Press.

Feyerabend, F. (1975) *Against Method: An Outline of an Anarchistic Theory of Knowledge*. London: Verso.

Fischer, F. and Forester, J. (eds) (1993) *The Argumentative Turn in Policy Analysis and Planning*. Durham, NC and London: Duke University Press.

Forester, J. (1999) *The Deliberative Practitioner*. Cambridge, MA: MIT Press.

Forrester, J. W. (1971) *World Dynamics*. Cambridge, MA: Wright-Allen Press.

Friedman, Y. (1971) *Vers une architecture scientifique* [Towards a scientific architecture]. Paris: P. Belfond.

Friedmann, J. (1973) *Retracking America: A Theory of Transactive Planning*. Garden City, NY: Anchor Press/Doubleday.

Goodman, R. (1971) *After the Planners*. New York: Simon and Schuster.

Gramsci, A. (1992) *Prison Notebooks*, ed. Joseph A. Buttigieg. New York: Columbia University Press.

Guggenberger, B. (1987) *Das Menschenrecht auf Irrtum: Anleitung zur Unvollkommenheit* [The Human Right to Err: Instruction for Imperfection]. München: Carl Hanser Verlag.

References

Haldane, J. B. S. (1985) *On Being the Right Size*. New York: Oxford University Press.

Harris, D. J. (2002) "Design Theory: From Scientific Method to Humanist Practice." Unpublished PhD dissertation, University of California, Berkeley.

Heath, T. (1984) *Method in Architecture*. New York: Wiley.

Hoos, I. R. (1969) *Systems Analysis in Public Policy: A Critique*. London: Institute of Economic Affairs.

Hoos, I. R. (2009) Alumna address, University of California, Berkeley, Department of Sociology. Available online at: <http://sociology.berkeley.edu/alumni> (accessed September 8, 2009).

Jones, J. C. (1970) *Design Methods: Seeds of Human Futures*. New York: Wiley-Interscience.

Jones, J. C. and Thornley, D. G. (eds) (1962) *Conference on Design Methods*. Oxford: Pergamon Press.

Kahneman, D. (2002) "Maps of Bounded Rationality." From *Les Prix Nobel. The Nobel Prizes 2002*, ed. Tore Frängsmyr. Stockholm: Nobel Foundation. Available online at: <http://nobelprize.org/nobel_prizes/economics/laureates/2002/kahneman-lecture.html> (accessed 10 September, 2009).

Kahneman, D. and Tversky, A. (1984) "Choices, Values and Frames." *American Psychologist*, 39: 341–50.

Kirschner, P. A., Buckingham Shum, S. and Carr, C. (eds) (2003) *Visualizing Argumentation: Software Tools for Collaborative and Educational Sense-making*. London/New York: Springer.

Krauch, H. (2006) "Beginning Science Policy Research in Europe: The Studiengruppe für Systemforschung, 1957–1973." *Minerva*, 44(2): 131–42.

Krippendorff, K. (2006) *The Semantic Turn: A New Foundation for Design*. Boca Raton, FL: Taylor and Francis CRC Press.

Kuhn, T. (1962) *The Structure of Scientific Revolutions*. Chicago: University of Chicago Press.

Langer, S. K. K. (1948) *Philosophy in a New Key: A Study in the Symbolism of Reason, Rite and Art*. New York: Penguin.

Latour, B. (1987) *Science in Action*. Cambridge, MA: Harvard University Press.

Lewin, K. (1936) *Principles of Topological Psychology*, trans. F. Heider and G. M. Heider. New York, London: McGraw-Hill.

Lewontin, R. (2000) *The Triple Helix*. Cambridge, MA: Harvard University Press.

Mandelbaum, S., Mazza, L. and Burchell, R. W. (eds) (1966) *Explorations in Planning Theory*. Rutgers, NJ: Center for Urban Policy Research, The State University of New Jersey.

Marschak, J. (1954) "Towards an Economic Theory of Organization and Information." In R. M. Thrall, C. H. Coombs and R. L. Davis (eds) *Decision Processes*. New York: John Wiley & Sons.

Meadows, D. H., Meadows, D. L., Randers, J. and Behrens III, W. W. (1972) *The Limits to Growth: A Report for the Club of Rome's Project on the Predicament of Mankind*. New York: Universe Books.

Moran, T. P. and Carroll, J. M. (eds) (1996) *Design Rationale: Concepts, Techniques, and Use*. Mahwah, NJ: L. Erlbaum Associates.

Pastore, N. (1949) *The Nature-Nurture Controversy*. New York: King's Crown Press.

Polanyi, M. (1958) *Personal Knowledge*. Chicago: University of Chicago Press.

Ponting, C. (1991) *A Green History of the World*. New York: Penguin.

Popper, K. (1959) *The Logic of Scientific Discovery*. New York: Basic Books.

Popper, K. (1966) *The Open Society and Its Enemies*. Vol. 2: *The High Tide of Prophecy: Hegel, Marx, and the Aftermath*, 5th edn, revised, Princeton, NJ: Princeton University Press.

Protzen, J. P. (1981) "Reflections on the Fable of the Caliph, the Philosopher and the Ten Architects." *Journal of Architectural Education*, 3(4): 2–8.

Protzen, J. P. and Verma, N. (1997) "On Rittel's Pathologies of Planning." *Planning Theory*, 1: 114–29.

RSAI (Regional Science Association International) (2008) Regional Science Association International—Home. Available online at: <www.regionalscience.org/>(accessed 8 September, 2009).

Reuter, W. D. (1992) "Introduction." In H. W. J. Rittel, *Planen Entwerfen, Design, Ausgewählte Schriften zu Theorie und Methodik* [Planning, Envisioning and Designing: Selected Writings on Theory and Method], ed. W. Reuter. Stuttgart, Germany: Kohlhammer.

Rith, C. and Dubberly, H. (2007) "Why Horst Rittel Matters." *Design Issues,* 23(1): 72–91.

Rittel, H. W. J. (1961) "Zu den Arbeitshypothesen der Hochschule für Gestaltung in Ulm" [On the Working Hypotheses of the School for Design at Ulm]. *WERK*, 48(8): 281–83.

Rittel, H. W. J. (1965) "Hierarchy vs. Team? Considerations on the Organization of Research of R&D Co-operatives." In *Economic Research Development*, ed. R. A. Tybout. Columbus, OH: Ohio University Press.

Rittel, H. W. J. (1966) "Some Principles for the Design of an Educational System for Design." In *Education for Architectural Technology*, ed. J. Passanneau. St Louis, MO: Washington University and the AIA Educational Research Project.

Rittel, H. W. J. (1972) "On the Planning Crisis: Systems Analysis of the First and Second Generations." *Bedriftsøkonomen*, 8: 390–97.

Rittel, H. W. J. (1976) "Der Sachzwäng–Ausreden für Entscheidungsmüde" [Coercive Facts: Excuses for the Decision-Weary]. In *Planen, Entwerfen, Design: Ausgewählte Schriften zu Theorie und Methodik*, ed. W. Reuter (1992). Stuttgart, Germany: Kohlhammer.

Rittel, H. W. J. (1986) "Design der Zukunft–wie stellt es sich in unseren Köpfen dar?" [Design for the Future: How is it Represented in Our Minds?]. Forumkongress des Internationalen Design Zentrum Berlin e.V. in Berlin in December 1986.

Rittel, H. W. J. (1992a) "Energie wird rar? Sachzwänge oder der Krieg um die Köpfe" [Energy is Becoming Scarce? Coercive Facts and the Battle for Ideas]. In W. D. Reuter (ed.) *Planen, Entwerfen, Design: Ausgewählte Schriften zu Theorie und Methodik*, Stuttgart, Germany: Kohlhammer.

Rittel, H. W. J. (1992b) *Planen, Entwerfen, Design: Ausgewählte Schriften zu Theorie und Methodik*, ed. W. D. Reuter. Stuttgart, Germany: Kohlhammer.

Rittel, H. W. J. and Kunz, W. (1973) "Das Umwelt-Planungs-Informationssystem UMPLIS" [The Environmental Planning Information System, UMPLIS]. *Städtebauliche Beiträge*, 2: 55–72.

Rittel, H. W. J. and Webber, M. M. (1973) "Dilemmas in a General Theory of Planning." *Policy Science*, 4: 155–69.

Schiller, F. (1759–1805) *Die Worte des Glaubens (The Word of the Faithful)*, st. 2 (1797).

Schön, D. (1983) *The Reflective Practitioner*. New York: Basic Books.

Simmons, M. R. (2000, October) "Revisiting the Limits to Growth: Could The Club of Rome Have Been Correct After All? An Energy White Paper." Available online at: <www.greatchange.org/ov-simmons,club_of_rome_revisted.pdf > (accessed 8 September, 2009).

Simon, H. (1947) *Administrative Behavior: A Study of Decision-making Processes in Administrative Organization*. New York: Macmillan.

Simon, H. (1969) *The Sciences of the Artificial*. Cambridge, MA: MIT Press.

Simon, H. (1984) "The Structure of Ill-structured Problems." In *Developments in Design Methodology*, ed. Nigel Cross. New York: John Wiley & Sons. (Originally published in 1973 in *Artificial Intelligence*, 4: 181–200.)

Singer, C. J., Holmyard, E. J. and Hall, A. R. (eds) (1958) *A History of Technology*. Vol. 4. Oxford: Clarendon.

Skinner, B. F. (1961) "The Design of Cultures." *Daedalus*, 90: 534–46.

Starr, K. (1963) *Product Design and Decision Theory*. Prentice-Hall Fundamentals in Engineering Design Series, Englewood Cliffs, NJ: Prentice-Hall.

Steinbuch, K. (1961) *Automat und Mensch* [Machine and Man]. Berlin: Springer-Verlag.

Tversky, A. and Kahneman, D. (1974) "Judgment Under Uncertainty: Heuristics and biases." *Science*, 185: 1124–31.

Venturi, R. (1966) *Complexity and Contradiction in Architecture*. New York: Museum of Modern Art.

Verma, N. (1996) "Pragamatic Rationality and Planning Theory." *Journal of Planning Education and Research*, 16: 5–14.

Verma, N. (1998) *Similarity, Connections and Systems: The Search for a New Rationality for Planning and Management*. Lanham, MD: Lexington Books.

Warner, W. L. (1960) *Social Class in America: A Manual of Procedure for the Measurement of Social Status*. New York: Harper.

References

Wildavsky, A. (1973) "If Planning is Everything, Maybe it is Nothing." *Policy Science*, 4: 127–53.

Winograd, T. and Flores, F. (1986) *Understanding Computers and Cognition: A New Foundation for Design*. New York: Addison and Wesley Publishing.

Wurster, W. (1960) *Bulletin 1960–1961*. Berkeley, CA, College of Environmental Design, University of California, Berkeley.

Author Index

Author Index

Subject Index